IMAGES
of America

SAN FRANCISCO RELOCATED

ON THE COVER: This 1908 photograph depicts a team of horses moving a Victorian house. In the early 1900s, two-horse teams were commonly used to move buildings. First, the house was jacked up off its foundation and supported by heavy wooden beams. Greased beams, serving as runners, helped the building inch along. As it progressed down the street, the planks and ties left behind were manually picked up by workers and carried to the front of the moving building to become the new track. A capstan (basically, a drum) was mounted in the middle of the street, and a pulley connected the structure to a cross beam between the runners. The horses walked around in a circle and pulled on a pulley connected to the capstan, stepping over the cable. The cable wound up on the capstan, and the house moved along. The horse-pull method was favored into the 1930s, even though gasoline-powered trucks were available, because horses could simply step over the cable each time, which was something a truck could not do. San Francisco Heritage identified this photograph's location as Steiner Street approaching Washington Street. (Courtesy of the Milwaukee Public Museum.)

IMAGES
of America

SAN FRANCISCO RELOCATED

Diane C. Donovan

ARCADIA
PUBLISHING

ISBN 978-1-4671-3371-5

Published by Arcadia Publishing
Charleston, South Carolina

Printed in the United States of America

Library of Congress Control Number: 2015931845

For all general information, please contact Arcadia Publishing:
Telephone 843-853-2070
Fax 843-853-0044
E-mail sales@arcadiapublishing.com
For customer service and orders:
Toll-Free 1-888-313-2665

Visit us on the Internet at www.arcadiapublishing.com

*To Bill Donovan, who always said I could do anything,
and Beni Bacon, whose support, computer, and
photography skills helped make this book happen*

Contents

Acknowledgments

Perhaps the most surprising part of producing an Arcadia book is the collaborative effort involved; not just between people who are already familiar to one another, but also between strangers who come together with a shared common interest in contributing images and facts to a historical investigation.

Through this shared effort, history becomes a living, breathing process, changing with the debates, fact finding and fact checking, research discoveries, and dialogue surrounding each book chapter's evolution.

San Francisco Relocated would not have happened without the generous time, information, and images shared by this growing circle of new friends.

I am indebted to Vicky Walker of Bernal Heights Association for her ongoing support and familiarity with Arcadia's processes and requirements. Also, I am immensely grateful for the assistance of the following people: photographer Dave Glass, for his many unique images of the Western Addition's Victorian house moves; collectors John Freeman and friend Glenn Koch, for their extensive research and images; Peter Linenthal, of the Potrero Hill Archives Project, for images and support; Paul Rosenberg, for his enthusiastic kick-off for the book; and Evelyn Rose, of the Glen Park Neighborhood History Association, for her wholehearted encouragement.

Fellow Arcadia author Lorri Ungaretti generously contributed her time and provided key encouragement at a point of despair, Mike Shea contributed many images and much enthusiasm, Woody LaBounty, of Western Neighborhoods Project, provided a treasure trove of images and information, and Philip Brent Digital Art and Photography worked a bit of magic to return many of these images to life. Friend Barry Lawrence provided much expertise and insight on the photograph permission process.

And, let us not forget that were it not for my childhood landlord Joseph Caruso's willingness to chat with a small child about his house-moving pursuits, as well as his family's enthusiastic encouragement for sharing his efforts and the origins of his house-moving involvement, the entire story of the Portola District and other small-time neighborhood movers might have remained untold.

It truly takes a village to produce an Arcadia book; it is an intersection of community, history, and generosity at its best. *San Francisco Relocated* could not have been written without this community's support, and I thank you all!

INTRODUCTION

Why write a book about San Francisco's house-moving past? And why move a house in the first place? Who were these "urban cowpokes," as one reporter described them, whose businesses revolved around picking up and moving houses? All three questions ultimately formed the nexus of *San Francisco Relocated.*

I was about nine years old when my parents moved to the Portola District, renting a common row house that seemed to hold no special attributes. It was not a Victorian, it could not be described as "ornate" by any manner of means, and it did not stand out from any other house on the block. It was sandwiched beside two other houses with the usual San Francisco propensity for allowing only a few inches of space between buildings.

Had it not been for hours of hanging on the back fence listening to our landlord tell stories about how he had made a thriving business out of buying up "houses that needed moving" and relocating them onto vacant lots, I would have never even known that a building could be picked up and moved.

Our house on Sweeny Street was one of those houses; its twin next to us was another. Joseph Caruso moved numerous homes throughout the Portola District, his center of operations. He was just a small-time contractor who, it turned out, was one of the last San Francisco house-moving entrepreneurs in the waning years of the city's moving history.

Now fast forward 40 years, when an amazing photograph of a two-story Victorian house being moved downhill via a team of draft horses and some wooden rollers caught my eye, releasing a floodgate of memories of Joseph Caruso and his unusual business.

As I investigated San Francisco's moved-building history, I was amazed to discover that the city's house-moving adventures were second only to Chicago's. It is also astonishing to note that the heyday of San Francisco's relocation actually occurred between 1850 and 1920, when so many houses were moved that San Franciscans came to consider them a nuisance and complained about the street-hogging houses that wandered irresponsibly from block to block in search of new lots as the city expanded and constantly revised its sidewalks, boundaries, and grid lines.

Mark Twain, one of the loudest (and most literary) of these protesters, used his position as a local reporter for San Francisco's *Daily Morning Call* to document the wayward buildings and their troublesome journeys through the streets of San Francisco: "An old two-story, sheet-iron, pioneer, fire-proof house, got loose from her moorings last night, and drifted down Sutter Street toward Montgomery."

An 1868 article in the *California Alta* documented the damage done to cobblestones and pavement by house-moving operations as follow: "The business of buying those old shells, moving them out of the fire limits, repairing or patching them up, and selling them on long credit, at round prices, has become a regular trade, which is followed by a number of persons with profit to themselves, but loss to the general public." The *California Alta* called for regulation, fines, and even imprisonment.

And sometimes, the city supervisors took matters into their own hands, as when they decreed that, on Golden Gate Avenue, "no permit shall ever be issued allowing the moving of any house along said street for any distance whatever, and no housemoving shall, ever, be done on said street, either along, upon or across the same."

Now, we come to the crux of the matter—why move a structure instead of tearing it down and rebuilding elsewhere?

In 1900s San Francisco, building materials were expensive to procure; so once built, it was no light matter to demolish a building. A house-moving industry sprung up to address the growing need of relocating structures throughout the city. A renegade bunch of house-herding cowboys, who tended to rebel against regulations, hoisted up and pulled buildings down the streets of San Francisco via draft horse, rollers, and capstans.

Moving houses was generally a popular venture in other cities at the turn of the century; however, homes on the East Coast were largely built of brick, making them too heavy and difficult to move on a regular basis in contrast to the sturdy, comparatively lighter redwood structures of San Francisco. Also, San Francisco's streets were regularly rerouted, redone, and regraded to cope with the city's growth, so there was simply more impetus for house moving in San Francisco than in the rest of the nation.

In 1900, the city proposed licensing and taxing these house movers and house-raisers, which resulted in movers protesting about the interference of government in small business and the accusations of house movers due to unjust taxes that favored larger companies over smaller independents.

In the mid-1800s to 1910, there were minimal overhead electrical or telegraph wires to worry about; but in June 1905, house mover D.J. Sullivan went to court for cutting electrical wires without permission (a crime that could be deemed either a felony or a misdemeanor at the judge's discretion). His act reflected an ongoing war between house-moving companies and the San Francisco Gas and Electrical Company, which eventually was resolved by a court injunction requiring house movers to post bonds for damages before moving structures.

All manner of buildings were moved in San Francisco over the decades that followed, from two-story Victorian structures to churches, earthquake shacks, and commercial buildings.

Today, the business of moving buildings in San Francisco is all but dead, killed off by a combination of traffic, density, and the preponderance of services that cannot be interrupted, however temporarily, to make way for a moving building. Contrast the increased challenges and costs of house moving (and its associated liability) with the ready availability of building materials and the (comparatively) easier process of obtaining a building or remodel permit in the city and it is easy to see why the heyday of San Francisco's relocation has long since passed.

San Francisco Relocated is not intended as a definitive history; it should be noted that many more buildings were moved in the city than appear here.

It is a story for anyone who wants to know how the city was shaped, and it is a tribute to those unsung heroes of San Francisco—the house movers and structural engineers—who attempted the impossible. It assures that their lasting legacy will not be forgotten.

As the daughter of a longtime house mover said, "House moving has been good to our family. We owe the life that we have been able to live to it, along with the hard work by our father and his guts to take on such a crazy profession! As my CPA once said to me, 'Who in the world would ever think of taking a house, such a big and enormous thing, and move it and decide that that is what they want to do for a living? That's just crazy!' I had never thought about it that way."

It is a crazy profession, it is exciting, and it ultimately changed San Francisco forever.

Within any history, there are mysteries. Some moving jobs have been identified as being within San Francisco, but little else is known about them. On my website lies your chance to contribute to their stories and solve these UMOs, or "unidentified moving objects." If you have any information or new findings on UMOs, please e-mail sfrelocated@gmail.com. Your research will help add to San Francisco's history by identifying these mysterious wanderers and will be posted on the book's website at www.sfrelocated.com.

One

A City on Rollers
San Francisco's Early Heyday of Moving Houses

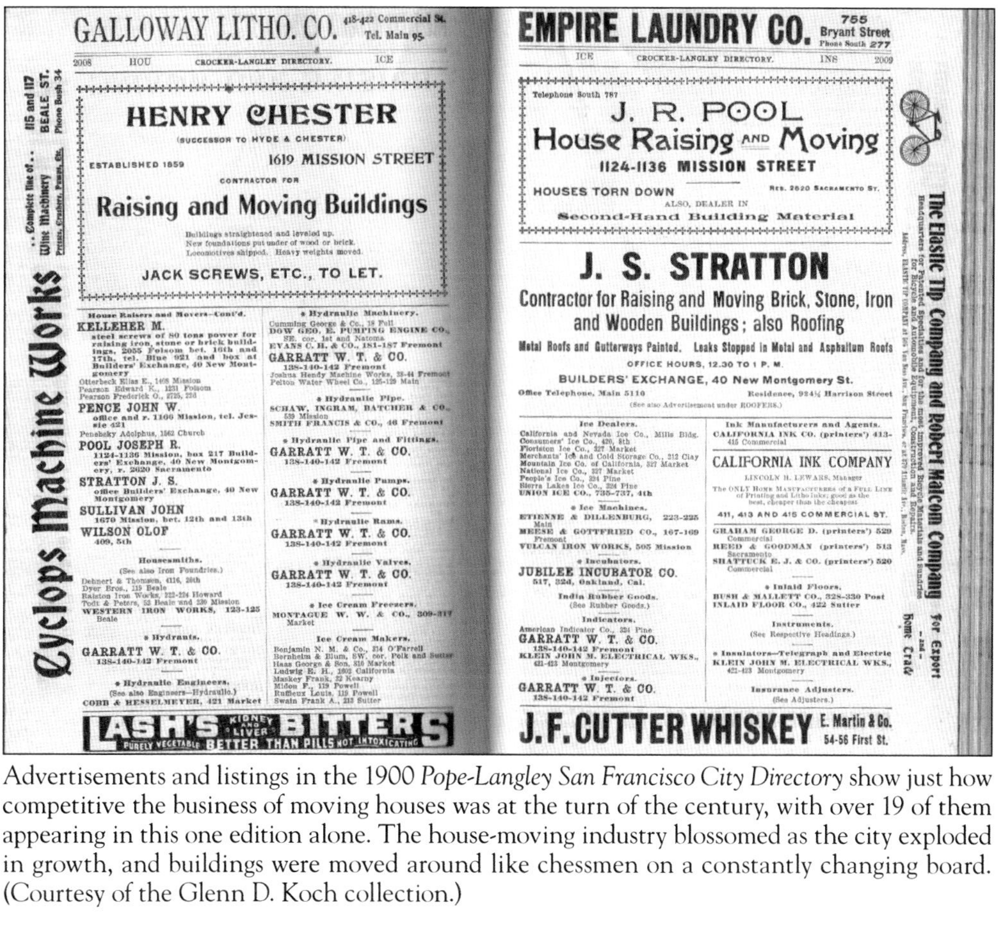

GALLOWAY LITHO. CO. 418-422 Commercial St. Tel. Main 95.

2008 HOU CROCKER-LANGLEY DIRECTORY. ICE

Cyclops Machine Works .. Complete line of .. Wine Machinery Presses, Crushers, Pumps, Etc. 115 and 117 BEALE ST. Phone Bush 34

HENRY CHESTER
(SUCCESSOR TO HYDE & CHESTER)
ESTABLISHED 1859 1619 MISSION STREET
CONTRACTOR FOR
Raising and Moving Buildings
Buildings straightened and leveled up.
New foundations put under of wood or brick.
Locomotives shipped. Heavy weights moved.
JACK SCREWS, ETC., TO LET.

House Raisers and Movers—Cont'd.
KELLEHER M. steel screws of 80 tons power for raising iron, stone or brick buildings, 2055 Folsom bet. 16th and 17th, tel. Blue 921 and box at Builders' Exchange, 40 New Montgomery
Otterbeck Elias E., 1408 Mission
Pearson Edward K., 1231 Folsom
Pearson Frederick O., 2725, 23d
PENCE JOHN W. office and r. 1100 Mission, tel. Jessie 421
Penebsky Adolphus, 1562 Church
POOL JOSEPH R. 1124-1136 Mission, box 217 Builders' Exchange, 40 New Montgomery, r. 2620 Sacramento
STRATTON J. S. office Builders' Exchange, 40 New Montgomery
SULLIVAN JOHN 1670 Mission, bet. 12th and 13th
WILSON OLOF 409, 5th

Housesmiths.
(See also Iron Foundries.)
Dehnert & Thomsen, 4116, 20th
Dyer Bros., 119 Beale
Ralston Iron Works, 222-224 Howard
Todt & Peters, 53 Beale and 230 Mission
WESTERN IRON WORKS, 123-125 Beale

* Hydrants.
GARRATT W. T. & CO. 138-140-142 Fremont

* Hydraulic Engineers.
(See also Engineers—Hydraulic.)
COBB & HESSELMEYER, 421 Market

* Hydraulic Machinery.
Cumming George & Co., 18 Fell
DOW GEO. E. PUMPING ENGINE CO., SE. cor. 1st and Natoma
EVANS C. H. & CO., 181-187 Fremont
GARRATT W. T. & CO. 138-140-142 Fremont
Joshua Hendy Machine Works, 38-44 Fremont
Pelton Water Wheel Co., 125-129 Main

* Hydraulic Pipe.
SCHAW, INGRAM, BATCHER & CO., 539 Mission
SMITH FRANCIS & CO., 46 Fremont

* Hydraulic Pipe and Fittings.
GARRATT W. T. & CO. 138-140-142 Fremont

* Hydraulic Pumps.
GARRATT W. T. & CO. 138-140-142 Fremont

* Hydraulic Rams.
GARRATT W. T. & CO. 138-140-142 Fremont

* Hydraulic Valves.
GARRATT W. T. & CO. 138-140-142 Fremont

* Ice Cream Freezers.
MONTAGUE W. W. & CO., 309-317 Market

Ice Cream Makers.
Benjamin N. M. & Co., 214 O'Farrell
Bernheim & Blum, SW. cor. Polk and Sutter
Haas George & Son, 816 Market
Ludwig E. H., 1802 California
Maskey Frank, 32 Kearny
Midon F., 119 Powell
Ruffieux Louis, 119 Powell
Swain Frank A., 213 Sutter

LASH'S KIDNEY AND LIVER BITTERS PURELY VEGETABLE BETTER THAN PILLS NOT INTOXICATING

EMPIRE LAUNDRY CO. 755 Bryant Street Phone South 277

ICE CROCKER-LANGLEY DIRECTORY. INS 2009

Telephone South 787
J. R. POOL
House Raising AND Moving
1124-1136 MISSION STREET
HOUSES TORN DOWN RES. 2620 SACRAMENTO ST.
ALSO, DEALER IN
Second-Hand Building Material

J. S. STRATTON
Contractor for Raising and Moving Brick, Stone, Iron and Wooden Buildings; also Roofing
Metal Roofs and Gutterways Painted. Leaks Stopped in Metal and Asphaltum Roofs
OFFICE HOURS, 12.30 TO 1 P. M.
BUILDERS' EXCHANGE, 40 New Montgomery St.
Office Telephone, Main 5110 Residence, 924½ Harrison Street
(See also Advertisement under ROOFERS.)

Ice Dealers.
California and Nevada Ice Co., Mills Bldg.
Consumers' Ice Co., 420, 8th
Floriston Ice Co., 327 Market
Merchants' Ice and Cold Storage Co., 212 Clay
Mountain Ice Co. of California, 327 Market
National Ice Co., 327 Market
People's Ice Co., 324 Pine
Sierra Lakes Ice Co., 324 Pine
UNION ICE CO., 735-737, 4th

* Ice Machines.
ETIENNE & DILLENBURG, 223-225 Main
MEESE & GOTTFRIED CO., 167-169 Fremont
VULCAN IRON WORKS, 505 Mission

* Incubators.
JUBILEE INCUBATOR CO. 517, 32d, Oakland, Cal.

India Rubber Goods.
(See Rubber Goods.)

Indicators.
American Indicator Co., 324 Pine
GARRATT W. T. & CO. 138-140-142 Fremont
KLEIN JOHN M. ELECTRICAL WKS., 421-423 Montgomery

* Injectors.
GARRATT W. T. & CO. 138-140-142 Fremont

Ink Manufacturers and Agents.
CALIFORNIA INK CO. (printers') 413-415 Commercial

CALIFORNIA INK COMPANY
LINCOLN H. LEWARS, Manager
The ONLY HOME MANUFACTURERS of a FULL LINE of Printing and Litho Inks; good as the best, cheaper than the cheapest
411, 413 AND 415 COMMERCIAL ST.

GRAHAM GEORGE D. (printers') 529 Commercial
REED & GOODMAN (printers') 513 Sacramento
SHATTUCK E. J. & CO. (printers') 520 Commercial

* Inlaid Floors.
BUSH & MALLETT CO., 328-330 Post
INLAID FLOOR CO., 422 Sutter

Instruments.
(See Respective Headings.)

* Insulators—Telegraph and Electric
KLEIN JOHN M. ELECTRICAL WKS., 421-423 Montgomery

Insurance Adjusters.
(See Adjusters.)

The Elastic Tip Company and Robert Malcom Company For Export – and – Home Trade
Headquarters for Patented Specialties and for the most improved Bicycle Materials and Sundries for Bicycle and Automobile Equipment, Construction and Repairs.

J. F. CUTTER WHISKEY E. Martin & Co. 54-56 First St.

Advertisements and listings in the 1900 *Pope-Langley San Francisco City Directory* show just how competitive the business of moving houses was at the turn of the century, with over 19 of them appearing in this one edition alone. The house-moving industry blossomed as the city exploded in growth, and buildings were moved around like chessmen on a constantly changing board. (Courtesy of the Glenn D. Koch collection.)

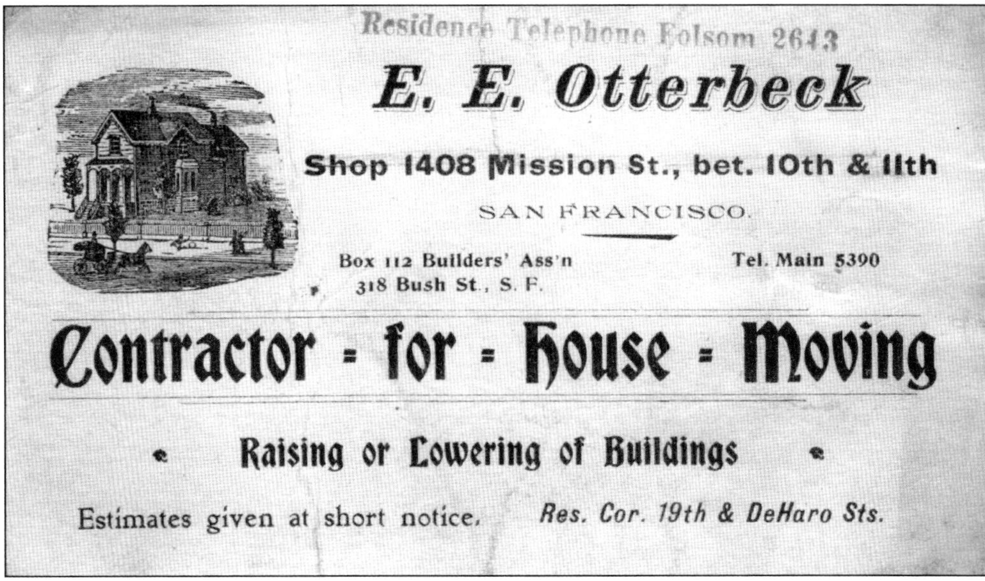

This image of yet another house-moving company advertises the skills of E.E. Otterbeck, who raised, lowered, and moved buildings. Otterbeck became involved in the ongoing war over house mover licensing and, in 1904, requested a repeal of the ordinance requiring a license, declaring it was designed to lock out small house-moving businesses. (Courtesy of Potrero Hill Archives Project.)

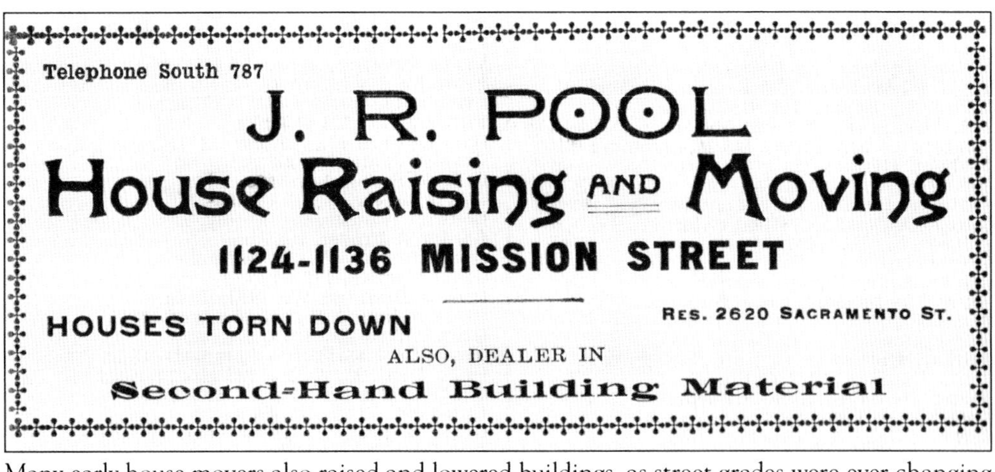

Many early house movers also raised and lowered buildings, as street grades were ever changing at the time. In addition to house moving and raising, J.R. Pool's services also included demolition and the salvaging and selling of second-hand building materials. Because lumber and building materials were hard to come by, moving a structure was often preferred over demolition. (Courtesy of the Glenn D. Koch collection.)

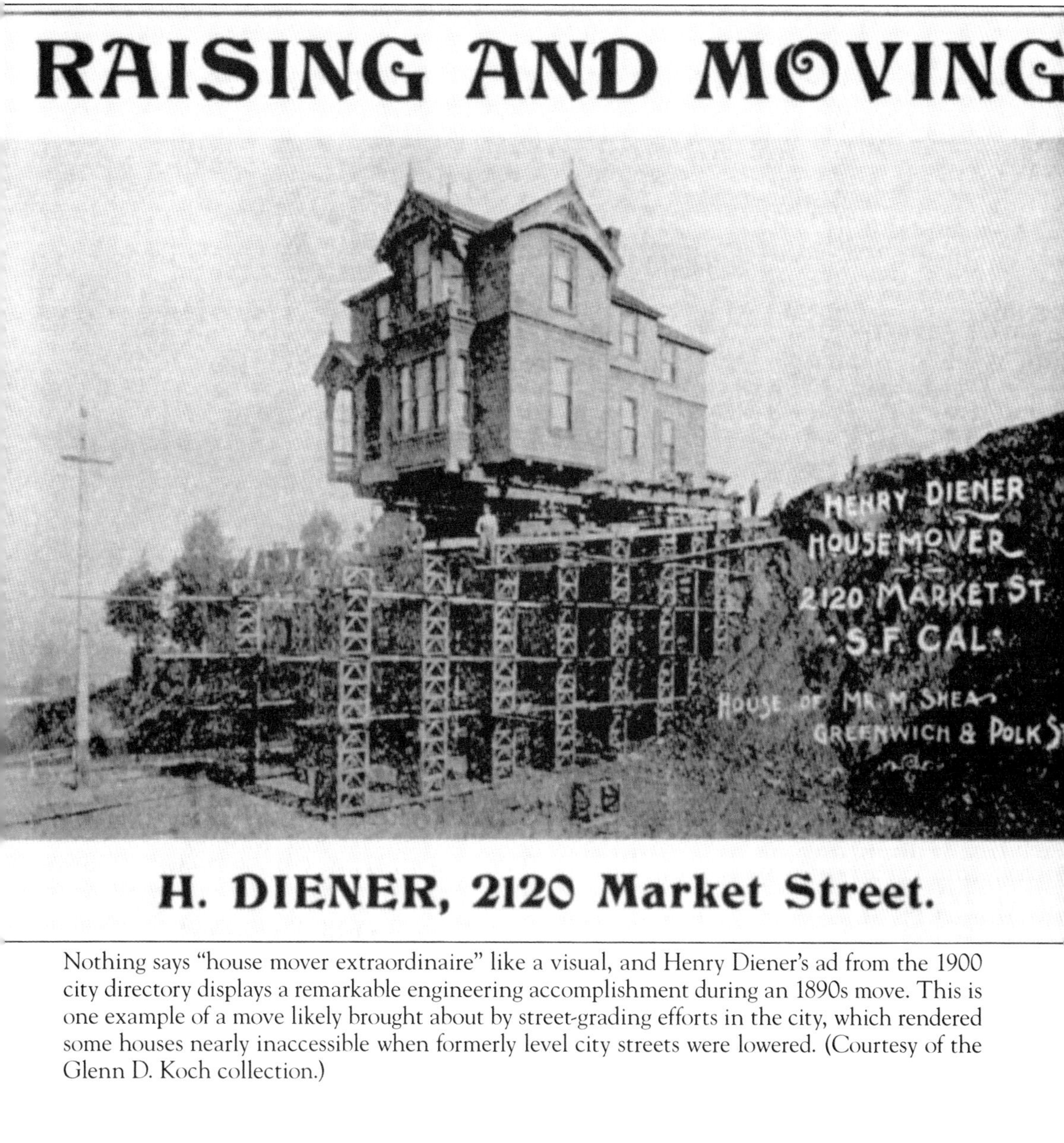

Nothing says "house mover extraordinaire" like a visual, and Henry Diener's ad from the 1900 city directory displays a remarkable engineering accomplishment during an 1890s move. This is one example of a move likely brought about by street-grading efforts in the city, which rendered some houses nearly inaccessible when formerly level city streets were lowered. (Courtesy of the Glenn D. Koch collection.)

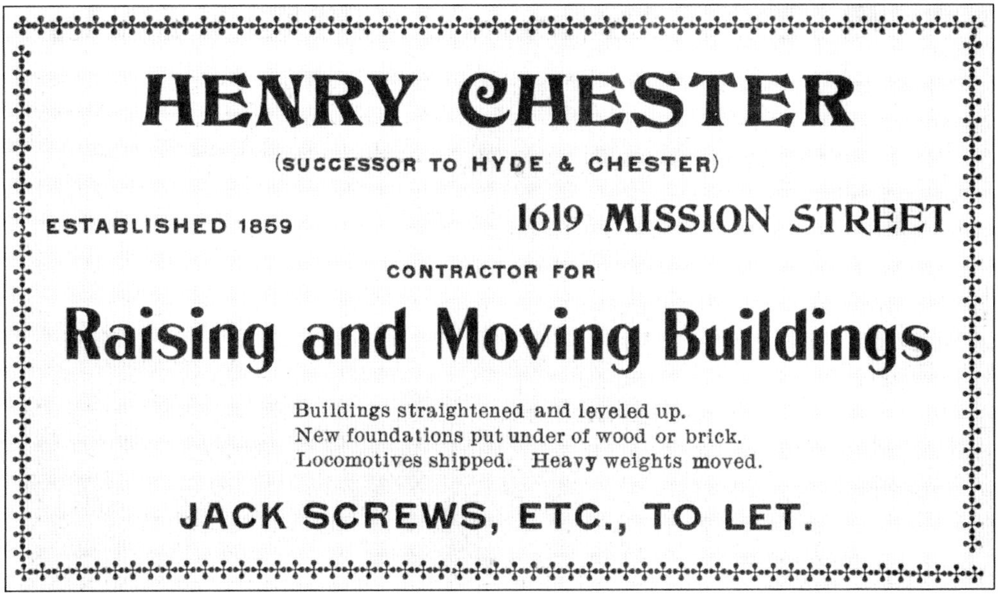

One of many house-moving court cases involved house movers Henry Chester and Patrick Gleason, who alleged that a new tax favored consortia of movers and stifled independents. Some 11 firms had joined together as one umbrella group in order to only pay a single tax. Chester and Gleason formed their own firm as copartners of San Francisco Housemovers' Company No. 1, under which they then obtained a single license. (Courtesy of the Glenn D. Koch collection.)

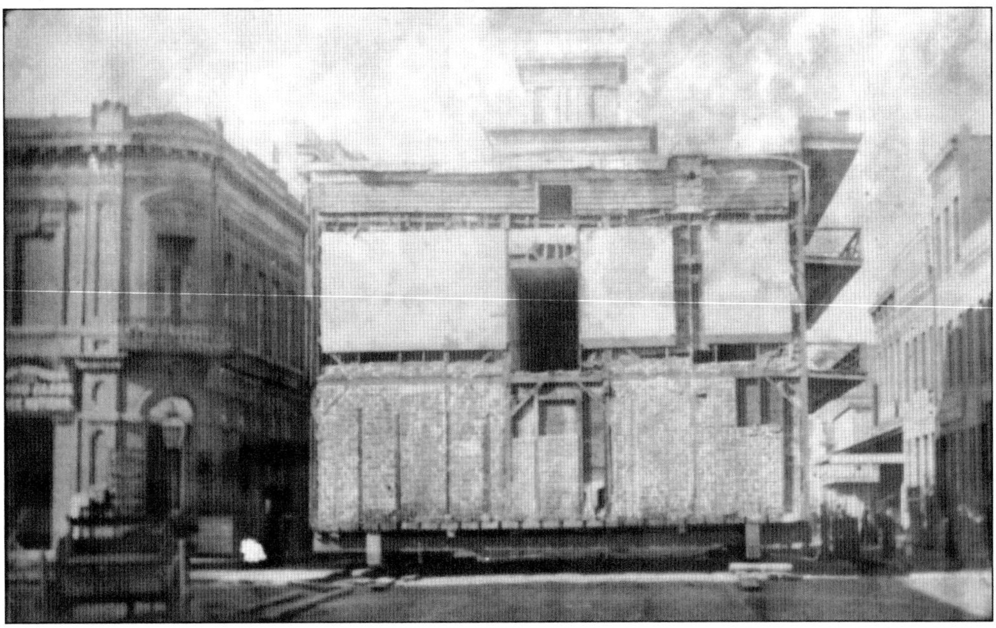

In 1866, this building blocked the whole street. Mark Twain, in the *San Francisco Daily Morning Call*, decried these increasingly common scenarios. He wrote, "For several days a vagrant two-story frame house has been wandering listlessly about Commercial Street, above this office, and she has finally stopped in the middle of the thoroughfare, and is staring dejectedly toward Montgomery street, as if she would like to go down there, but really do not feel equal to the exertion." (Courtesy of the Library of Congress.)

Mayor Frank McCoppin was the first official to publicly decry the impact of moving houses, blaming the city's deteriorating streets on "excessive house moving." An 1858 news report stated, "Pavements are cut up into ruts by the weight of the buildings hauled over them and teams are driven over the sidewalks to the damage, and sometimes total destruction, of planking and curbstones. Not infrequently the moving of a single old frame, worth lest than $100, will cost three times that amount of injury, for which the public have the whole bill to foot." (Courtesy of Philip Brent Digital Art and Photography.)

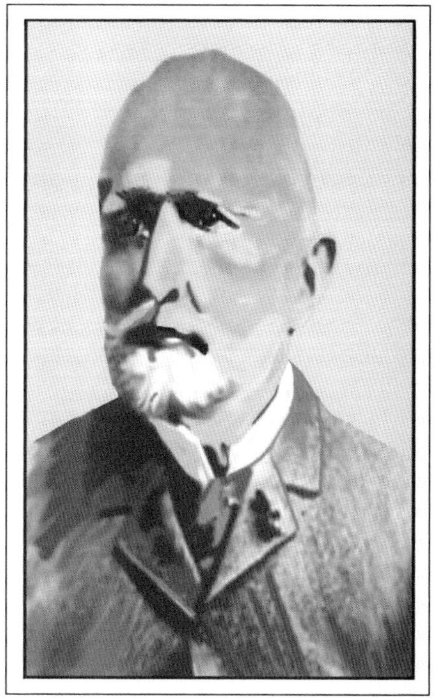

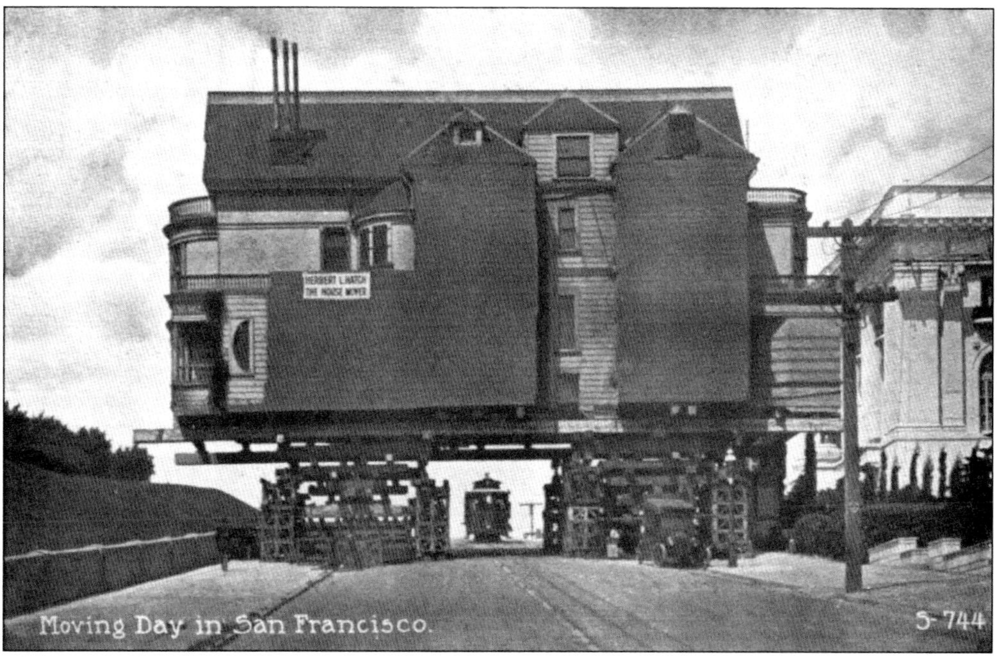

This is one of history's as-yet-unsolved mysteries. One collection identifies it as a building moved for the Spreckles Mansion in the 1890s, but the Spreckles residence (seen here on the right) was not built until 1913. Additionally, newspaper accounts from July 1913 report that Herbert L. Hatch sought permission to move an unnamed home in this same vicinity. The house sits at Washington Street between Octavia and Gough Streets. (Courtesy of the Glenn D. Koch collection, permission courtesy of the San Francisco Metropolitan Transit Authority.)

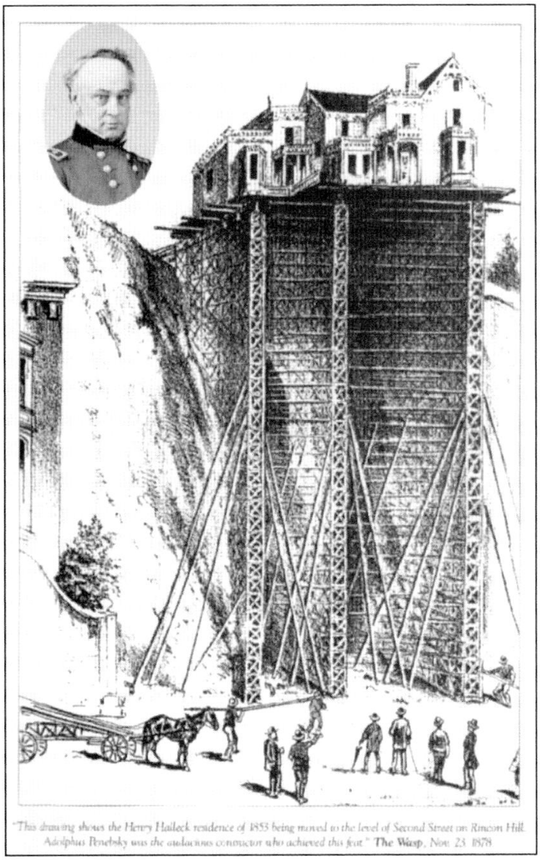

Street grading Rincon Hill left some lavish buildings, such as Henry Halleck's home, high and dry. This artist's rendering, illustrated originally in the *Wasp* on November 23, 1878, shows Henry Halleck's residence supported by box cribs during its move to the level of Second Street. Cribbing is often used in building moves, along with pneumatic or hydraulic shoring. House owner General Halleck's image is in the upper-left corner. (Courtesy of Philip Brent Digital Art and Photography.)

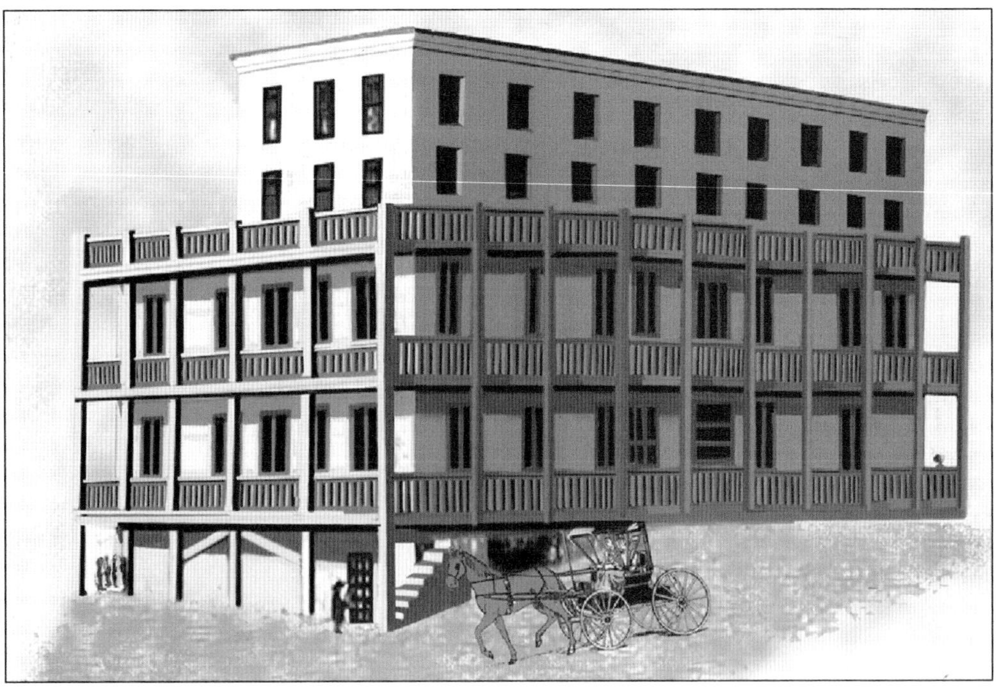

This is a digital rendering of what was the Graham House. The four-story wooden building, lined on two sides by continuous balconies, was shipped in sections from Baltimore and set up on the corner of Kearny and Pacific Streets. It was purchased for $150,000 on April 1, 1850, to serve as San Francisco City Hall. Executive and judicial offices were placed on the upper floors. It burned to the ground in the fire of June 1851. (Courtesy of Philip Brent Digital Art and Photography.)

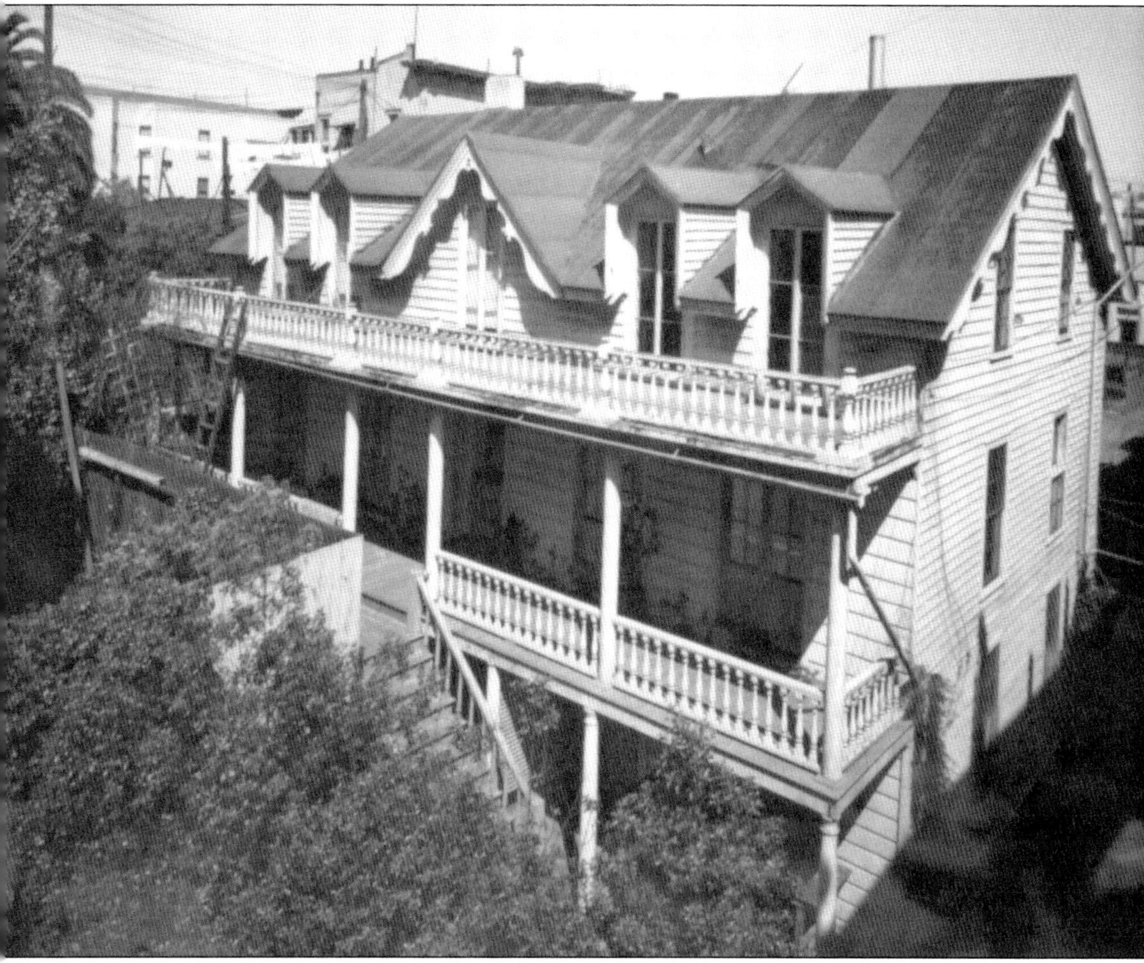

The Phelps House was shipped in pieces to San Francisco via Cape Horn. A 1934 account states that it was "built in 1850 and brought round the Horn from Maine, there being no sawmills here at the time." However, Abner Phelps's great-granddaughter maintained that the house had been purchased in New Orleans in 1850 and was shipped in sections from Louisiana. (Courtesy of the San Francisco History Center, San Francisco Public Library.)

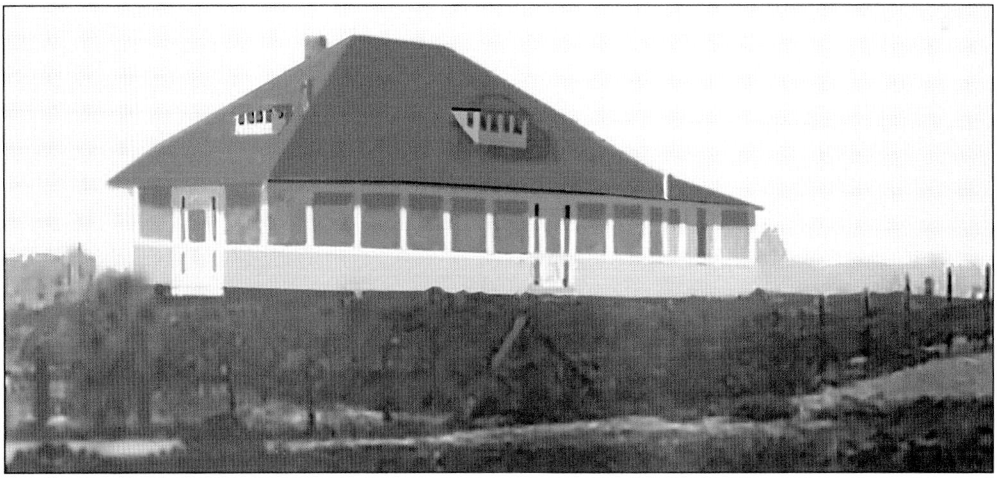

This is a digital rendering of what is today's Turk Station Lodge. In 1910, the plantation-style home was moved from the docks in San Francisco to its present location at Turk Station in Coalinga. The house was originally destined for an unknown location in the Pacific Rim, but the deal fell through. The owners of Pleasant Valley Farming Company purchased the home, and a mule train moved it to its present site. (Courtesy of Philip Brent Digital Art and Photography.)

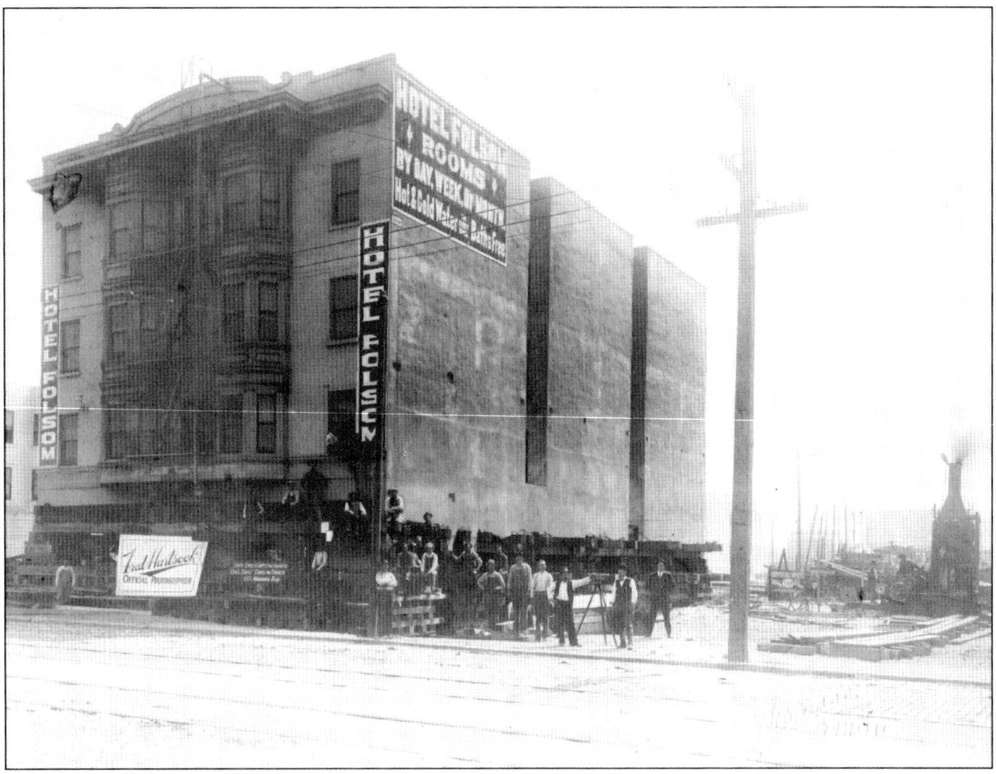

Soon after it was completed in 1907, the Hotel Folsom began sinking in the unstable South of Market soil. It was moved one lot over while pilings were driven into the ground to stabilize it, and a new foundation was created (along with a new commercial first floor, seen in this photograph) on the now-reinforced lot. Then the building was returned to the site. It remains a hotel today, with a new name. (Courtesy of the John Freeman collection.)

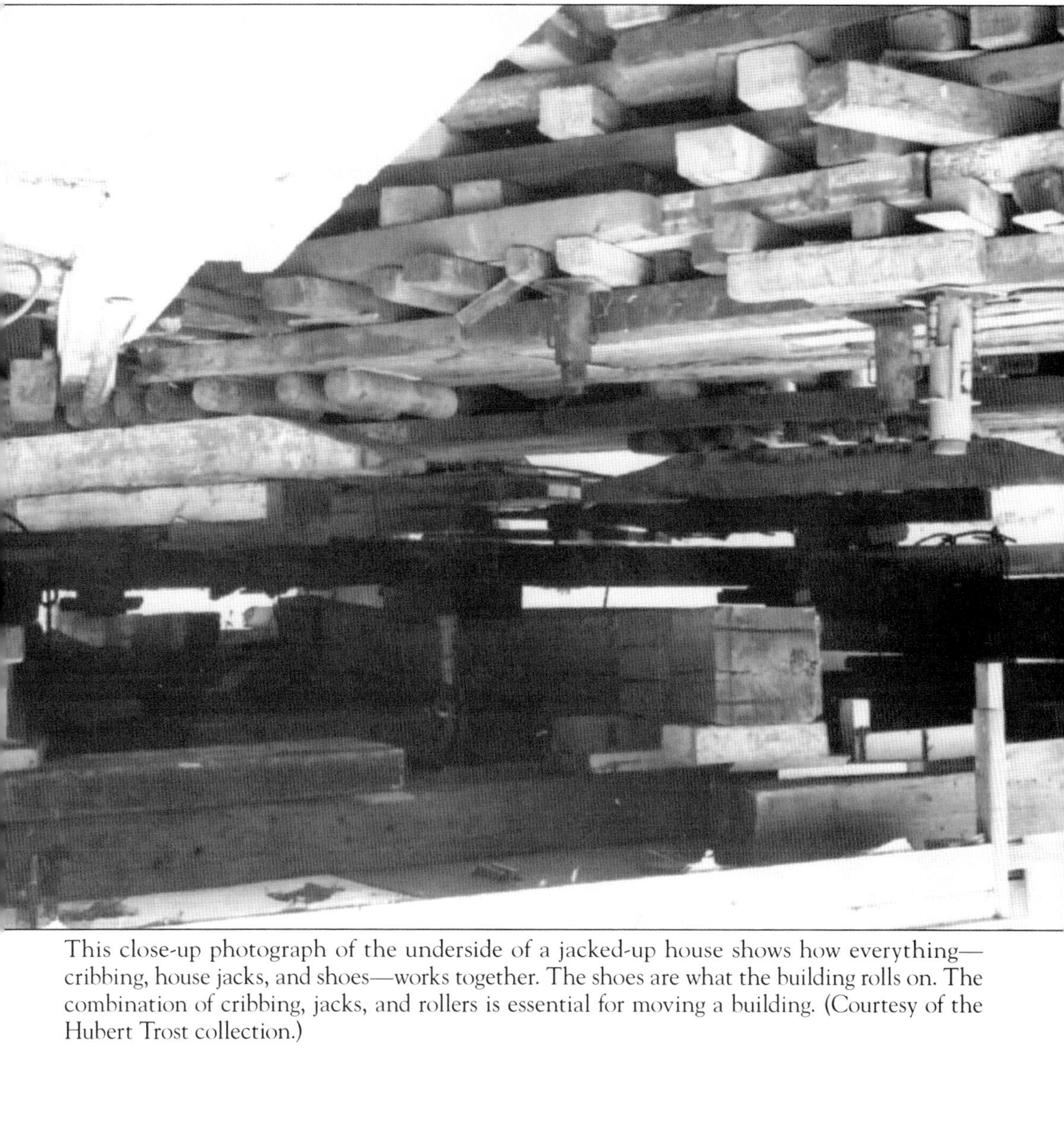

This close-up photograph of the underside of a jacked-up house shows how everything—cribbing, house jacks, and shoes—works together. The shoes are what the building rolls on. The combination of cribbing, jacks, and rollers is essential for moving a building. (Courtesy of the Hubert Trost collection.)

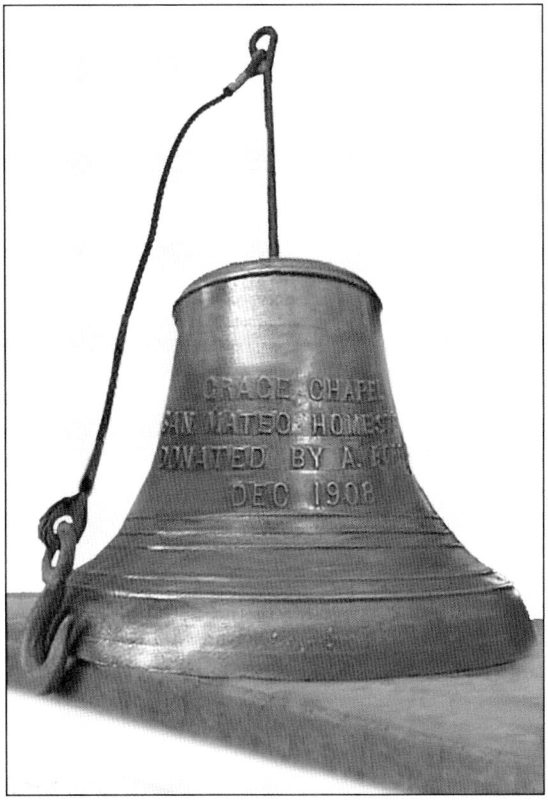

Buildings were not the only things moving in 1908 San Francisco. The W.T. Garrett & Co. foundry created a 300-pound bell for Grace Church, located at El Camino and Highway 92. In the 1950s, the Hillbarn Theater used the bell to end intermissions. In 1968, it moved to Foster City. In 2004, it was stolen. In 2010, it was discovered at a scrap shop in San Leandro and returned to Foster City. (Courtesy of Philip Brent Digital Art and Photography.)

In 1912, the Union Iron Works office building stood in the way of a new powerhouse, prompting the biggest moving effort of its times. The company picked up the 10-foot-deep, 50-foot-high, four-story building, placed it on the barge seen here, and floated it to nearby Hunter's Point. When a yard packed with heavy materials limited access to the barge, the workers simply jacked the structure nine feet high and moved the building over the obstacles. (Courtesy of the John Freeman collection.)

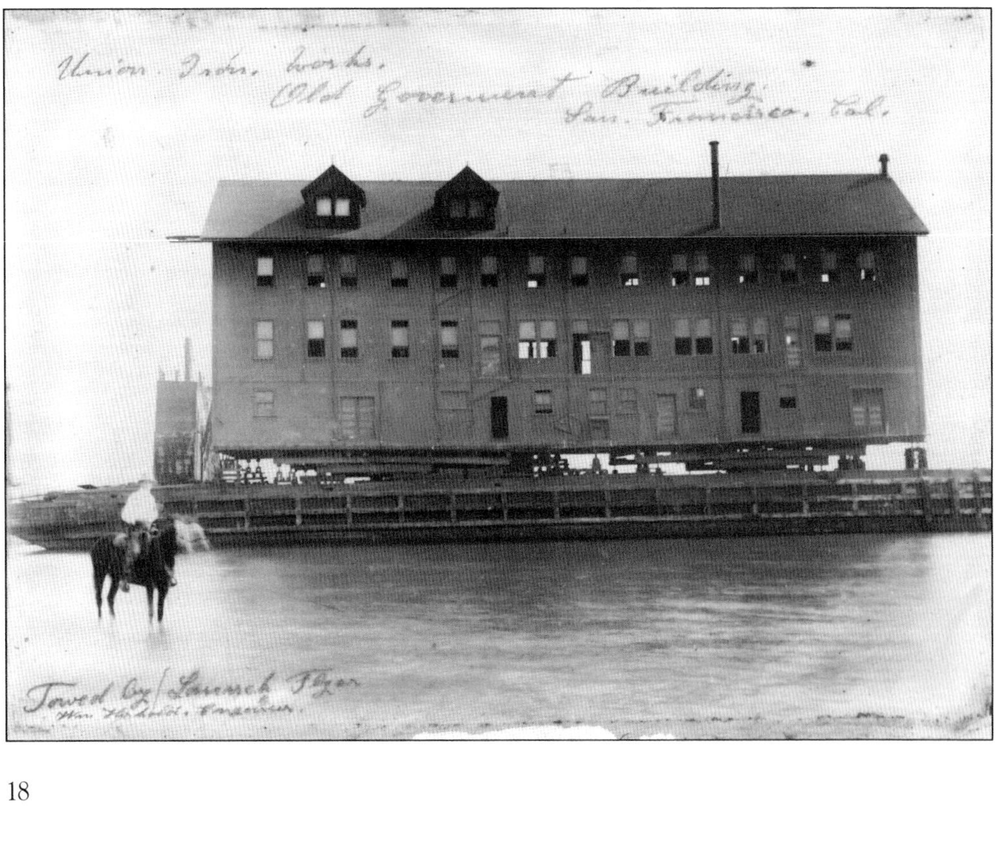

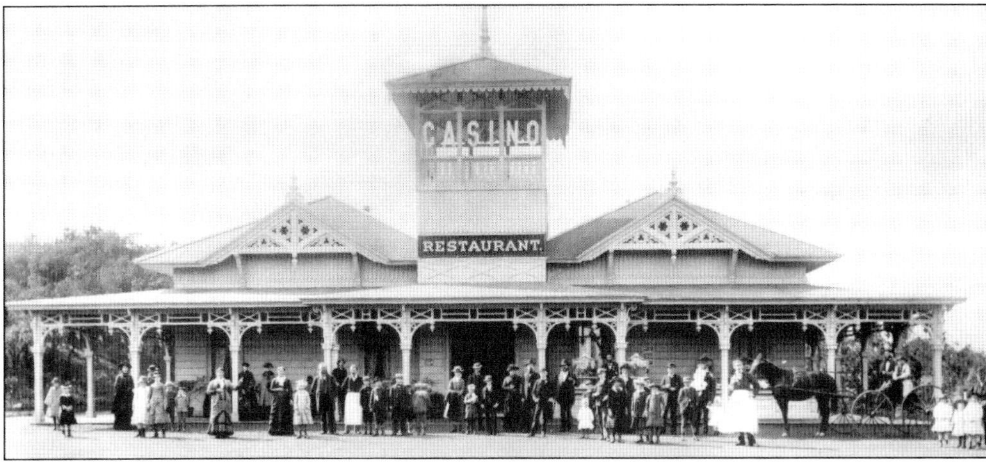

In 1882, the Daeman brothers built the Casino Restaurant and Bar in Golden Gate Park. This is a photograph of the original Casino. While it was a moneymaker for the family who later leased it, its reputation for serving liquor conflicted with the city's image of a family-oriented tourist attraction, and the pressure was on to move it away from the center of park activities. (Courtesy of a private collection.)

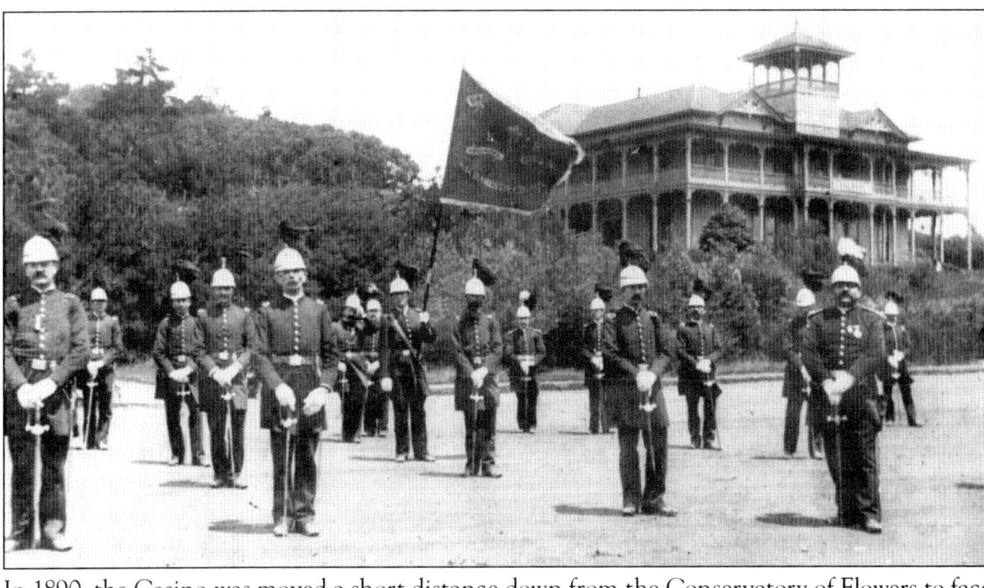

In 1890, the Casino was moved a short distance down from the Conservatory of Flowers to face today's John F. Kennedy Drive and was raised up one story. Still, its reputation as a saloon rankled those who viewed it as an immoral establishment. In this location, its service as a casino was very short-lived. It temporarily became a museum until the two-story Casino was moved to the end of the speedway to become a clubhouse. (Courtesy of a private collection.)

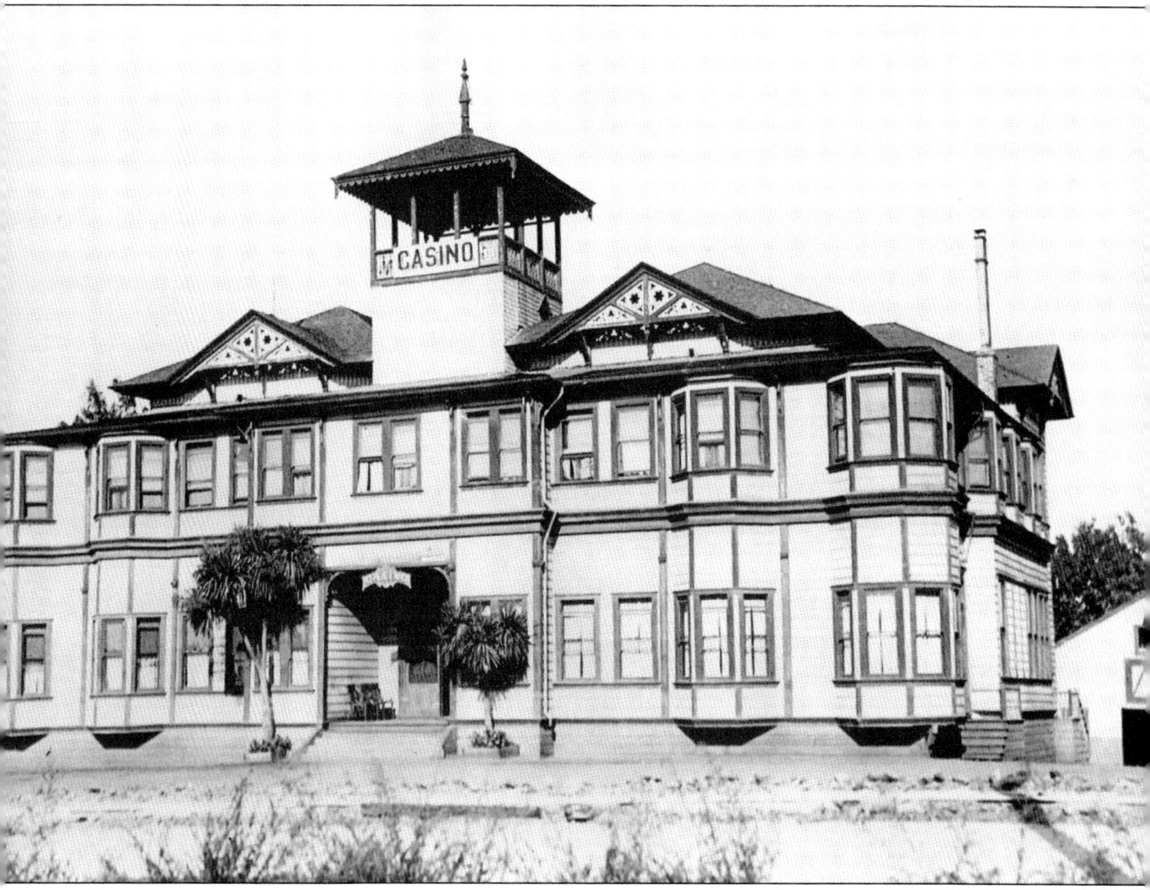

Here is the revamped Casino with its new second story. In 1896, Stewart Menzies bought the building and moved it out of the park to the corner of Twenty-Fourth Avenue and Fulton Street, where he ran it as a popular and lively roadhouse—a much more acceptable venture when removed from the public eye of Golden Gate Park. (Courtesy of a private collection.)

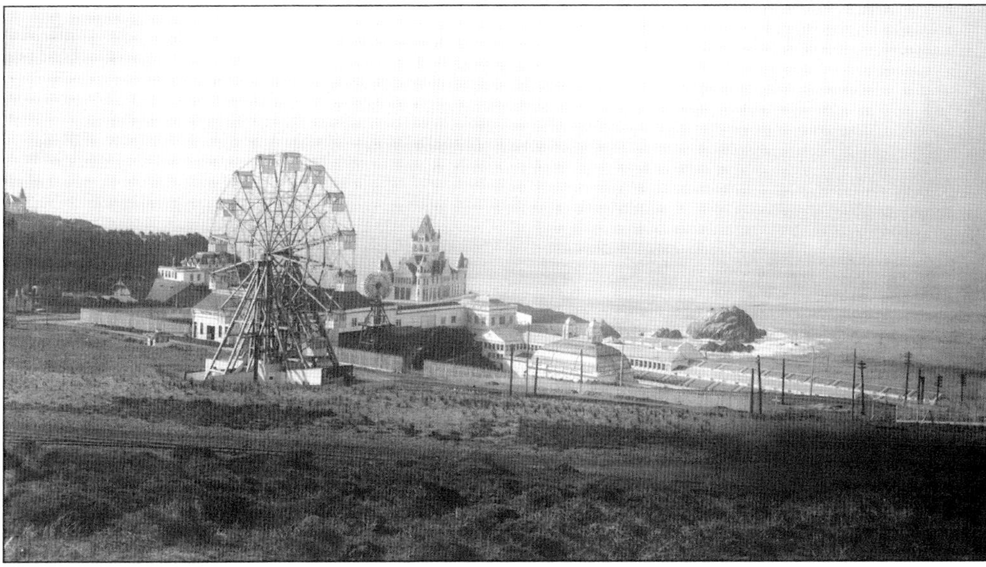

The Firth Wheel was one of the most popular crowd-pleasers at the 1894 California Midwinter International Exposition. George Ferris originally invented the ride for the Columbian Exposition. M.H. de Young got J.K. Firth & Co. to make him a smaller one for the exposition. After the exposition ended, Sutro arranged for it to be transported to his property. Mover James Bain was killed in the process. (Courtesy of the Dennis O'Rorke collection.)

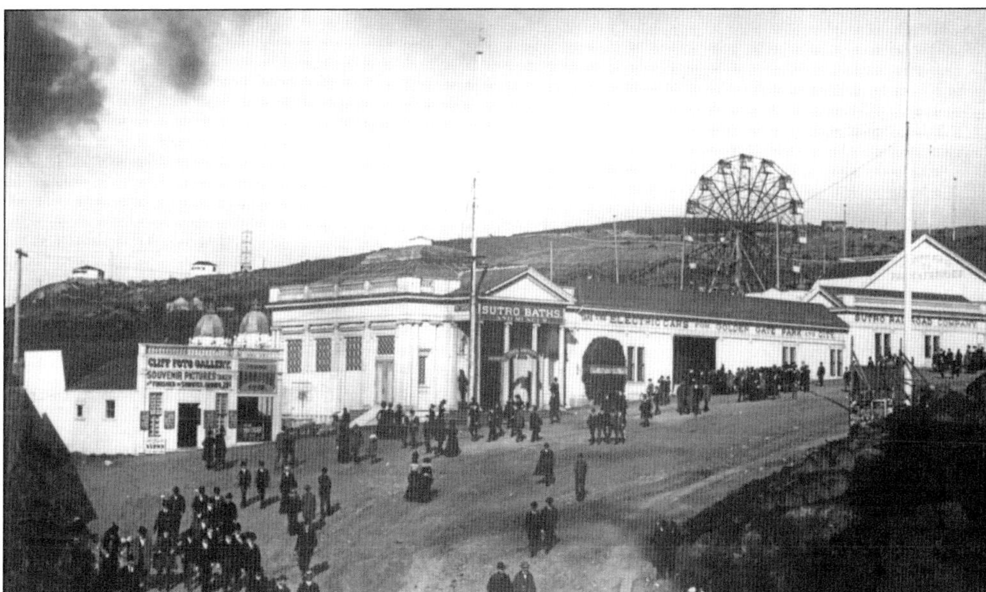

The Firth Wheel installed at Adolph Sutro's midway complex was 100 feet in diameter, had 16 carriages, and offered dramatic seaside views for those who took its 20-minute-long ride. The massive wheel, illuminated by hundreds of electric lights, even acted as a beacon for ships approaching the Golden Gate at night. Seventeen years later, Sutro's investment proved unprofitable, and the wheel was torn down after years of neglect. (Courtesy of the Dennis O'Rorke collection.)

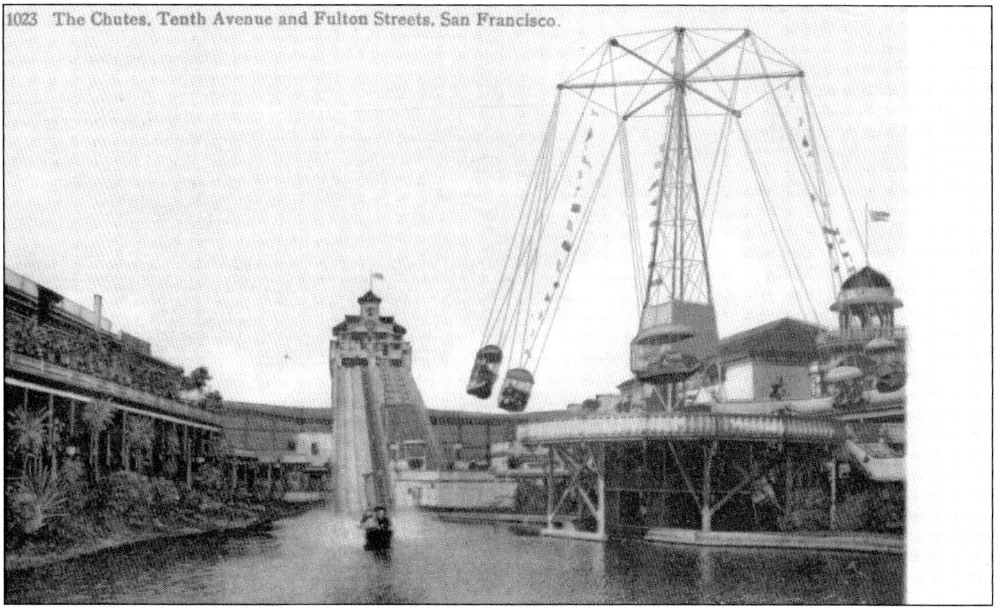

An amusement park does not move like a building; it must be disassembled and rebuilt each time. The Chutes saw three locations between its 1895 opening on Haight Street and its final location at Fillmore and Fulton Streets in 1911. Attractions were modified to suit their new locales, and some never were reassembled. This postcard depicts the Chutes at Tenth Avenue and Fulton Street in its second location, from 1902 to 1908. (Author's collection.)

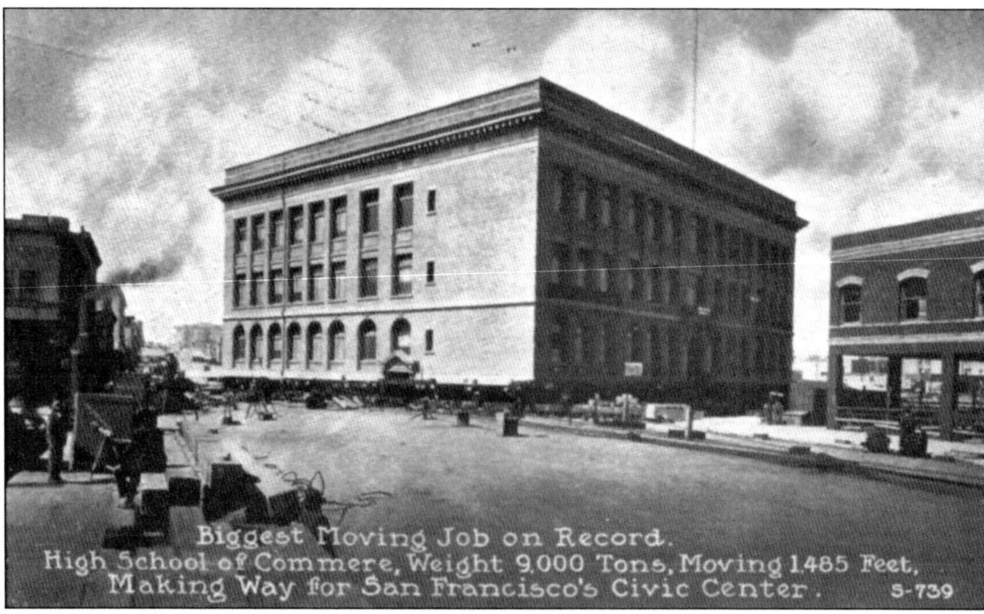

In 1913, the proposal of a new civic center in San Francisco prompted the move of a huge structure weighing some 9,000 tons, billed as "the biggest moving job on record." The 67,000-square-foot building, designed by architect Newton Tharp in 1907, was completed in 1910. Only two years later, in 1913, Commercial High, also known as High School of Commerce (misspelled on this postcard), was moved to 170 Fell Street. This vintage postcard shows the building jacked up and ready to go. (Courtesy of the Lew Baer collection, www.postcard.org.)

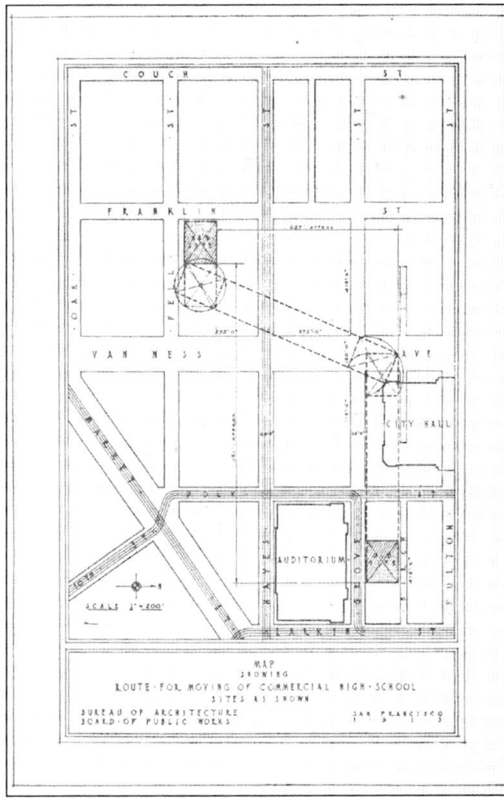

This 1913 map shows Commercial High's curious route. Its original location was mid-block on Grove Street. The building was moved across vacant land one and a half blocks to Van Ness Avenue, rotated 22.5 degrees in the middle of the intersection of Grove Street and Van Ness Avenue, and crossed two vacant blocks to mid-block on Fell Street, where it was rotated again before being placed on the northeast corner of Fell and Franklin Streets. (Courtesy of the John Freeman collection.)

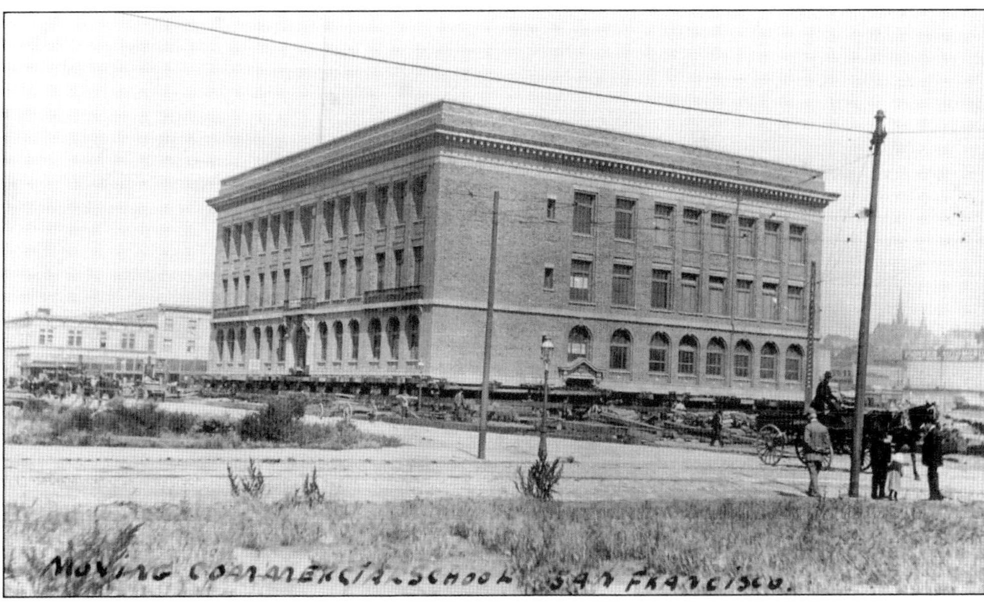

Many rollers, as seen in this photograph, were necessary in order to move a building the size of Commercial High. Movers used laurel rollers that were four feet long and eight inches in diameter. The shoes rested on these rollers and were extra long at the heavier front of the building to lend added support. Steam donkeys provided the power to pull the cables. (Courtesy of the John Freeman collection.)

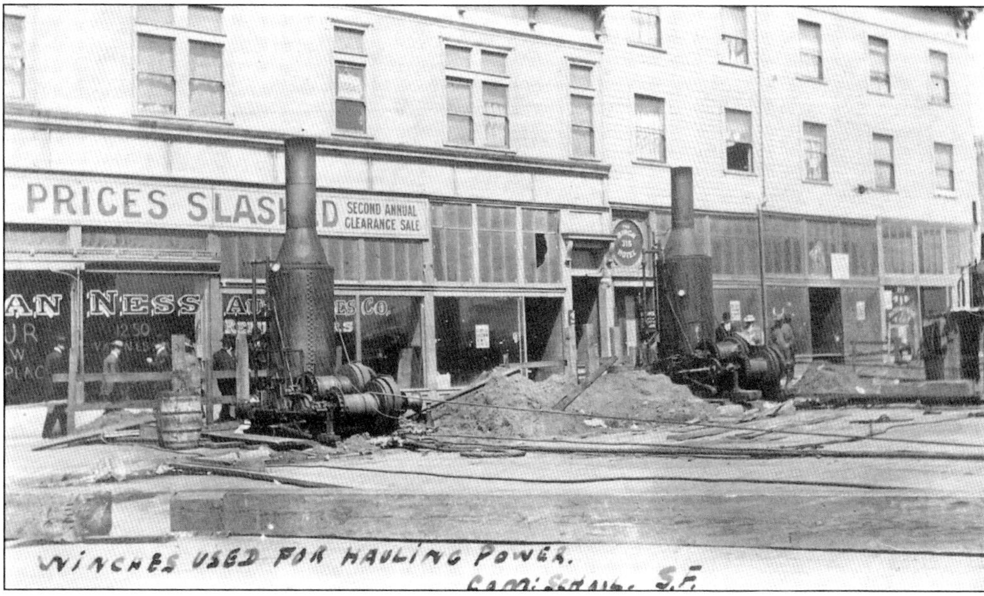

This photograph shows how steam donkeys were used for winching and pulling buildings during moves. The 50-horsepower, double-spooled donkey engines pulled one-fourth-inch cable. This tackle pulled on the main cable, which was seven-eighths of an inch thick and rated at 27 tons. The main cable pulled on the eveners, which applied force at the rear of the building to actually push it, preventing the platform from being pulled apart during the move. (Courtesy of the John Freeman collection.)

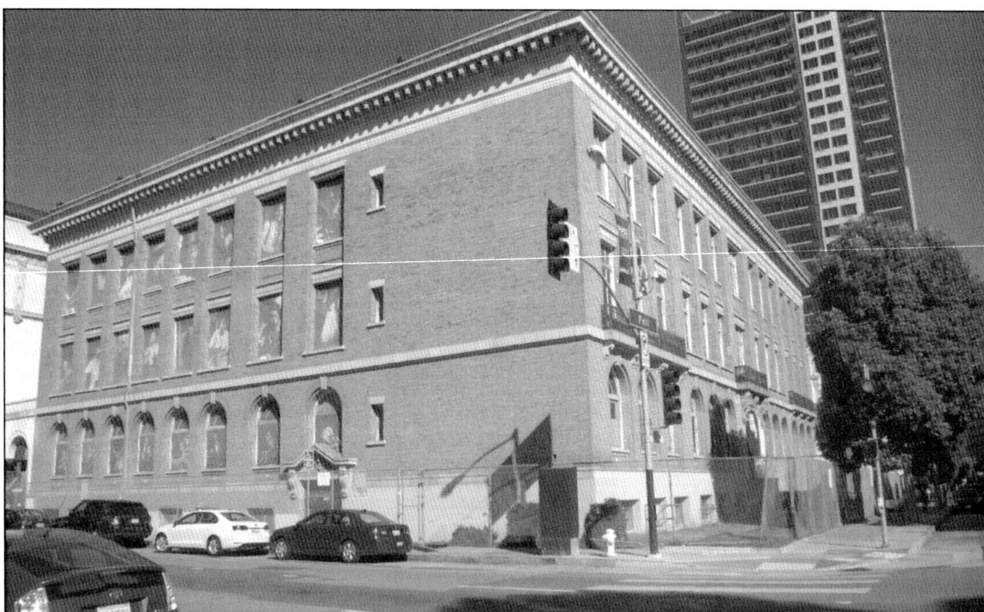

The Newton J. Tharp Commercial School was named in honor of Tharp's many design contributions. In 1951, the school housed the San Francisco Unified School District's administrative offices, but in 1989, the building was damaged in the Loma Prieta earthquake. Unable to qualify for federal money to retrofit it because the damage was not quite up to the red-tag criteria, the school at 170 Fell Street remains boarded up and unsafe for use. (Photograph by Beni C. Bacon.)

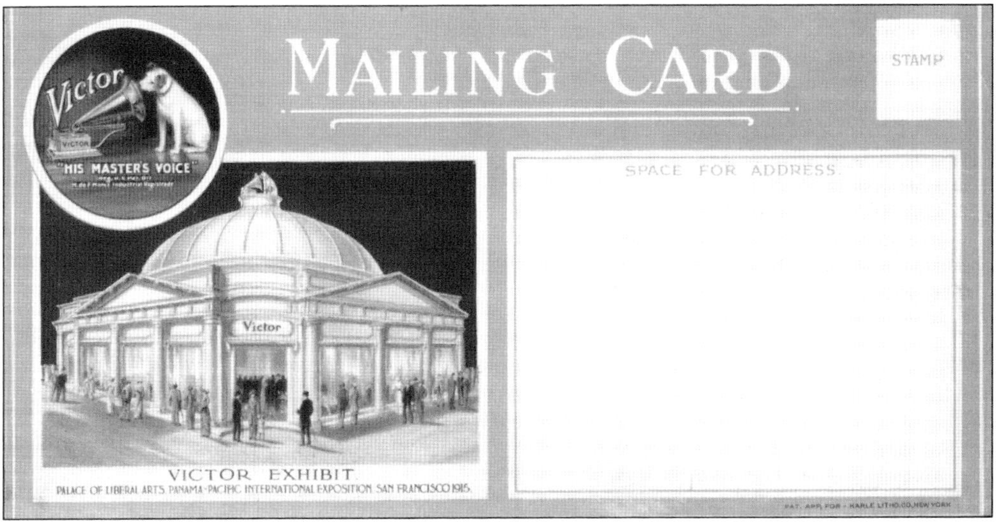

This postcard is the only surviving image of the Victor Talking Machine Company's pavilion inside the Palace of Liberal Arts, before it was moved from the Panama–Pacific International Exposition (PPIE). The talking machine represented high technology in 1915. Regularly scheduled piano and vocal recitals alternated with recordings chosen from a library of over 7,000 78-rpm discs played on the turntables of two hand-painted Victrola consoles. (Courtesy of the Glenn D. Koch collection.)

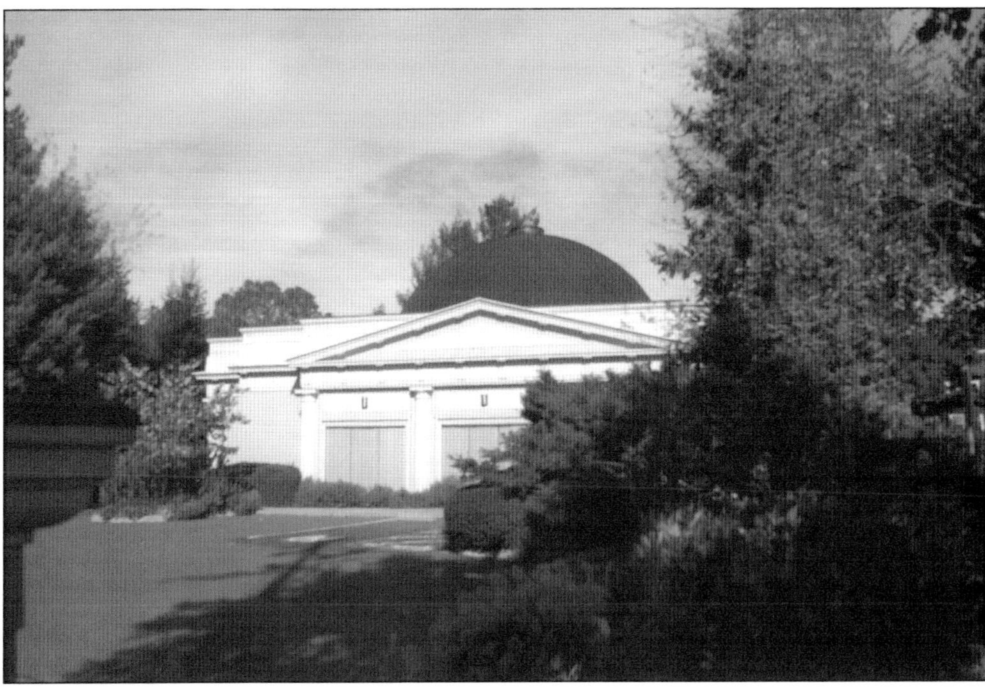

When the exposition ended in 1916, the pavilion was dismantled, barged across San Francisco Bay to San Rafael, and floated up the San Rafael Canal to the home of Leon Douglass, who eventually sold it to the San Rafael Improvement Club for $500. Members had it moved a second time to its current location. This image shows the back end of the pavilion building, which is behind a fence and surrounded by shrubbery. (Photograph by Beni C. Bacon.)

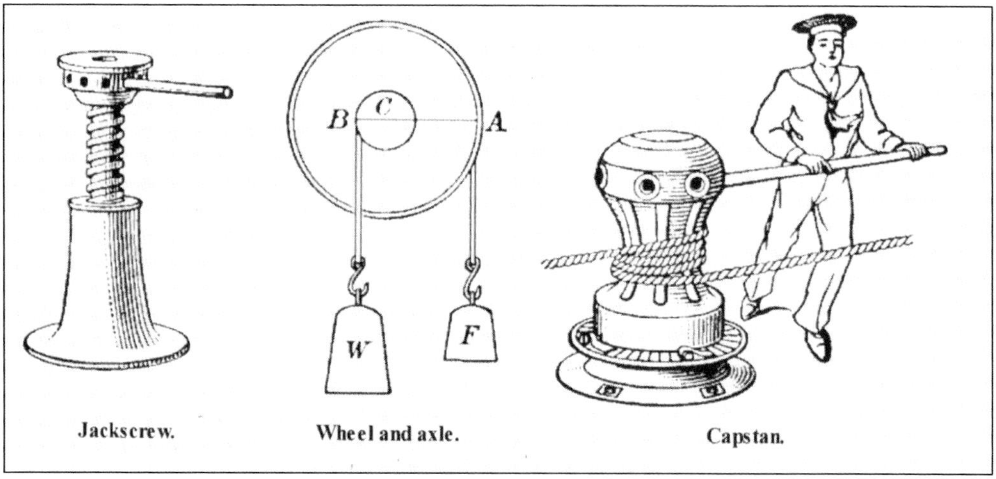

Early moving equipment consisted of jackscrews, capstans, cables, and winches. Hydraulic, computer-assisted jacks are used today, but early lower-tech jackscrews were manually turned to lift the structure off its foundation. Capstans turned via two-horse teams. As the horses circled, stepping over the cable each time, the cable would slowly pull up on the capstan and move the house. Horses were preferred until the 1940s, when trucks began using gear-driven winches powered by engines. This image from *Mechanics* magazine, published in London in 1824. (Courtesy of the Glenn D. Koch collection.)

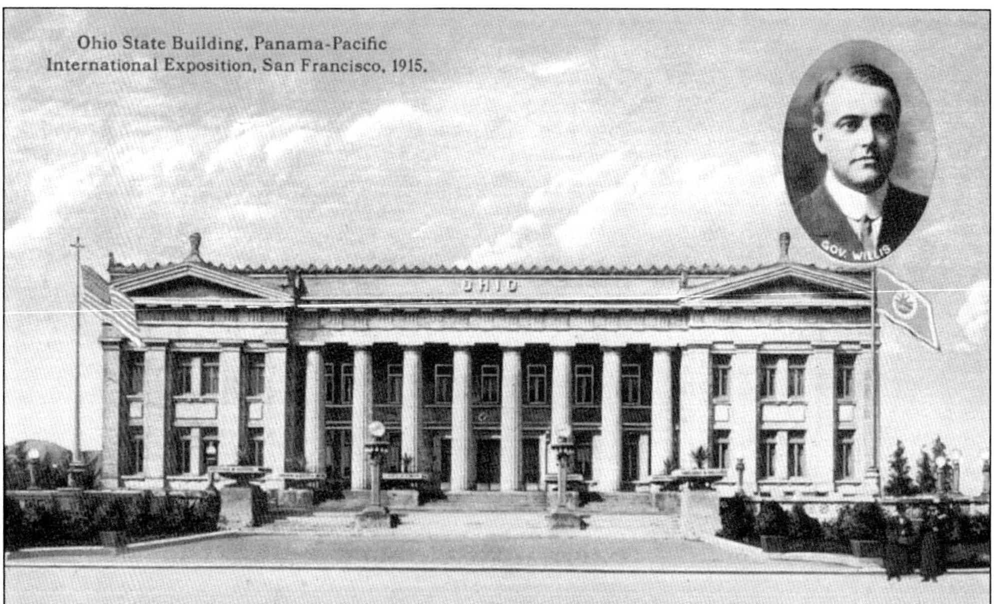

The Ohio State Building at the 1915 Panama–Pacific International Exposition was a replica of the state's capitol building in Columbus. After the fair ended, it was purchased by group of investors who barged it 30 miles down the San Francisco Bay to the San Carlos Harbor to make it into a clubhouse. Mover Herbert L. Hatch stated that the 800-ton, 133-by-85-foot Ohio State Building was the "largest, heaviest piece of freight ever transported on salt water." (Courtesy of the Glenn D. Koch collection.)

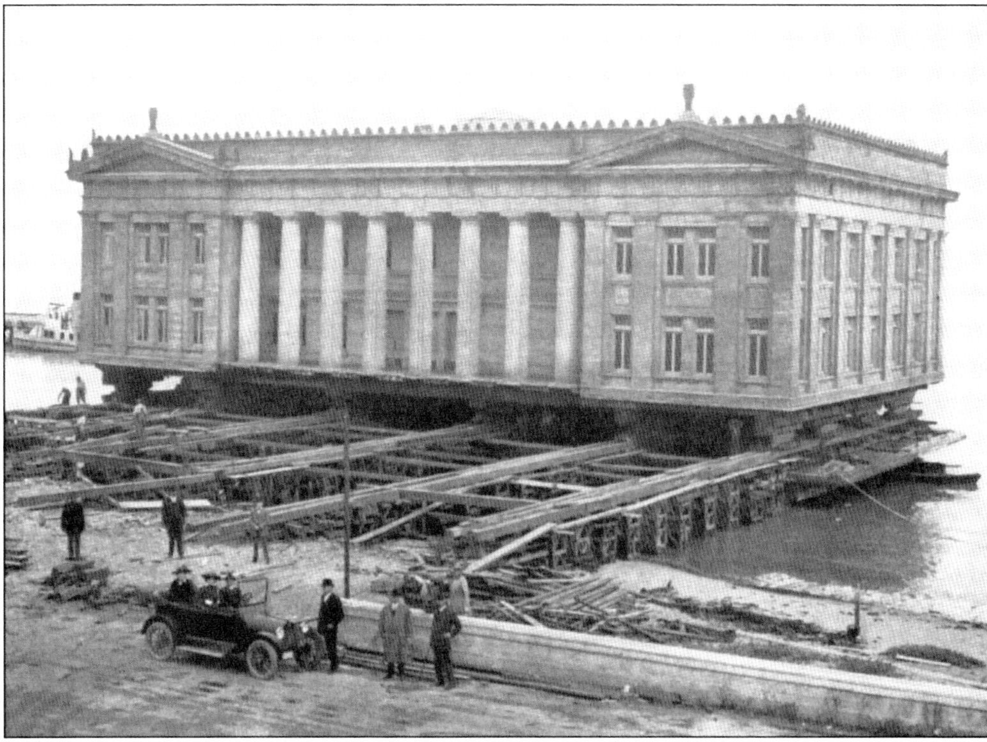

The Ohio State Building was one of the largest of the state buildings at the PPIE. Here, it is being moved from shore onto the barges at the water's edge. The building sat 600 feet back from the beach at the exposition. It had to be raised (using 170 jackscrews) and moved (via 250 rollers). It was pulled onto the barges by horses hitched to house-moving capstans. (Courtesy of the Glenn D. Koch collection.)

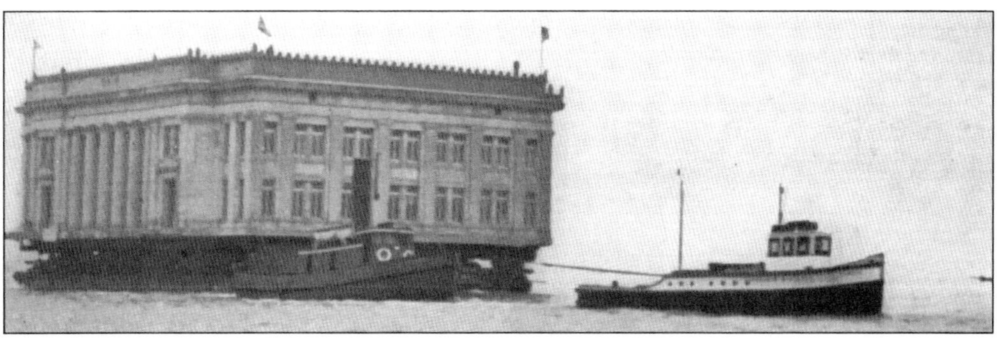

At low tide, the Ohio State Building was lowered onto two 500-ton barges. When the tide rose, several tugboats moved it downstream, but unusually strong winds carried the barge past its destination, and it almost collided with the Dumbarton Bridge. It was moved into position at high tide and settled onto its foundation when the tide went out. Filled land created the base for a new ground floor, converting the building from two stories to three. (Courtesy of the Glenn D. Koch collection.)

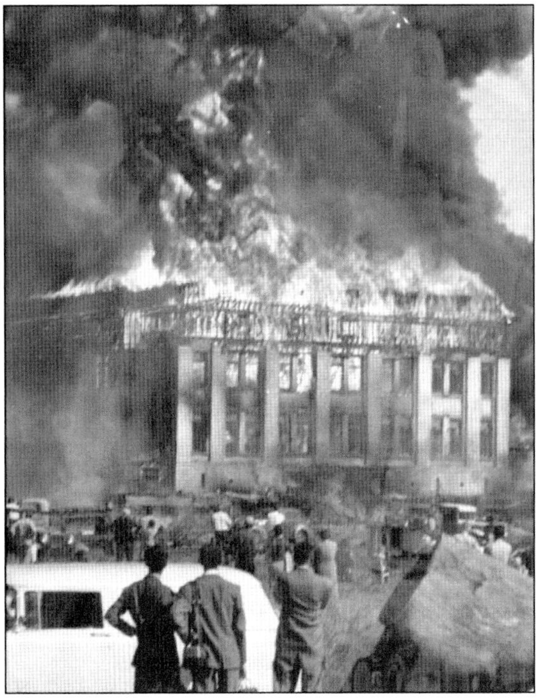

When the country club ran out of funds, the building was abandoned. Charles Cooley, who operated an airport next door, bought it but then decided to sell his airport. The building was slated to be moved again, but a dispute arose over how long it was taking. On December 14, 1956, the Ohio State Building was intentionally burned to the ground as the fastest way of clearing the property. This photograph captures its final fate. (Courtesy of the San Francisco History Center, San Francisco Public Library.)

The Lumbermen's Building and House of Hoo Hoo was moved from the PPIE to Monte Vista, about 40 miles south of San Francisco. The building was 100 feet long, covered in bark, and originally contained a lumbermen's exhibit. In 1916, it was taken apart, moved by the lumbermen, and reconstructed on the top of Inspiration Point. (Courtesy of the Glenn D. Koch collection.)

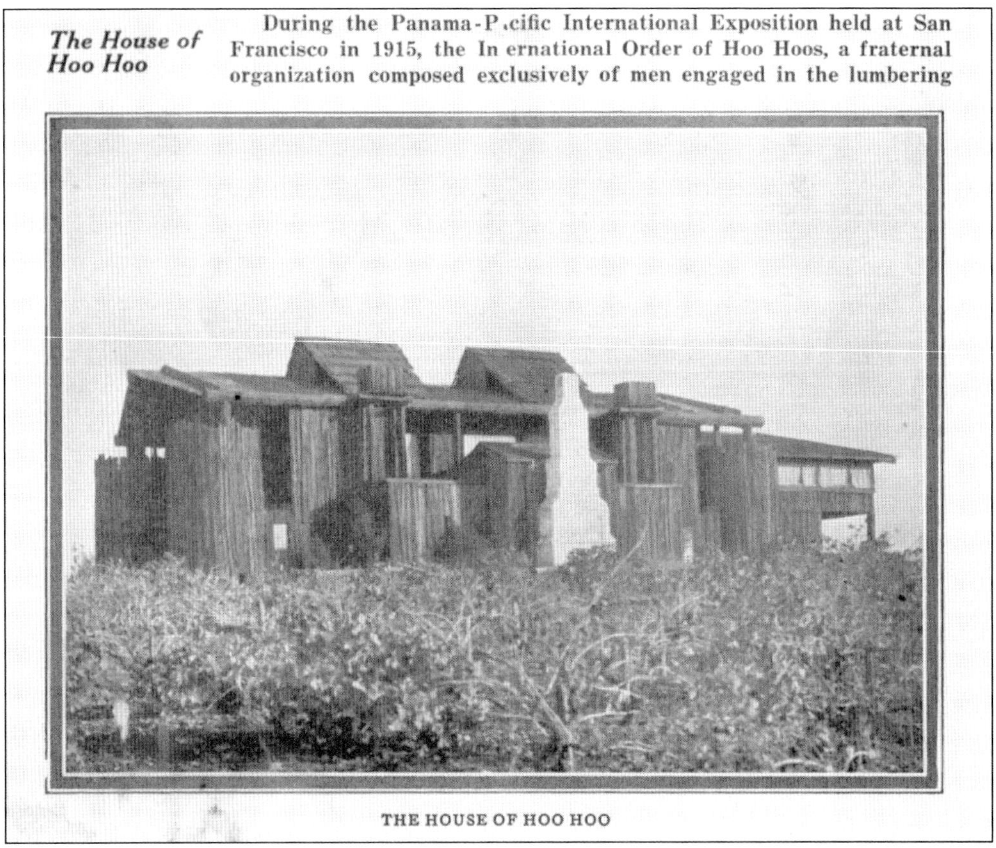

The House of Hoo Hoo

During the Panama-P.cific International Exposition held at San Francisco in 1915, the In ernational Order of Hoo Hoos, a fraternal organization composed exclusively of men engaged in the lumbering

THE HOUSE OF HOO HOO

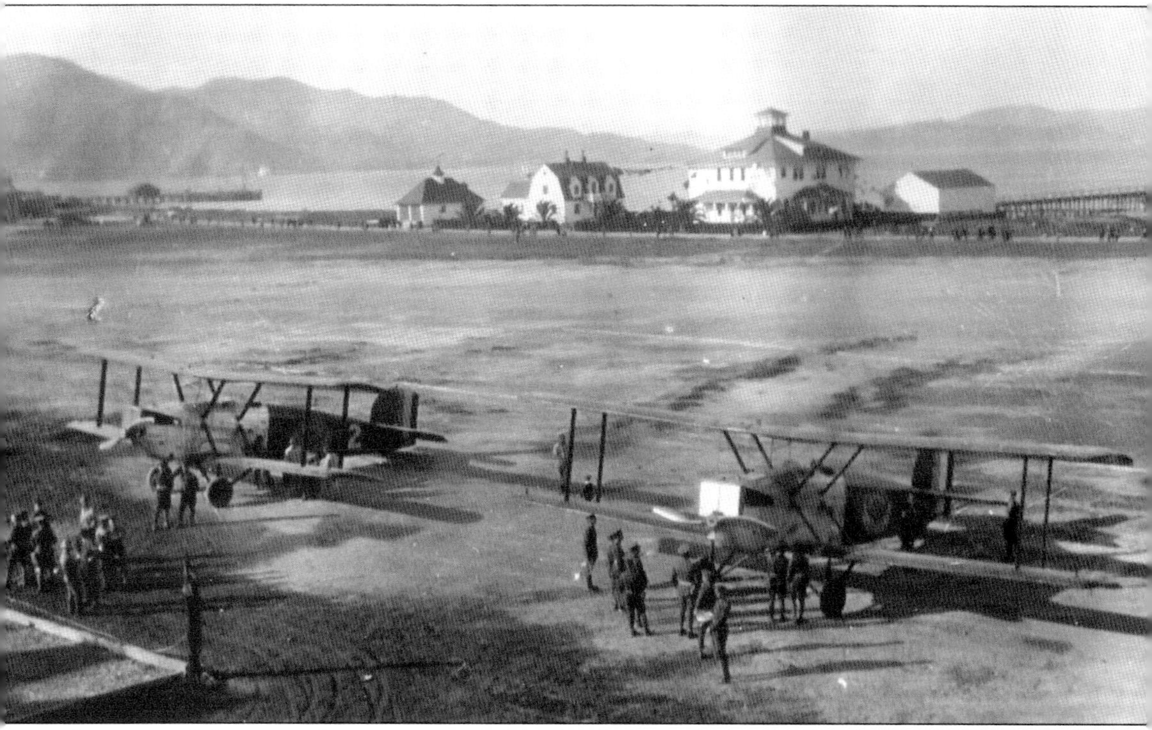

In 1914, work began on the construction of the Panama–Pacific International Exposition grounds on the San Francisco waterfront, including the lower Presidio. The Fort Point Coast Guard Station became an obstacle to the exposition's plans for building a planked auto racetrack on the same site. This image shows the building in the background prior to the move, with the old airfield in the foreground. (Courtesy of the Robert W. Bowen collection and the Presidio Trust.)

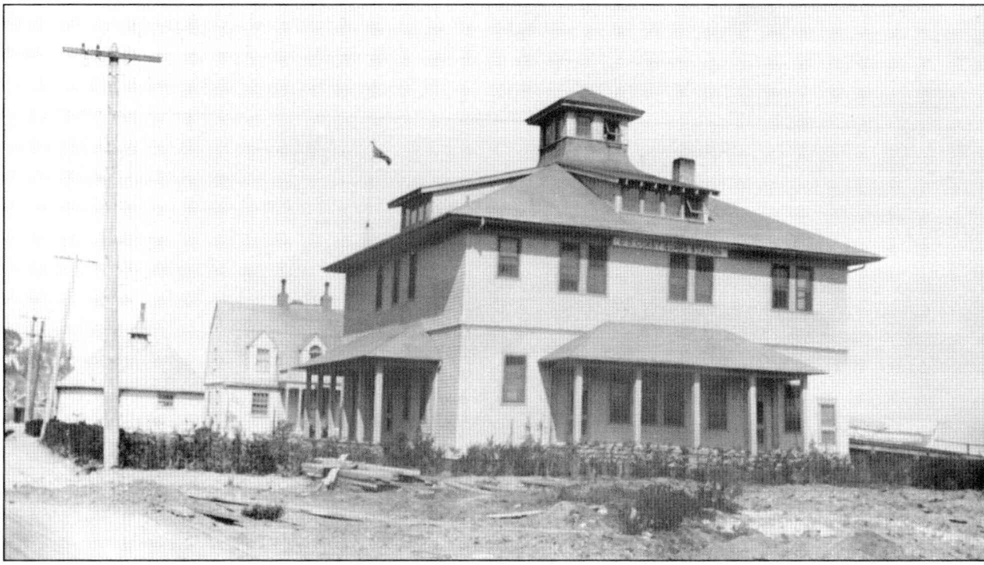

The PPIE bore the cost of moving the station 700 feet to its present location. It also cost the exposition $19,000 to install a new steel boat launch at the new site. This is another pre-move photograph of the old 1887 Coast Guard station, first established at the west end of Crissy Field and decommissioned in 1990. (Courtesy of the Robert W. Bowen collection and the Presidio Trust.)

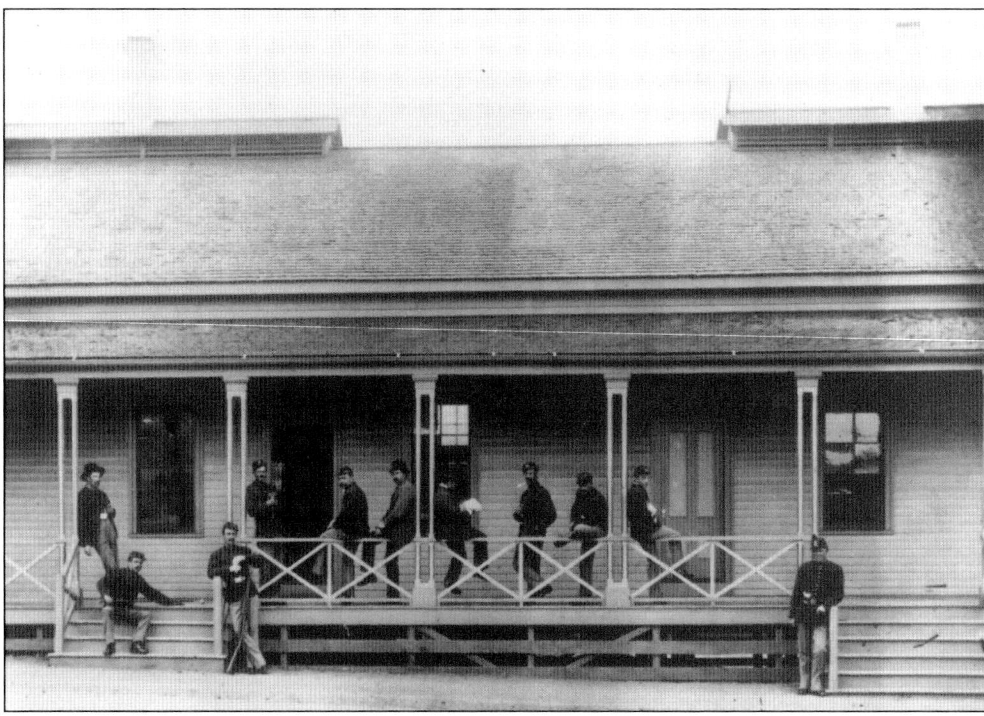

While today vertical moves in San Francisco are some of the last major building moves taking place in the city, vertical moves were also an integral part of early building relocation projects. This is the original barracks building in the Presidio, constructed in 1862 as part of the first major expansion of the Presidio. (Courtesy of the Presidio Trust.)

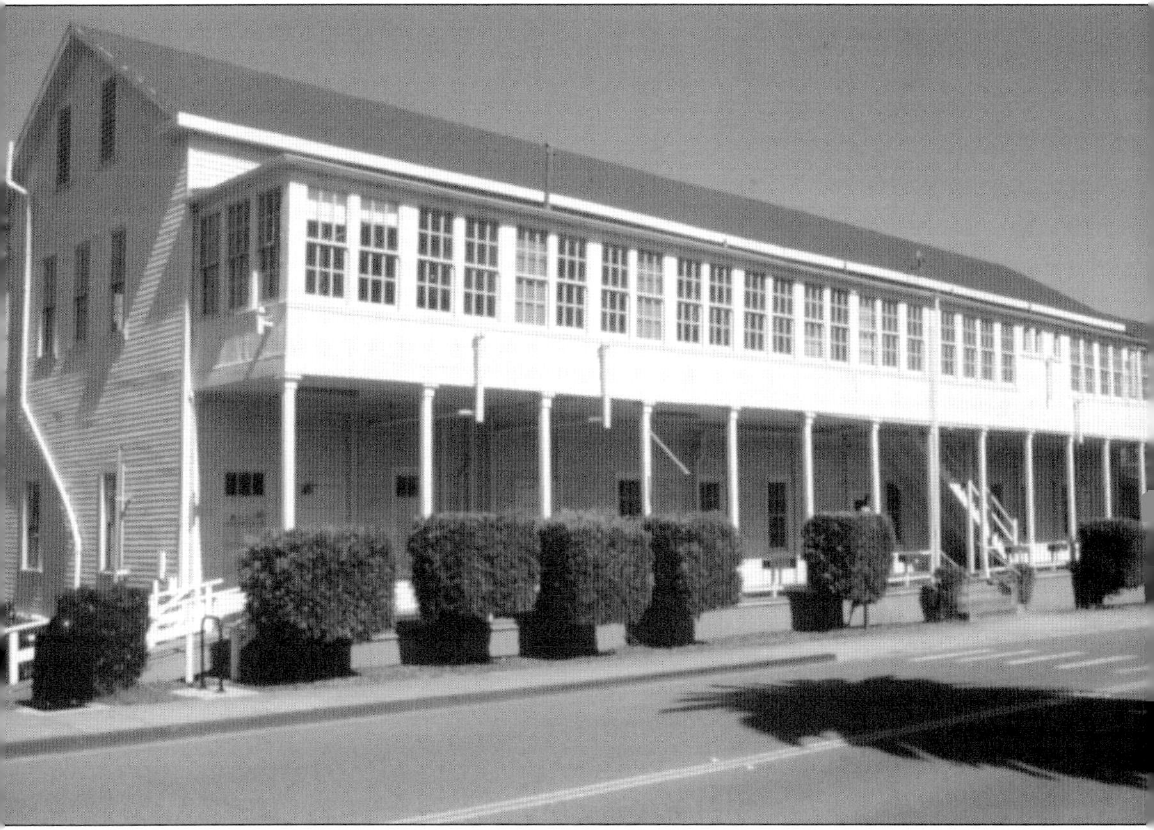

The specifics have been lost, but in 1885, the Presidio barracks received an additional story, either by removing the roof and making a new story on top of the old one or by jacking up the original building and constructing a new first floor. If the former is the case, very little of the original 1882 design is left. This is a modern photograph of the barracks today. (Courtesy of the Presidio Trust.)

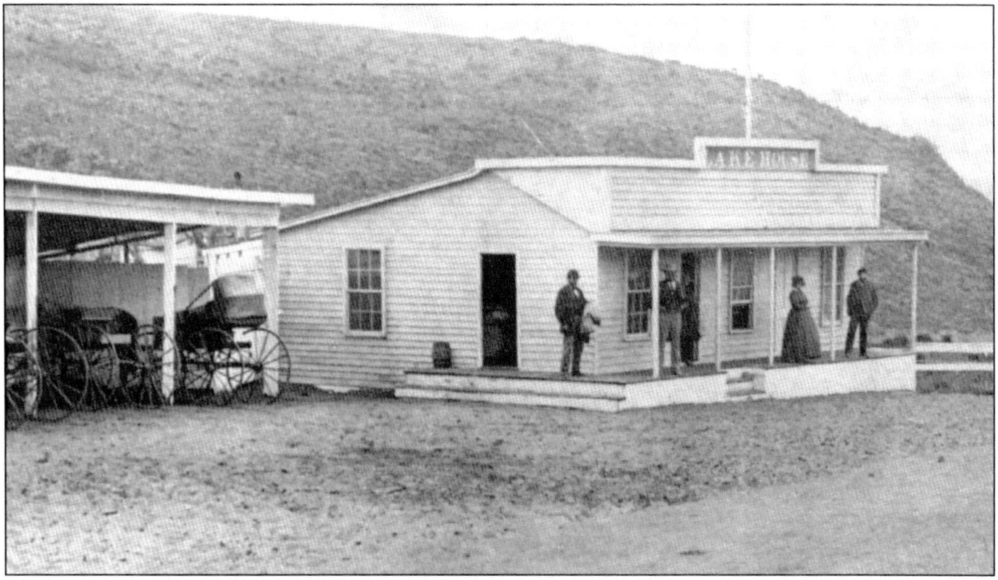

In the 1870s, John Middleton Sr. moved the Lake House, which was to be used as his residence, from Lake Merced to Bryant and Second Streets. This move was likely the longest move on rollers ever undertaken by a San Francisco house. Curiously, there were two lake houses. This photograph's identification is not definitive, but it most likely shows the earlier residence, which was moved by original owner Don DeHaro's son-in-law from the south of the lake. (Courtesy of a private collection.)

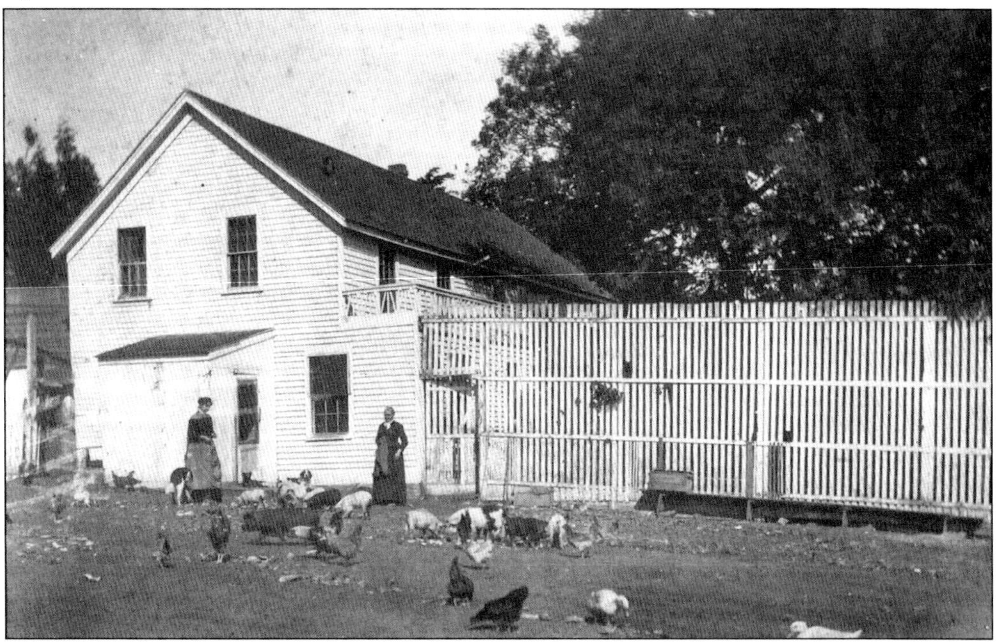

The lumber for the Schwerin family home was brought from France on three ships and then by wagon to Visitacion Valley, where Henry and Ottilia Schwerin raised eight children. The home was torn down in 1922. During the Gold Rush, there were hardly any men felling lumber. It was hard to get material to build a house, often prompting extraordinary measures. (Courtesy of the Taylor family collection and the Visitacion Valley History Project.)

Two

LIFE INTERRUPTED
THE EARTHQUAKE SHACKS

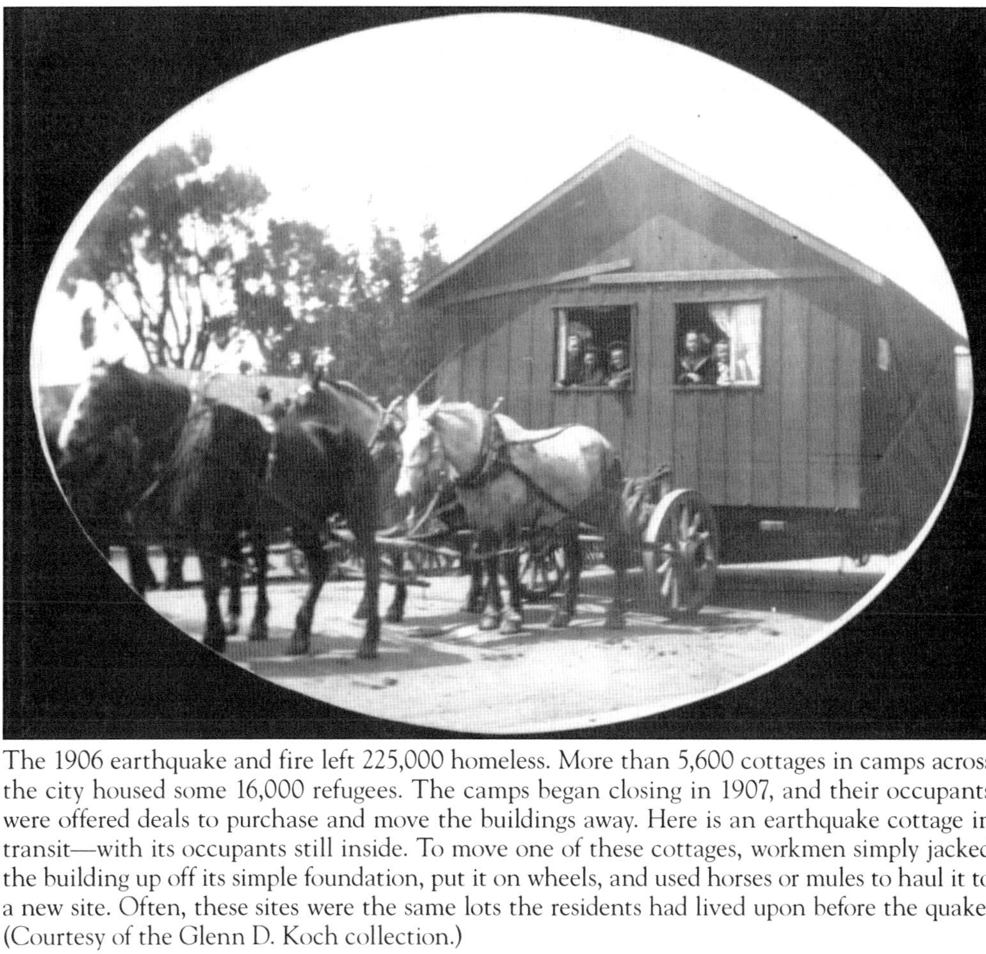

The 1906 earthquake and fire left 225,000 homeless. More than 5,600 cottages in camps across the city housed some 16,000 refugees. The camps began closing in 1907, and their occupants were offered deals to purchase and move the buildings away. Here is an earthquake cottage in transit—with its occupants still inside. To move one of these cottages, workmen simply jacked the building up off its simple foundation, put it on wheels, and used horses or mules to haul it to a new site. Often, these sites were the same lots the residents had lived upon before the quake. (Courtesy of the Glenn D. Koch collection.)

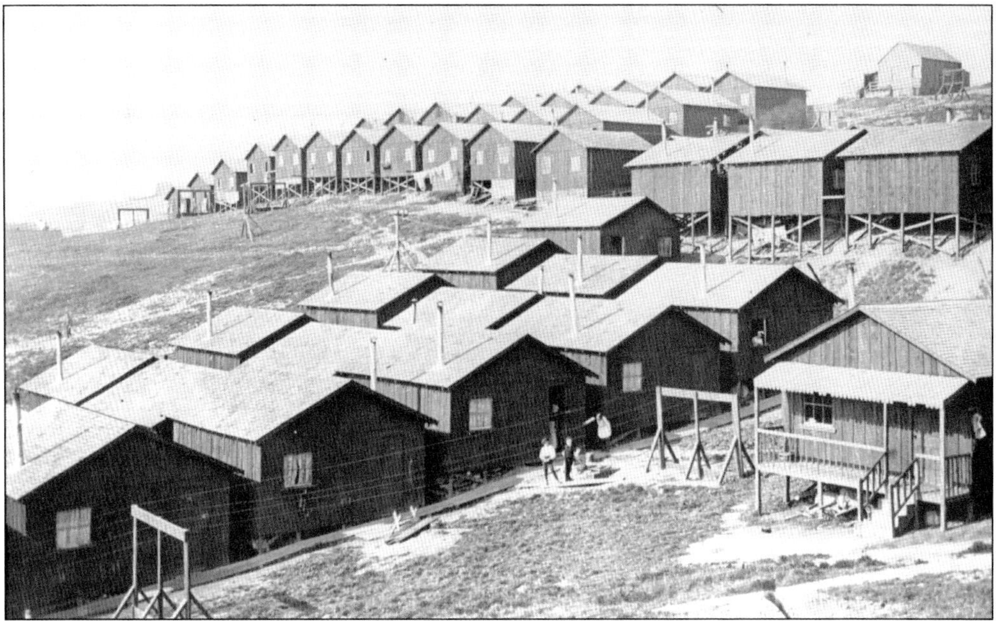

This photograph portrays an early Potrero Hill "earthquake shack" community near Twentieth and Pennsylvania Streets. The communities were dissolved in 1907, and little green houses traveling up and down the streets were common sights. The shacks were moved throughout the city, and some were even carried via train as far away as Santa Cruz, some 60 miles south. (Courtesy of the Ellie Baine collection, Potrero Hill Archives Project.)

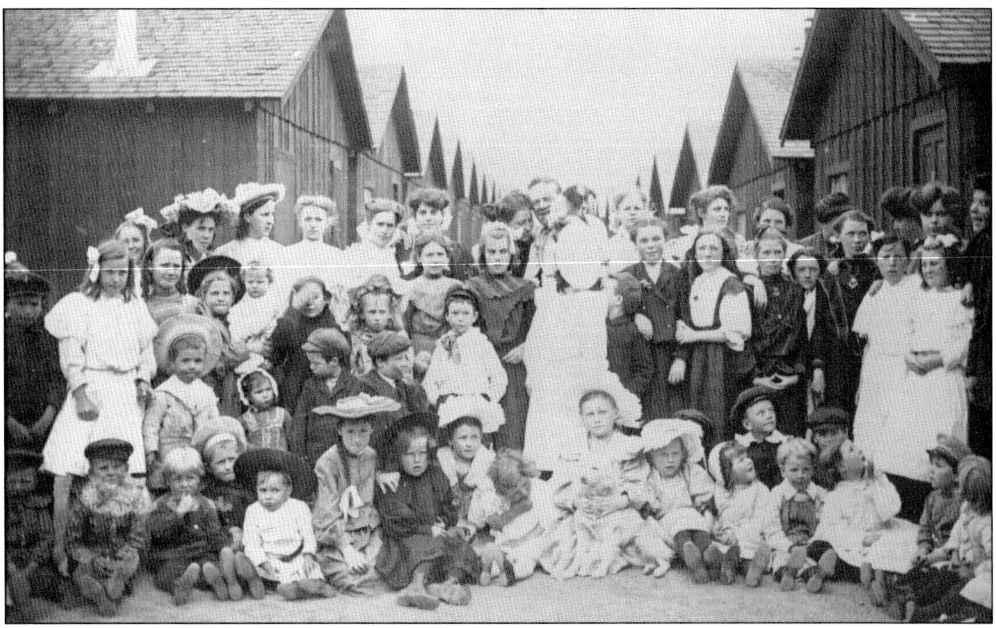

Many families lived in these sturdier structures, replacing tents, and they were intended as temporary homes to help survivors through the winter. Some were just 10 by 14 feet. Stoves cost extra, and toilets were communal facilities built in the parks. Shack tenants, in an early lease option plan, paid $2 per month toward the final $50 cost of the structure. (Courtesy of the Ellie Baine collection, Potrero Hill Archives Project.)

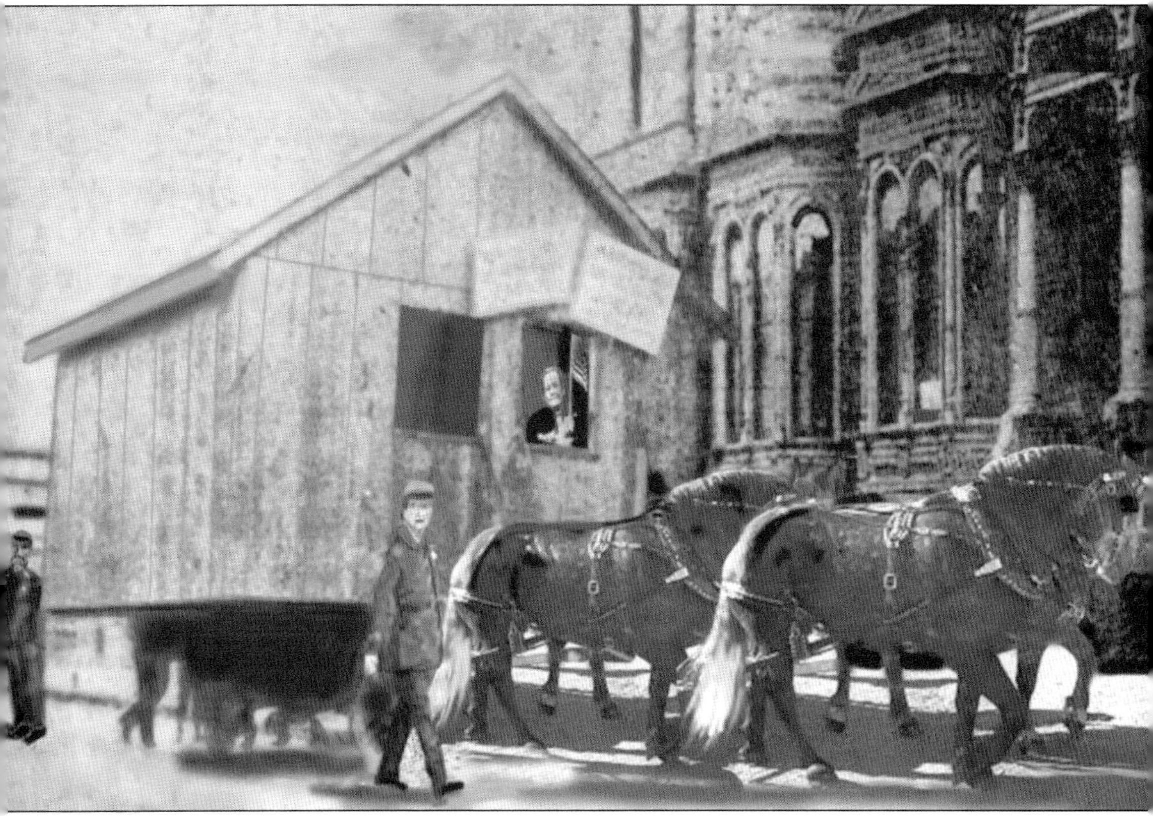

The efforts of the Relief Corporation to provide temporary housing to earthquake survivors was not without its controversy, as demonstrated on November 3, 1906, by Mary Kelly, a resident of the Jefferson Square refugee camp since the April quake. When she refused to pay rent on her "earthquake cottage," the executive officer of the department of camps forcibly lifted her cottage onto a truck and hauled it away to another camp. Mary Kelly refused to abandon her home and was carried through the streets of San Francisco via horse and wagon, still inside her house and loudly demanding a share of the relief fund and fair distribution of food and supplies. This artist's digital rendering of a 1906 newspaper photograph shows her shack in transit, a journey of some five miles across town from Jefferson Square to the Ingleside Camp. (Courtesy of Philip Brent Digital Art and Photography.)

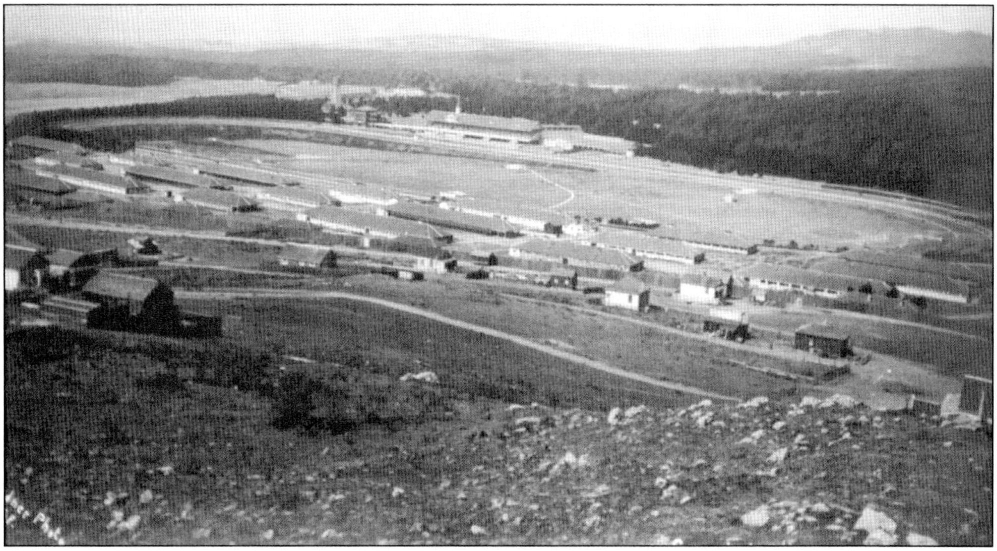

Camp Ingleside wanted no part of Mary Kelly either, so she sat at the gates in her cottage, which was firmly roped to the truck that had brought it there. Hundreds of people observed the house-laden truck blocking the road. While there, Kelly told her story to many who would never have heard of Kelly or her cause if it had not been for the novel moving operation of the Relief Corporation. (Courtesy of the San Francisco History Center, San Francisco Public Library.)

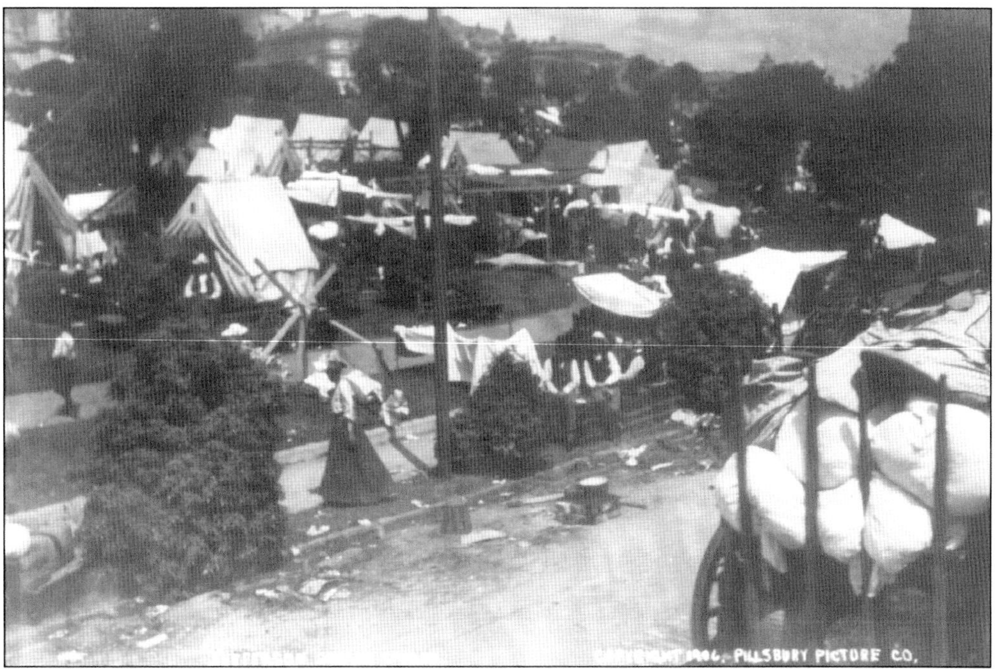

The Jefferson Square Camp, which originally housed Mary Kelly's cottage, consisted of a combination of tents and temporary buildings. A total of 26 official military camps housed as many as 40,000 homeless people from May 1906 to June 1908, when the last camp closed. These camps were transferred from the military to the Red Cross, which promoted progressive new relief methods. Ultimately, many refugees moved their cottages to lots where they became permanent homes. (Courtesy of the Library of Congress.)

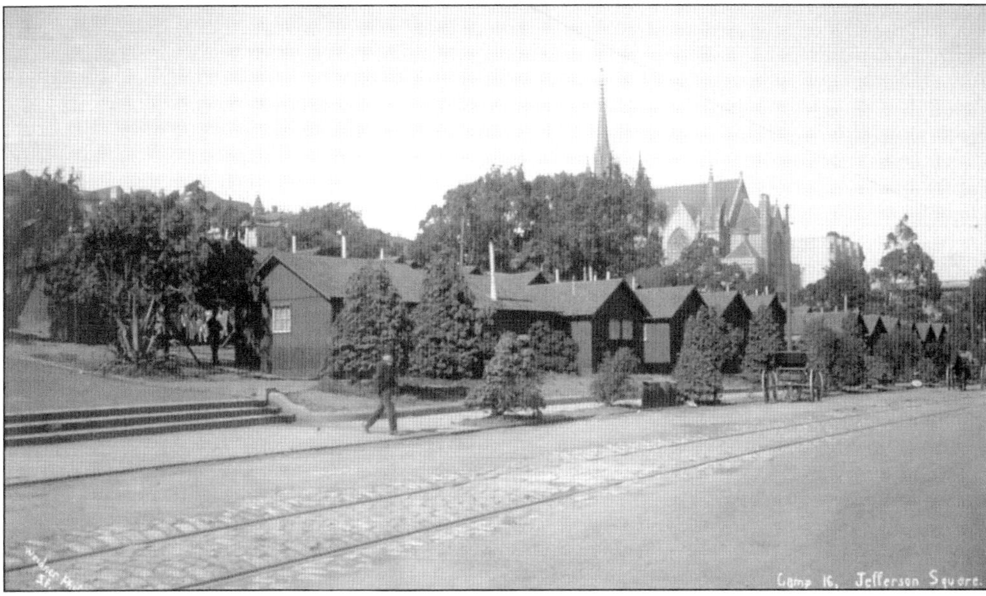

As the earthquake camps evolved from makeshift tents to temporary cottage housing, the quickly constructed structures began to look like real neighborhoods. This photograph of the Jefferson Square camp where Mary Kelly made her stand reflects a big change from the thrown-together tent camps of only a few months earlier. (Courtesy of the Western Neighborhoods Project.)

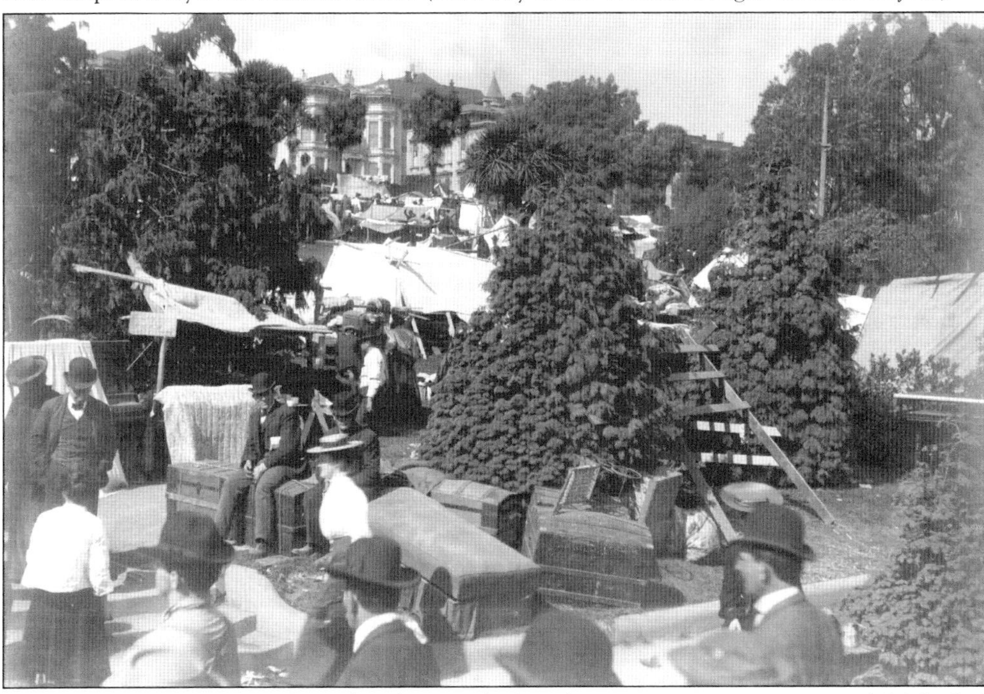

Refugees had little shelter from the elements before the cottages were constructed. Makeshift tents provided only minimal protection against the elements, so the cottages were a big step up. This photograph shows how refugees lived in the streets before the cottages were built. W.J. Street took this photograph in 1906. (Courtesy of the Anne T. Kent California Room, Marin County Free Library.)

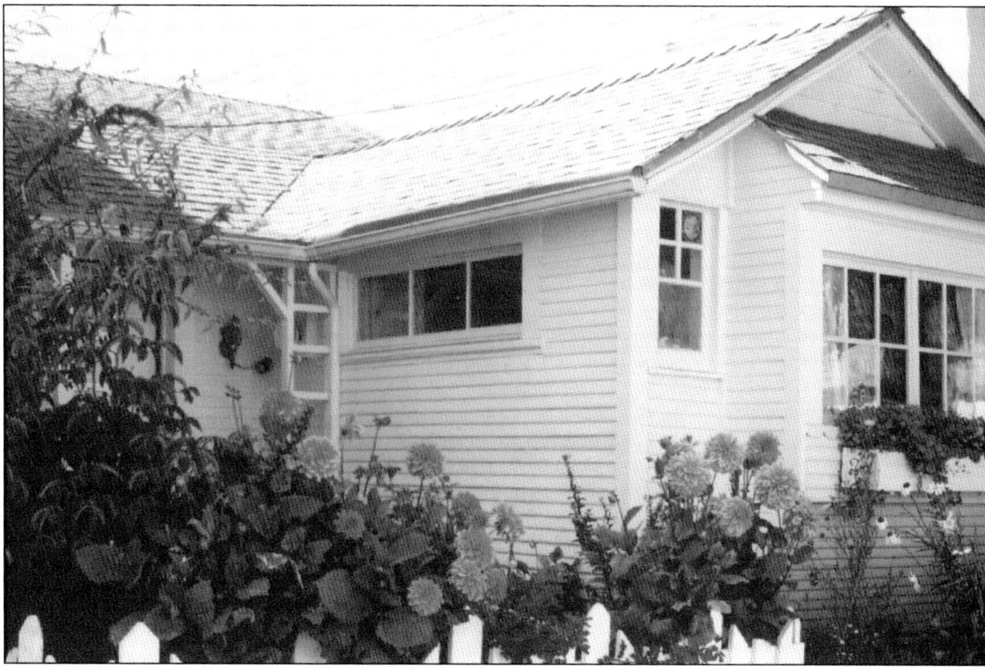

This surviving shack in the Sunset District on Twenty-Fourth Avenue has been remodeled. In the early 1980s, Jane F. Cryan lobbied for the identification and preservation of earthquake cottages after discovering that the building she was living in was an amalgamation of three or four such original cottages. This cottage was declared a city landmark in 1984. (Courtesy of the Lorri Ungaretti collection.)

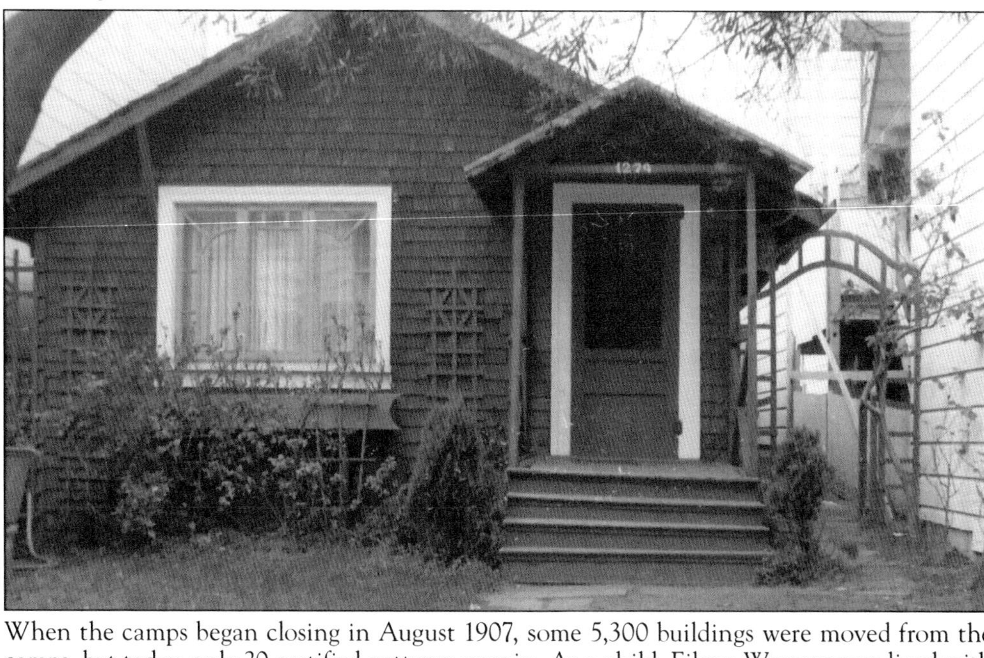

When the camps began closing in August 1907, some 5,300 buildings were moved from the camps, but today, only 20 certified cottages remain. As a child, Eileen Wassermann lived with her family in this cottage, which no longer stands. (Photograph by Eileen Hershberg, courtesy of the Lorri Ungaretti collection.)

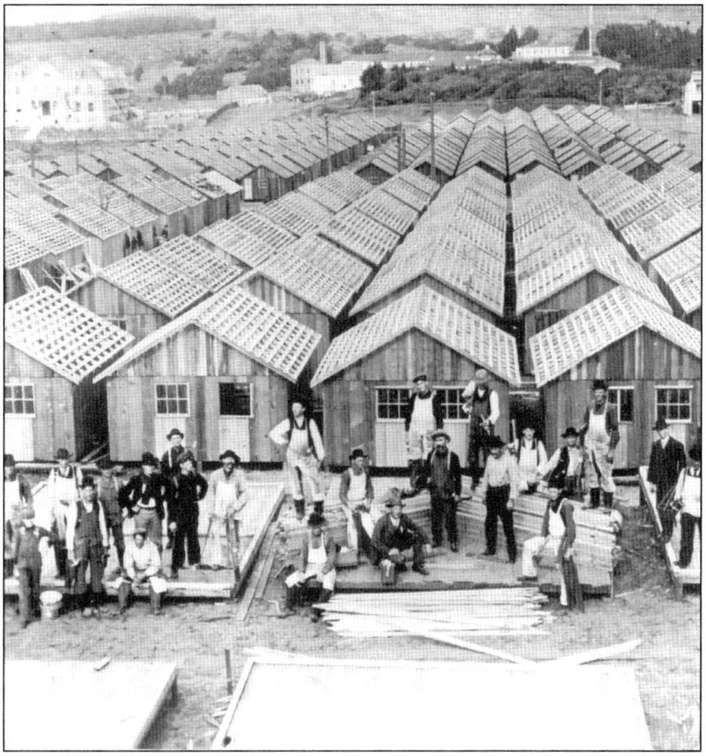

Camp Richmond, one of the larger communities, existed from 1906 to 1908. The cottages sported cedar-shingle roofs and were painted green to blend in with their environment. Shack tenants paid $2 per month toward the final $50 cost of the structure. When the Relief Corporation closed Camp Richmond, many refugees opted to move their new home to private lots. This photograph depicts the construction of Camp Richmond by union carpenters. (Courtesy of the Western Neighborhoods Project.)

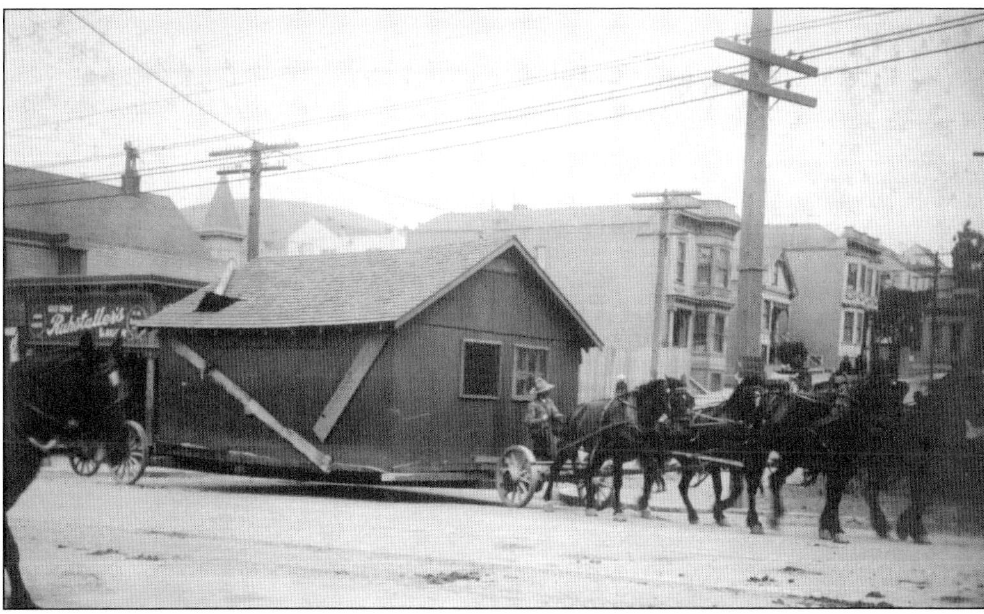

When the earthquake camps closed in 1907, over 5,000 structures were moved to private lots via horse and wagon. Those unable to afford such costs simply disassembled their homes and carried them away in pieces. An alternative perspective maintains that, despite the cottages' initial success, business interests exaggerated their public health problems in order to move shack communities to make way for more profitable buildings. (Courtesy of the San Francisco History Center, San Francisco Public Library.)

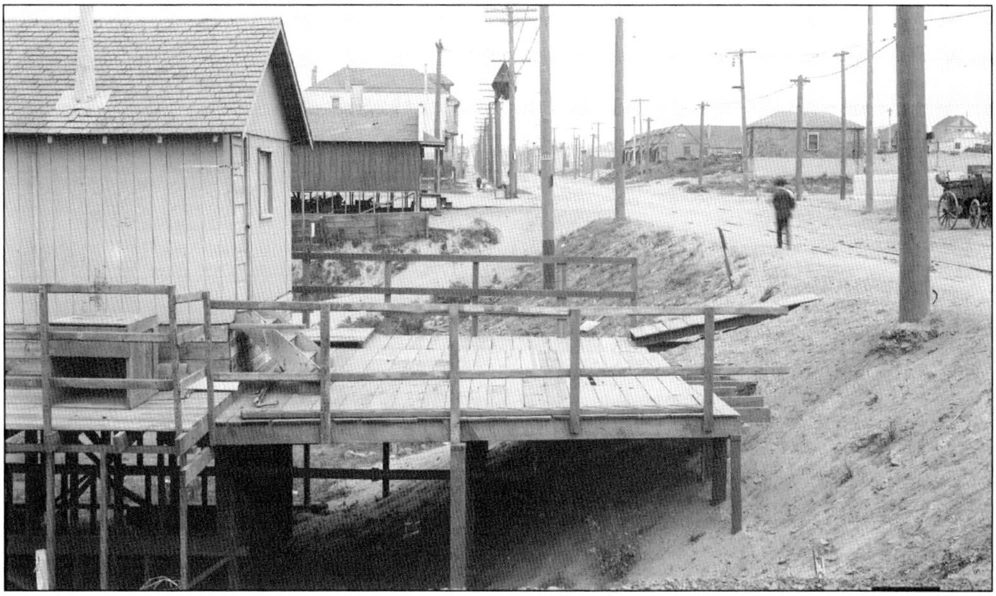

These two 1906 earthquake refugee cottages, located on California Street between Seventeenth and Eighteenth Avenues in 1908, offer a close-up view of how the original shacks became communities and homes, complete with porches, entryways, and amenities. The emergency shacks brought scores of new settlers to the area. Many wound up building permanent homes to replace the tents and temporary cottages. (Photograph by John Henry Mentz, courtesy of the San Francisco Municipal Transportation Agency.)

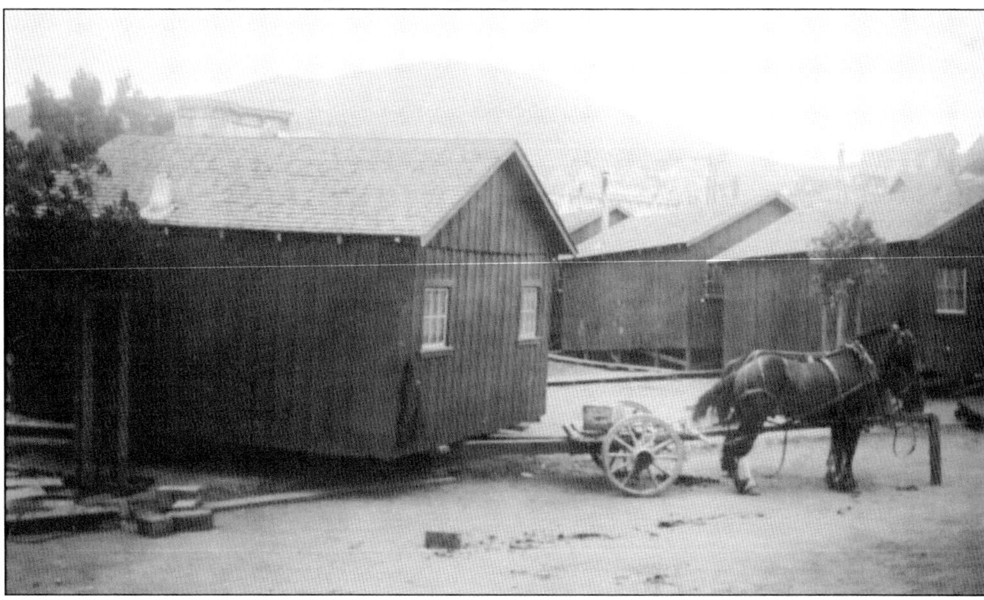

This 1906 photograph shows the refugee camp at Bernal Heights' Precita Park. Precita Park held 520 such shacks, of which 143 were three-room buildings. Earthquake shacks moved out of such camps to become permanent homes. According to the annual report of the American National Red Cross, some 5,000 cottages were built, and the "major portion of which have been reconstructed by residents into permanent homes." (Photograph by Charles Weidner, courtesy of the San Francisco History Center, San Francisco Public Library.)

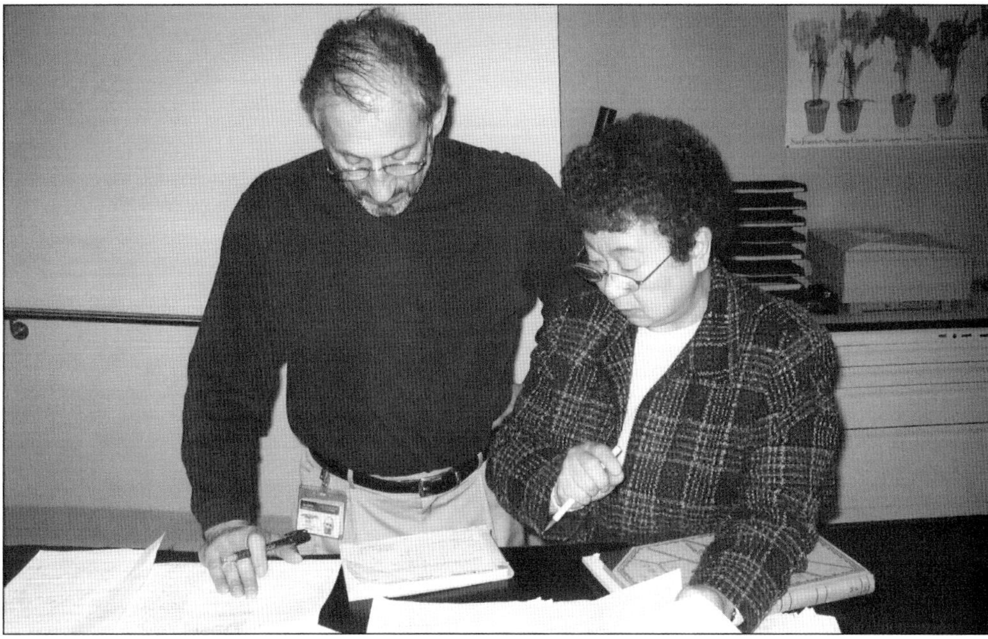

The story of the Kirkham Street earthquake shacks' moves begins with the permit process. This 2005 photograph shows Laurence Kornfeld and Anita Lee working on a permit. The ledger under Anita's elbow contains a record of all house moves in San Francisco during the last few decades. Sadly, the ledger was destroyed by the San Francisco Planning Department, likely because few houses are being moved today, so the department's wealth of permit history was deemed obsolete. (Courtesy of the Western Neighborhoods Project.)

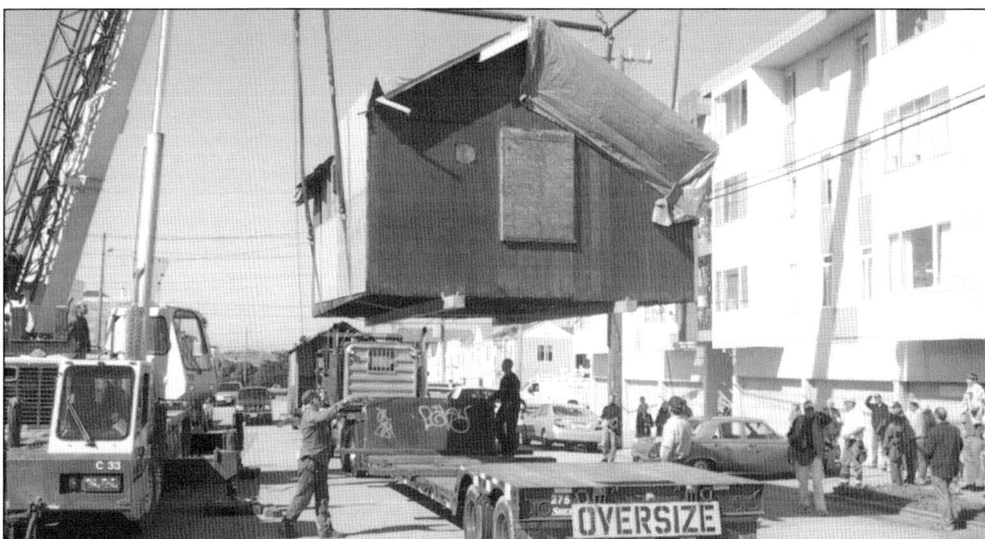

In 2002, two "eyesore" cottages, which were some of the last remaining earthquake shacks in the city, were slated for demolition. In 1997, of the 5,343 shacks moved from camps, only 19 remained standing. The 2005 struggle to move and preserve these shacks began when the Western Neighborhoods Project became involved in saving the Kirkham Street cottages. This shack is being airlifted to a truck to journey to a new home. (Courtesy of the John Freeman collection.)

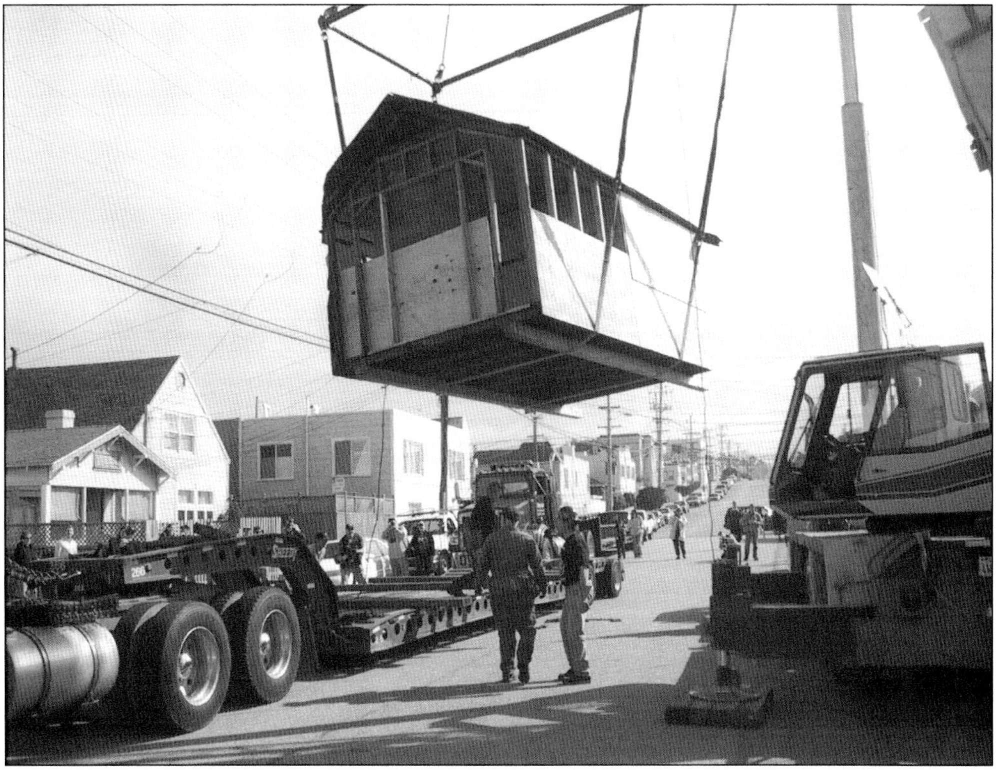

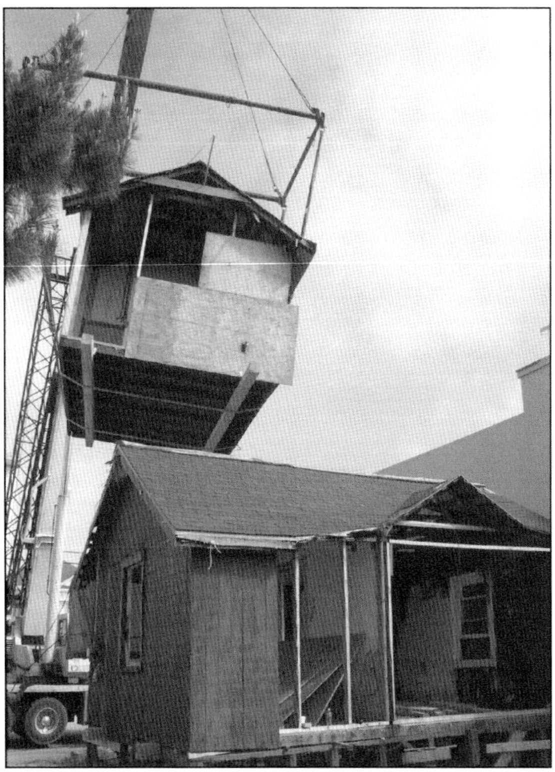

The Kirkham Street moves represented a huge community effort. Reed Walker of Ryan & Associates rallied fellow carpenters and Bay Area companies to donate their labor and coordinated the move with city agencies, Bluewater Services sent an entire team of experts out for three days to remove hazardous siding from the shacks free of charge, and moving trucks came from Sheedy Drayage, who moved the cottages safely to their new home. (Courtesy of the John Freeman collection.)

It took a lot of hard work to remove and restore this original earthquake shack from 1906–1907. The building was painstakingly renovated, displayed for the centennial, and now rests at the San Francisco Zoo's new Conservation Center, where it is open for public viewing. Most other remaining shacks have had major modifications or were built new as representations of an original shack. (Courtesy of the Western Neighborhoods Project.)

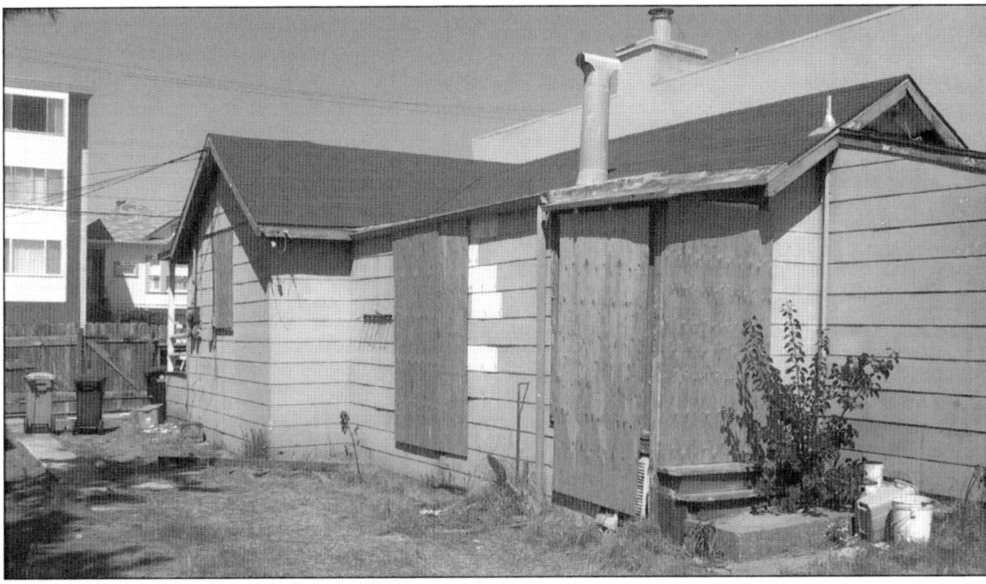

This 4329 Kirkham Street cottage from 2003 represents a Type B connected to a Type A cottage. Together with 4331 Kirkham, this house made up half of the four Kirkham shacks saved in 2004. The shacks, cobbled together to form two separate residences on one lot, had been in terrible shape for years. The back cottage did not even have heat and was reportedly condemned in the early 1970s. (Courtesy of the Western Neighborhoods Project.)

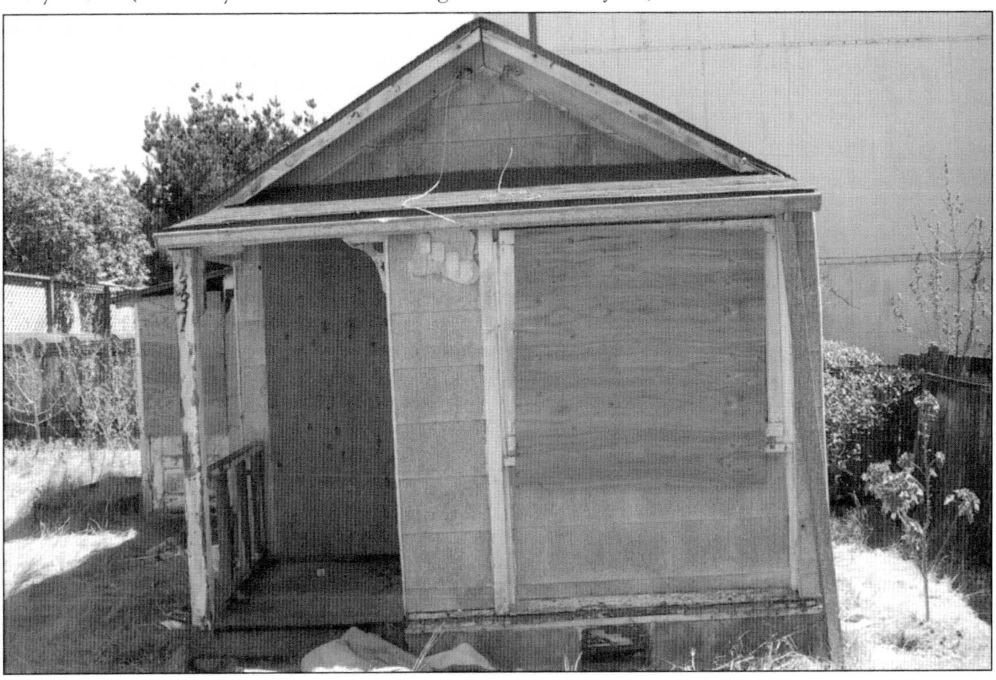

Asbestos siding had to be removed from some of the Kirkham Street shacks before they could be restored and moved. Decades of insulation and siding had to be removed, not to mention layers of linoleum. This 2004 photograph of 4331 Kirkham Street shows the shack after the removal of its later additions. It is a Type A shack set in a T formation. (Courtesy of the Western Neighborhoods Project.)

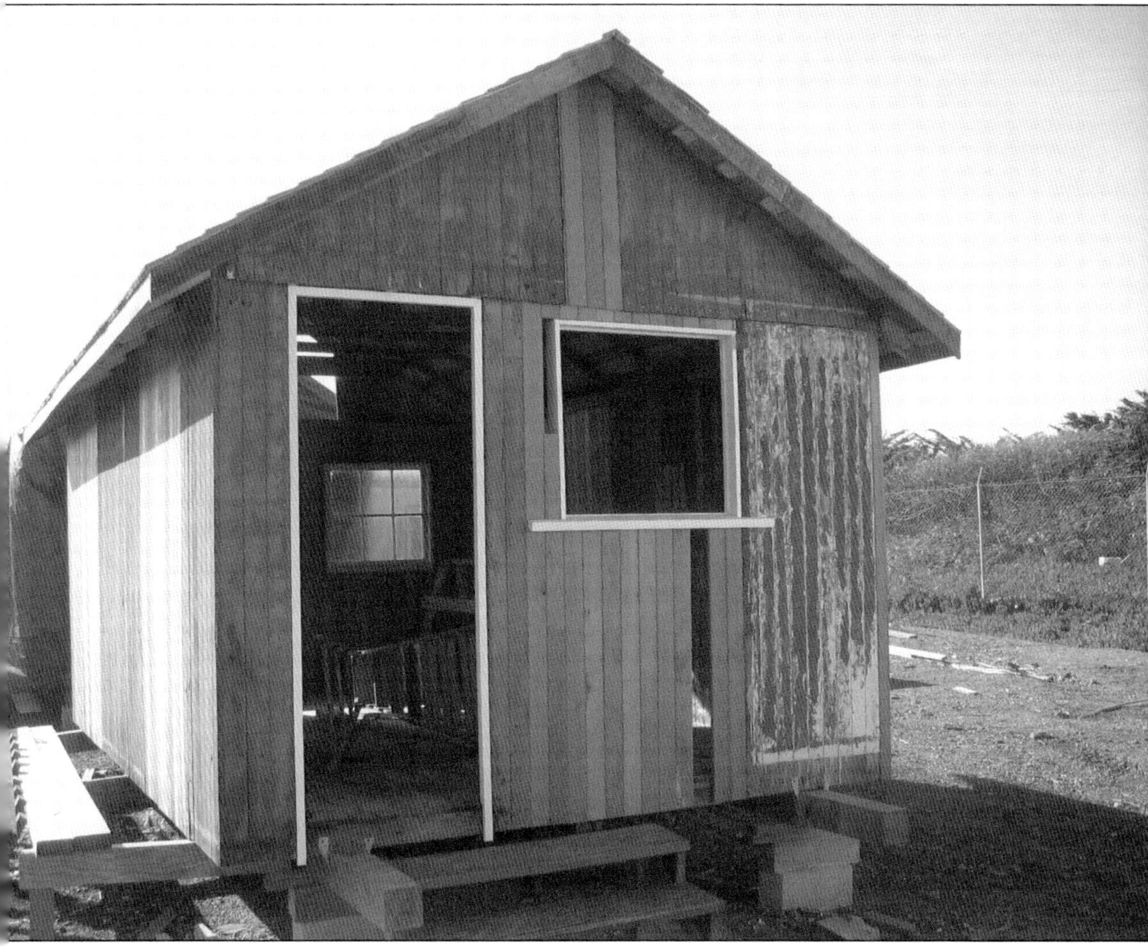

During the restoration process, windows were fabricated from original designs. Look inside the building of this 2005 photograph to see the window in place. On Kirkham Street, two brothers inherited a patch of land and its curious shacks. It was not until they applied for a demolition permit that they discovered their historic value. (Courtesy of the Western Neighborhoods Project.)

Three

Moving Prayers
The Churches That Followed Their Flock

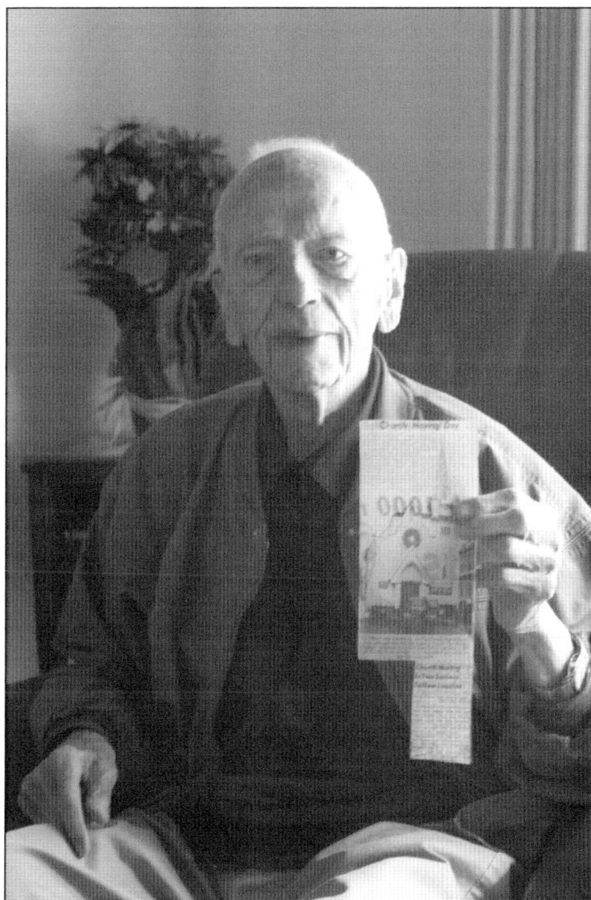

In 1949, Rev. Frank. A Jacobsen was faced with a dilemma: a small church and rapidly expanding flock. It would cost up to $5,000 to demolish the building, so he took out an ad in an interdenominational publication, and a Baptist church purchased it—for $5,000. Here, Reverend Jacobsen holds the article documenting Zion Church's move three blocks down the street. The move began on Friday and concluded Monday morning. (Photograph by Beni C. Bacon.)

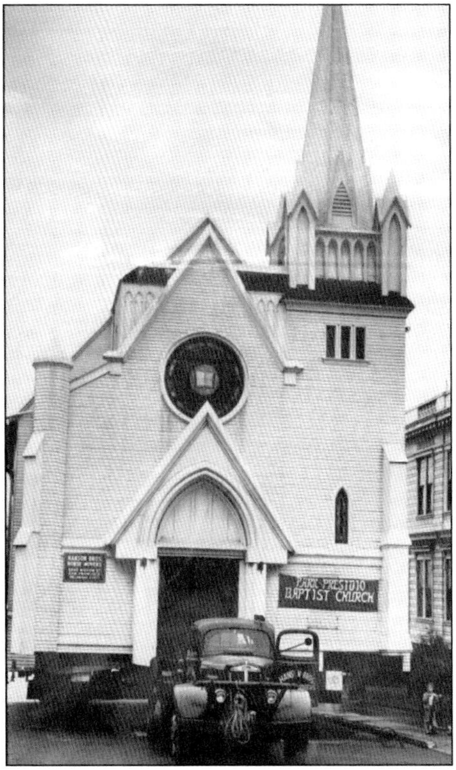

Reverend Jacobsen recalls the church move "took place in a day," but an eyewitness reports it rested in the street all weekend, blocking traffic as it sat at the corner of Balboa Street. There was a street barricade at Cabrillo Street. All the kids came out on Saturday and Sunday to play street games while the adults socialized; it was a regular block party made possible because a church blocked their street over the weekend. (Courtesy of the History Center, San Francisco Public Library.)

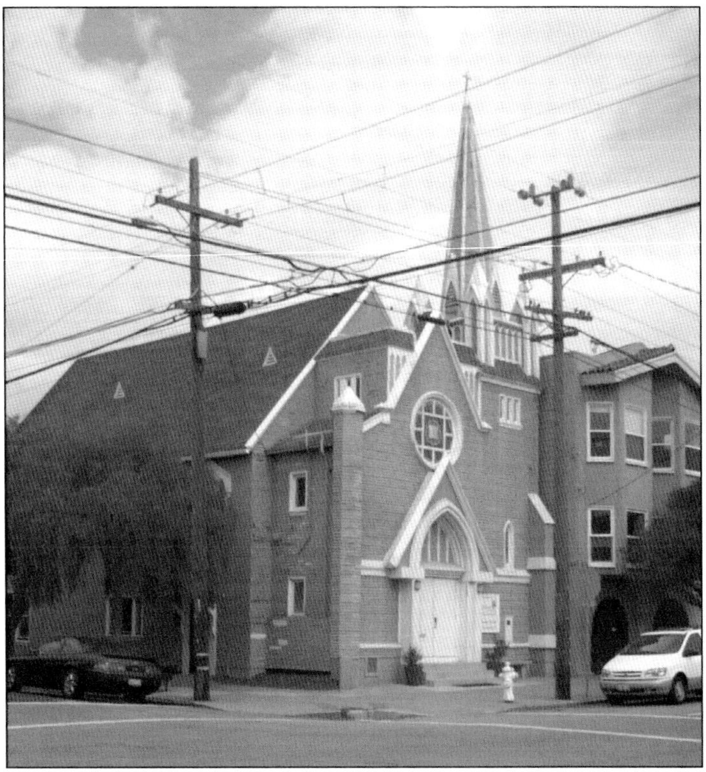

The former Zion Church still stands today on the corner of Cabrillo and Tenth Streets, but it is no longer a Baptist church. It became Christ Church at Park Presidio and still holds regular services. There is little to indicate its past, and no mention is made on its website of its moving history. (Photograph by Beni C. Bacon.)

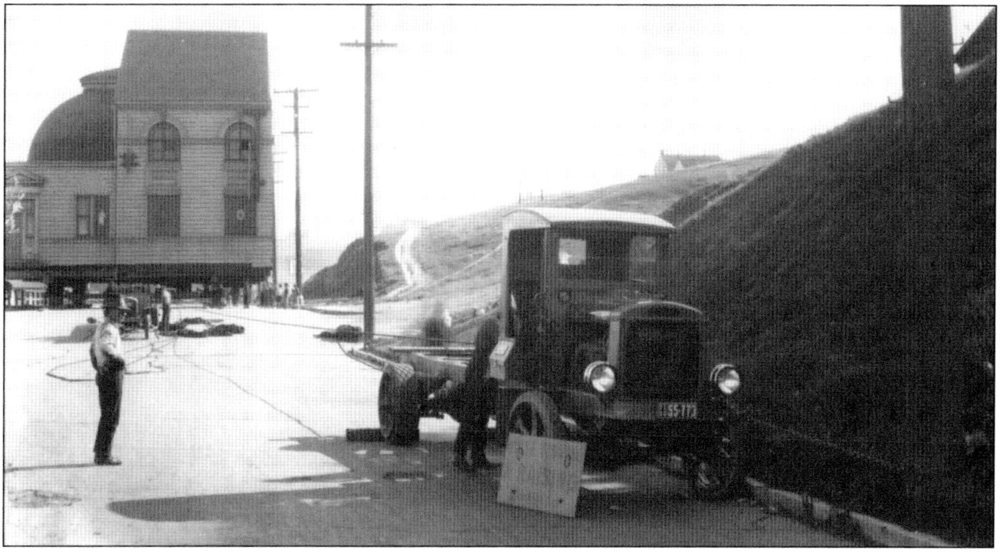

It is unusual to see half a church moving up the street, much less a whole one, but this photograph demonstrates how partial disassembly of a structure for moving purposes can be chosen, even for a larger building, to save labor costs while reducing the potential loss of a structure's fabric. St. Teresa's Church used this method to move its building in 1924. (Courtesy of the Potrero Hill Archives Project.)

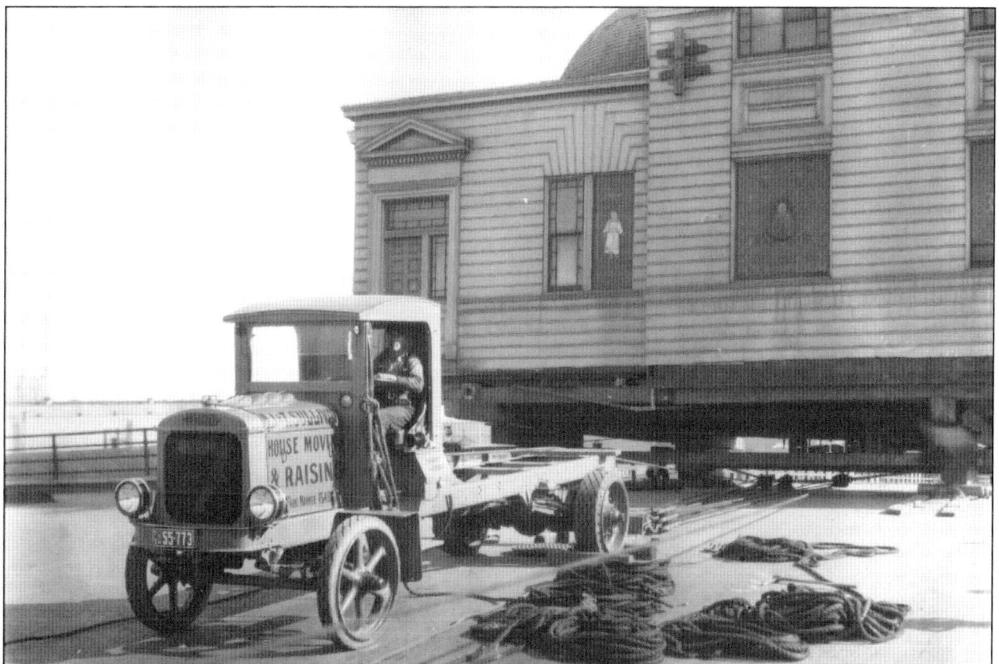

When St. Teresa's parishioners moved to homes higher on Potrero Hill as the area became increasingly industrialized, the church decided to follow them. The Sullivan house-moving company is still in business at this time, towing the church via rollers and truck. Each part of the church was moved independently to its present location at the northeast corner of Nineteenth and Connecticut Streets. (Courtesy of the Potrero Hill Archives Project.)

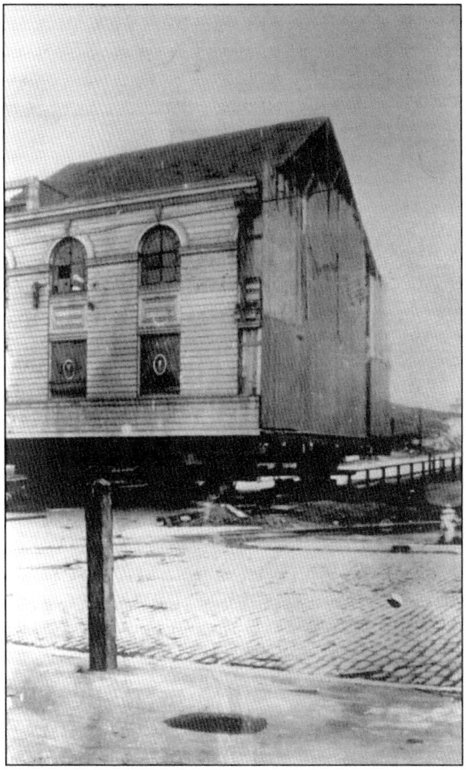

St. Teresa's is sitting on cribbing and ready for its move. A building that cannot move as a unit requires a partial disassembly, with an emphasis on handling the move in the largest pieces possible, and in this case, it had two big sections. Larger frame buildings require more bracing, since elements that originally supported two walls cannot support both walls when they are separated. (Courtesy of the Potrero Hill Archives Project.)

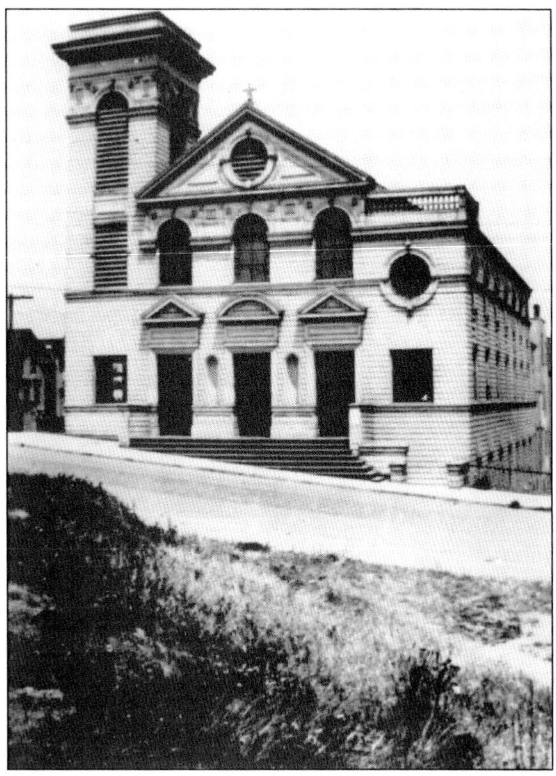

St. Teresa's two halves were rejoined on top of a new social hall and a new rectory at the corner of Nineteenth and Missouri Streets. Since its original move in 1924, the building has been remodeled numerous times, but it still stands and is open and active. The church celebrated 120 years as a parish in 2000. (Courtesy of the Potrero Hill Archives Project.)

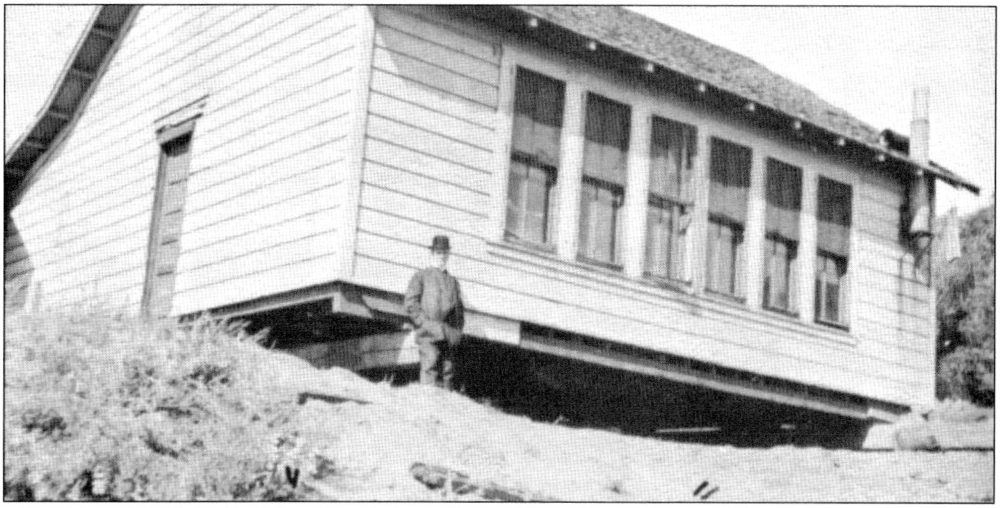

The 1909 Parkside School at Thirty-First and Taraval Streets was built as a one-room schoolhouse. When the city decided to build a new school, the mayor donated this building to the archdiocese, and it became part of the newly built St. Cecilia Church at Fifteenth Avenue and Taraval Street. In 1927, the parish hall was moved from Sixteenth Avenue and Taraval Street to newly acquired property and placed on the west side of Seventeenth Avenue. (Courtesy of Lorri Ungaretti, the Archdiocese of San Francisco Collection.)

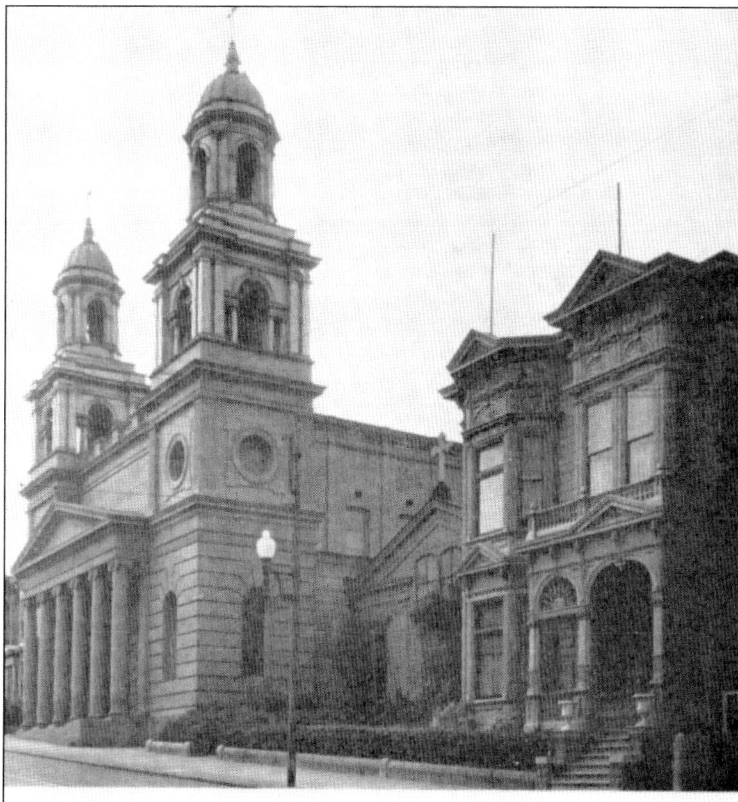

Present Holy Cross Church.

Holy Cross Church has a long and moving history. Shortly before the Palace Hotel was built in 1876, the church was moved to Eddy Street opposite Jefferson Square and renamed St. John's Church. In 1891, it was moved again to its present site, became Holy Cross Church, and was used as the parish church. This photograph of the present church is from 1937. (Courtesy of the Library of Congress.)

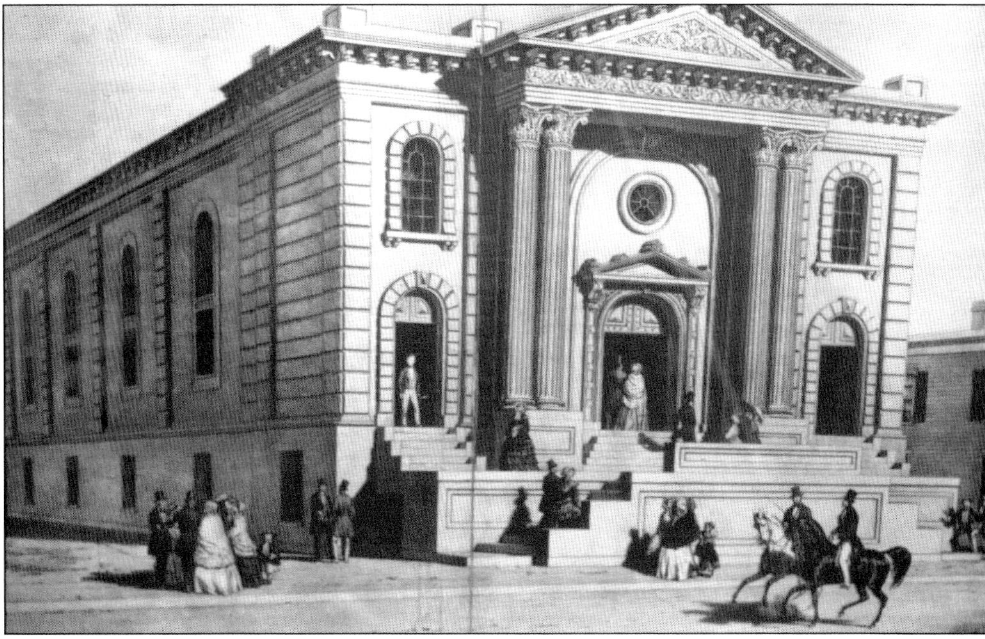

Calvary Presbyterian Church has moved twice since its initial 1854 location on Bush Street. This photograph is of an etching that was probably made by the architectural firm that designed the building. At the time, it was the largest Protestant church in California. As the city continued to rapidly expand westward, this first location became strictly commercial. In 1869, the church moved into a new building in the more residential Union Square area. (Photograph by Beni C. Bacon.)

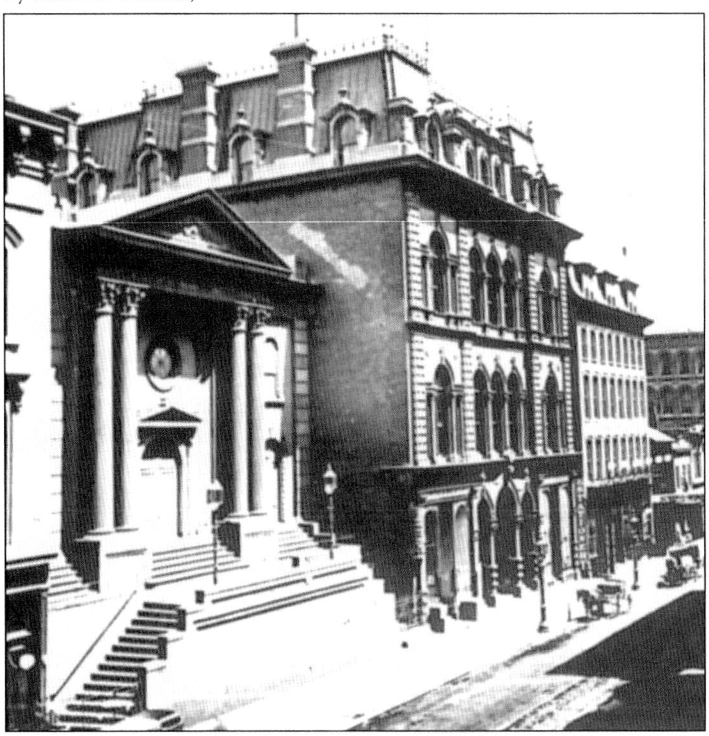

This photograph of Bush Street (looking toward Sansome Street) was taken sometime after 1869 and shows how the then-empty Calvary Church building was being squeezed out by larger commercial buildings. At some unknown date, the church building was torn down. In 1892, the current Mills Building was constructed on this former church site. (Courtesy of Calvary Presbyterian Church.)

This photograph captures the disassembly of Calvary Church on Union Square. Between 1900 and 1902, all the pews, metal balcony supports, much of the woodwork, the pipe organ, and over one million bricks were salvaged and reused in Calvary's third and current location, on the corner of Fillmore and Jackson Streets. During those two years, Calvary's congregation held their services jointly with members of St. John's Presbyterian Church. (Courtesy of Calvary Presbyterian Church.)

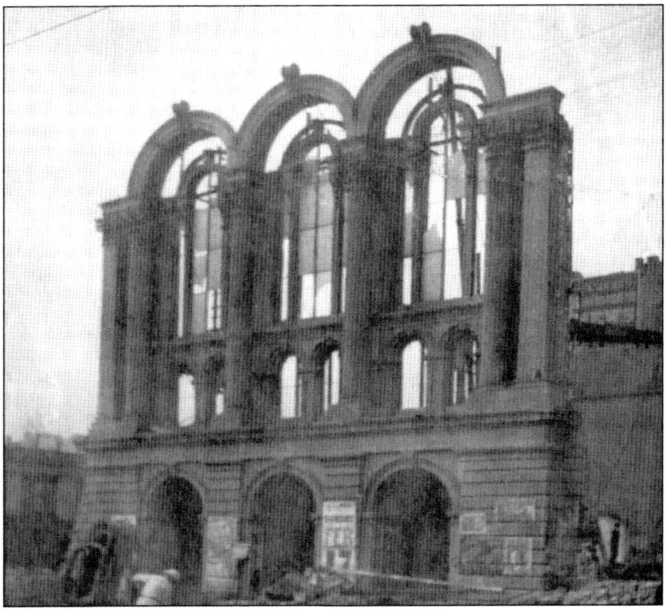

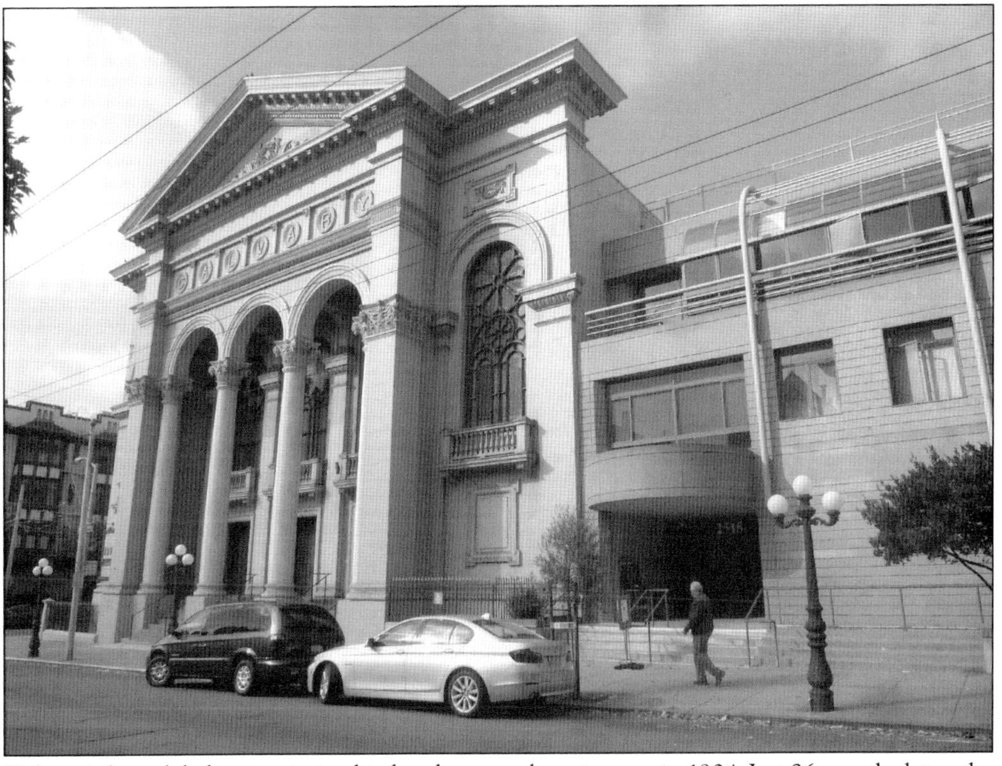

Calvary's formal dedication in its third and current location was in 1904. Just 26 months later, the 1906 earthquake and fire did terrible damage, devastating the Union Square area. But Calvary suffered no structural damage, and the fire did not come to its new home. The timing of the move from its prior location was extremely fortuitous. In 1978, Calvary Presbyterian Church was added to the National Register of Historic Places and named a San Francisco Historic Landmark. (Photograph by Beni C. Bacon.)

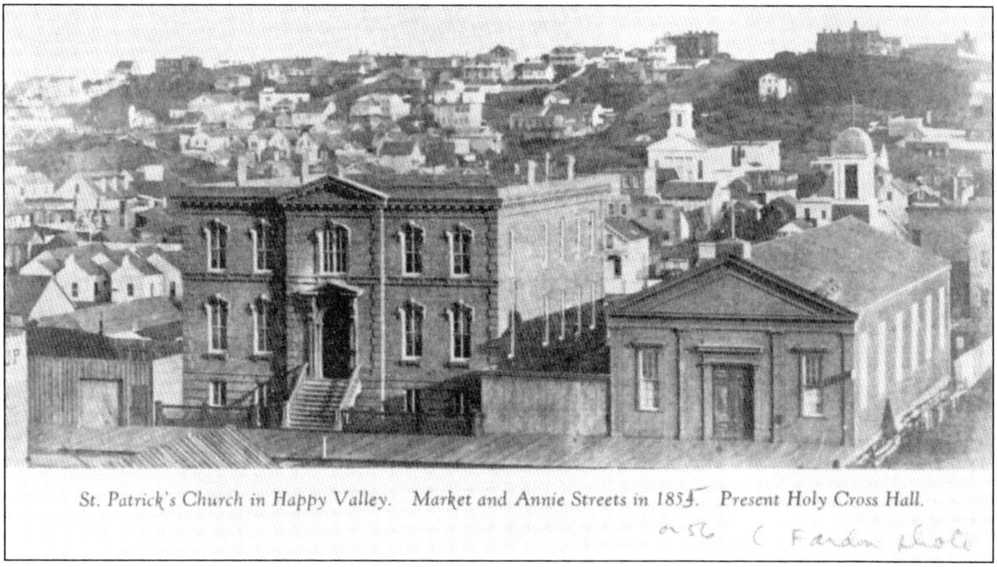

In 1872, St. Patrick's Church was moved to make way for the Palace Hotel, and in the 1890s, it moved a second time. It is the oldest frame church building still standing in San Francisco. Originally constructed in 1854 on Market Street between Second and Third Streets (where the Palace Hotel stands), it was the second church for the parishioners of St. Patrick. This 1855 photograph, taken by G.R. Fraden, shows its original location. (Courtesy of the Library of Congress.)

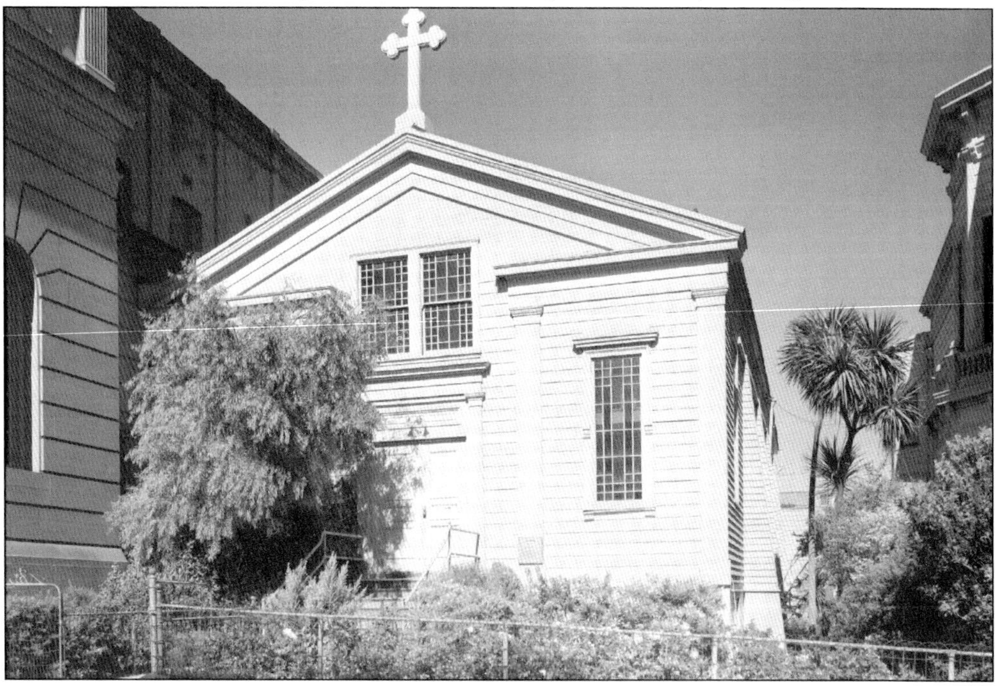

In 1873, St. Patrick's was moved to Eddy Street (between Laguna and Octavia Streets) to become the church building for St. John the Baptist Parish. In 1891, it moved to its present site to serve as the Holy Cross Parish until 1899, when a new church was consecrated and the old wooden church became the Parish Hall. This 1960 photograph shows the front of Holy Cross Parish Hall. (Courtesy of the Library of Congress.)

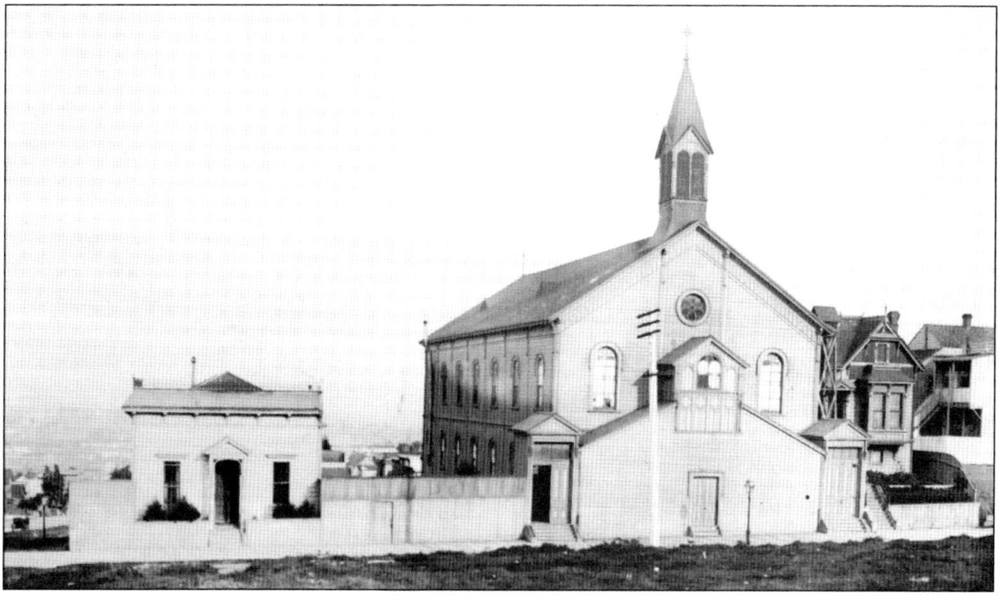

In 1885, Reverend Flood purchased a derelict, one-story Methodist church on Linden and Buchanan Streets. In 1886, he purchased the existing site of Sacred Heart and moved the building. In 1887, he commissioned a larger church and moved the old building to the back of the property where it became a parochial residence. This photograph, taken between 1888 and 1906, depicts the exterior of the building at Fell and Fillmore Streets. (Courtesy of the History Center, San Francisco Public Library.)

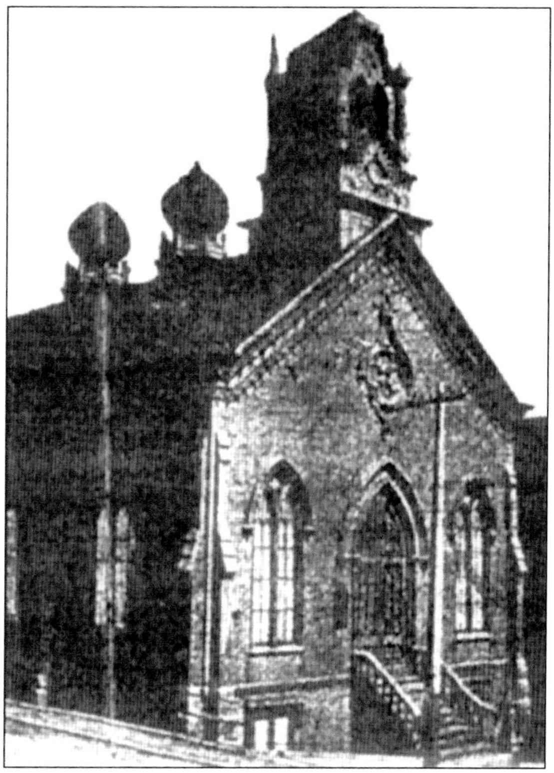

In 1852, the First Colored Baptist Church of San Francisco was founded to celebrate the abolishment of slavery in the West Indies. In 1854, church members purchased an old church and moved it to Dupont Street (now Grant Avenue) between Greenwich and Filbert Streets. This antique photograph shows their second Powell Street location. The congregation moved five more times, but the first moved building on Grant Avenue remained behind. (Courtesy of the Third Baptist Church of San Francisco.)

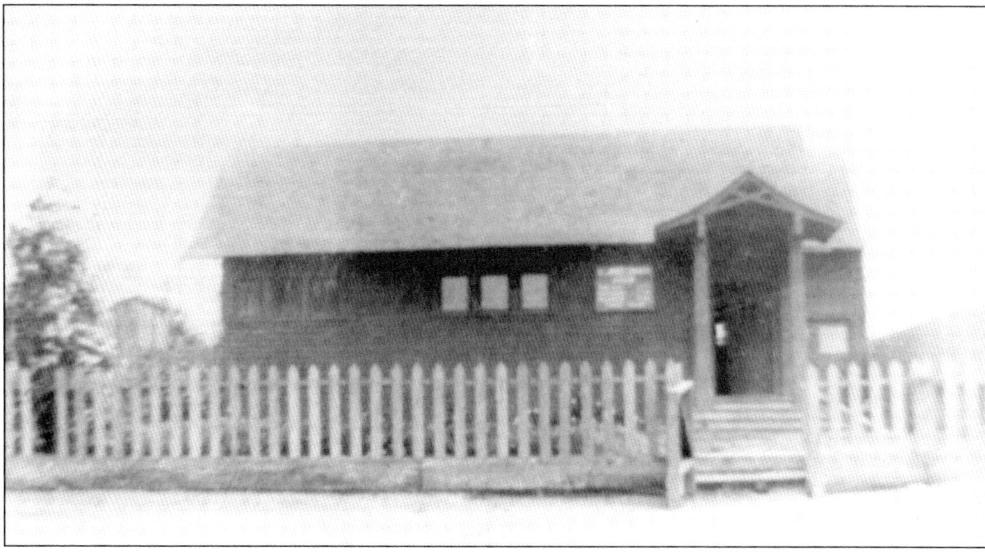

In 1906, the original St. James Presbyterian Church was built at 240 Leland Avenue. By 1922, the facilities were too small for the growing congregation, so plans were made to build a bigger church. This is an image of the original church. The present church at 240 Leland Avenue, designed by Julia Morgan, was completed in 1923. (Courtesy of the Visitacion Valley History Project.)

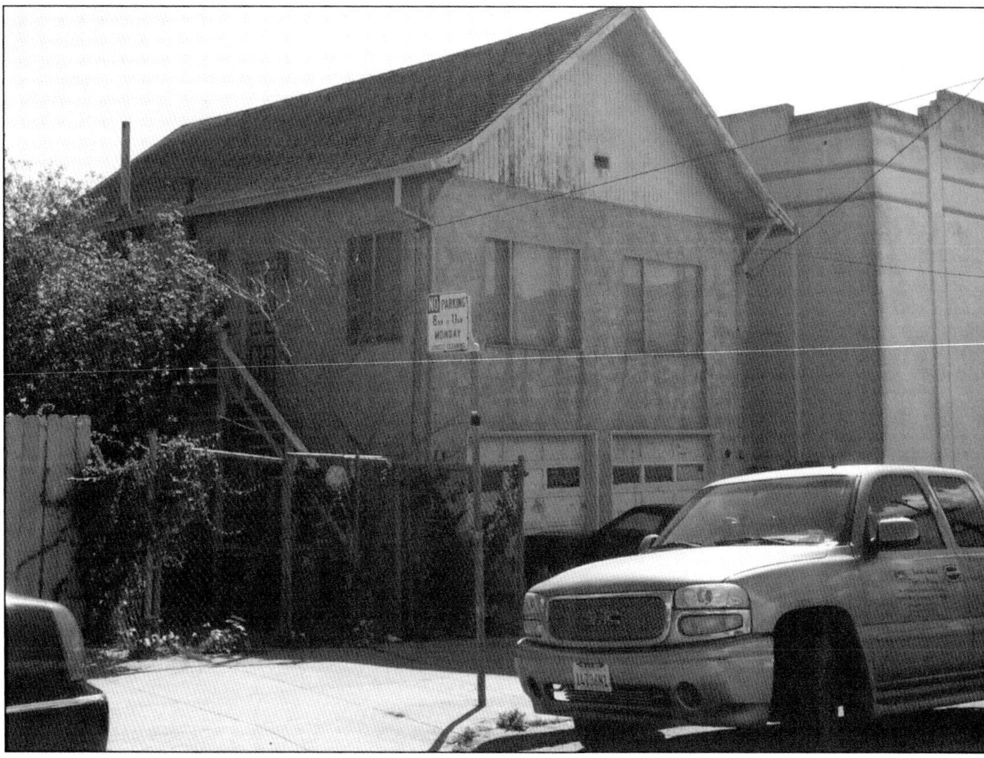

The original church moved around the corner to Schwerin Street, where it was converted to a private residence, as shown in this photograph. It stands at this location today, adjacent to Visitacion Valley Elementary School. The original gymnasium addition at the rear of the lot was not moved or saved. (Courtesy of the Visitacion Valley History Project.)

Four

"It's Getting Impossible." The Twilight Years of San Francisco's Relocation

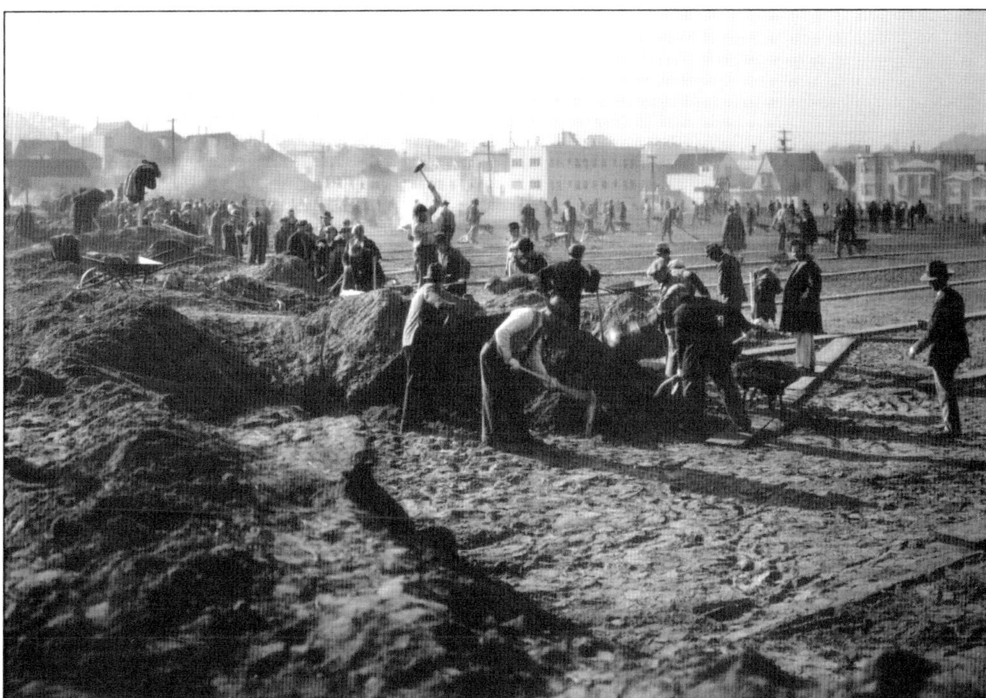

Workers are digging up the Odd Fellows Cemetery in preparation for its move on December 26, 1933. The cemetery opened in 1865 and consisted of some 30 acres bounded by Geary, Turk, Parker, and Arguello Streets. The push to remove the cemeteries from San Francisco's boundaries began in the late 1800s, encouraged by developers who foresaw that San Francisco's land would become too valuable to serve as burial grounds. (Courtesy of a private collection.)

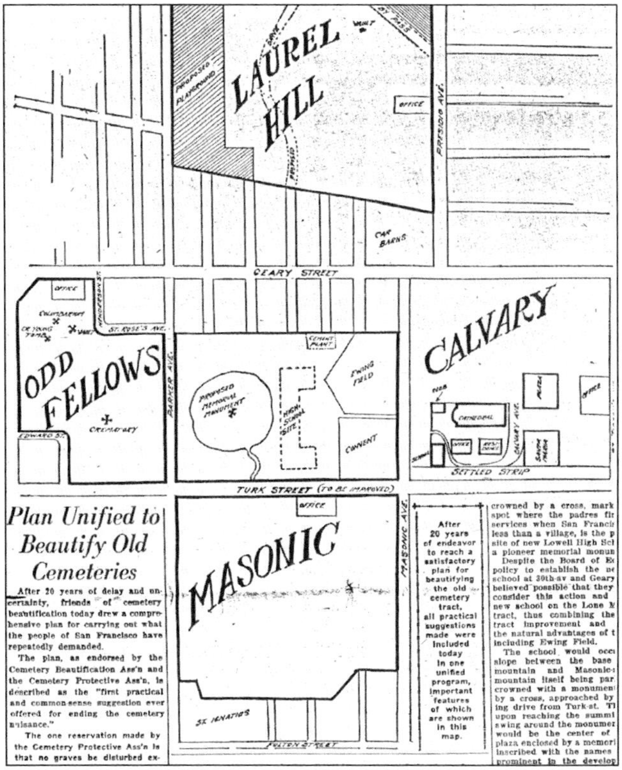

Plan Unified to Beautify Old Cemeteries

After 20 years of delay and uncertainty, friends of cemetery beautification today drew a comprehensive plan for carrying out what the people of San Francisco have repeatedly demanded.

The plan, as endorsed by the Cemetery Beautification Ass'n and the Cemetery Protective Ass'n, is described as the "first practical and common-sense suggestion ever offered for ending the cemetery nuisance."

The one reservation made by the Cemetery Protective Ass'n is that no graves be disturbed ex-

After 20 years of endeavor to reach a satisfactory plan for beautifying the old cemetery tract, all practical suggestions made were included today in one unified program, important features of which are shown in this map.

crowned by a cross, mark spot where the padres fir services when San Francis less than a village, is the p site of new Lowell High Sch a pioneer memorial monun

Despite the Board of Ed policy to establish the ne school at 30th-av and Geary believed possible that they consider this action and new school on the Lone M tract, thus combining the tract improvement and the natural advantages of t including Ewing Field.

The school would occ slope between the base mountain and Masonic- mountain itself being par crowned with a monumen by a cross, approached by ing drive from Turk-st. Th upon reaching the summi swing around the monumen would be the center of plaza enclosed by a memori inscribed with the names prominent in the develop

A 1930s cemetery map displays the locations of "the big four" cemeteries. In 1900, the board of supervisors prohibited further burials within city limits after 1901; thus, the revenue for burial charges and lot sales vanished for those cemeteries already in place. As the existing cemeteries deteriorated, the push for their removal became relentless. By the 1940s, the cemeteries had all moved away from San Francisco. (Courtesy of the Western Neighborhoods Project.)

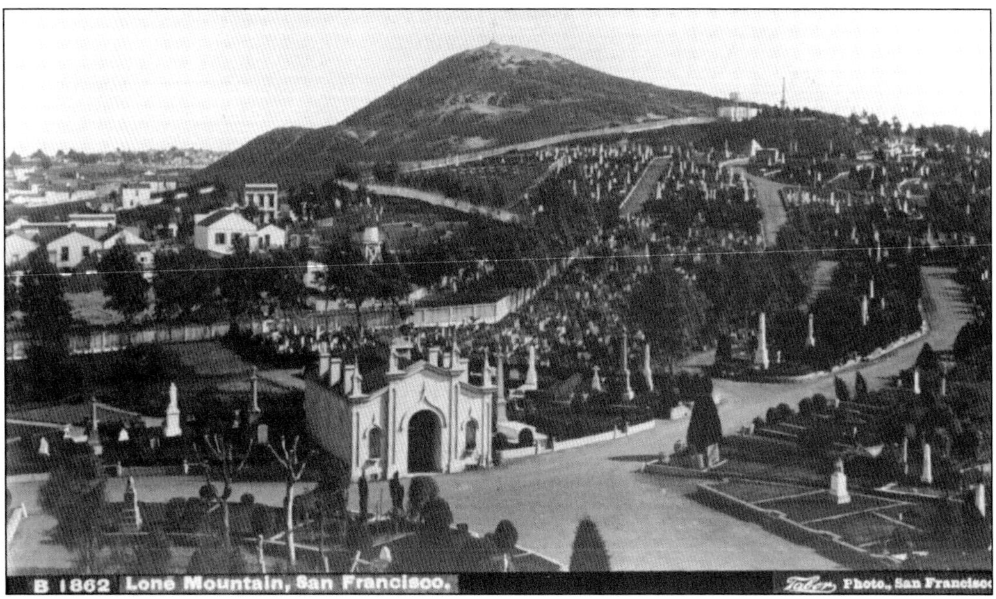

Lone Mountain Cemetery is shown in 1862; it was moved in 1937. From the 1920s to the 1940s, San Francisco's cemeteries were moved to Colma, the "cemetery city" south of town. There were two reasons for these moves: cemeteries attracted teenagers and vandals, and more importantly, real estate developers foresaw huge profits in relatively inexpensive land in prime neighborhoods. The health issue cited as a concern was actually a smokescreen. (Courtesy of the Western Neighborhoods Project.)

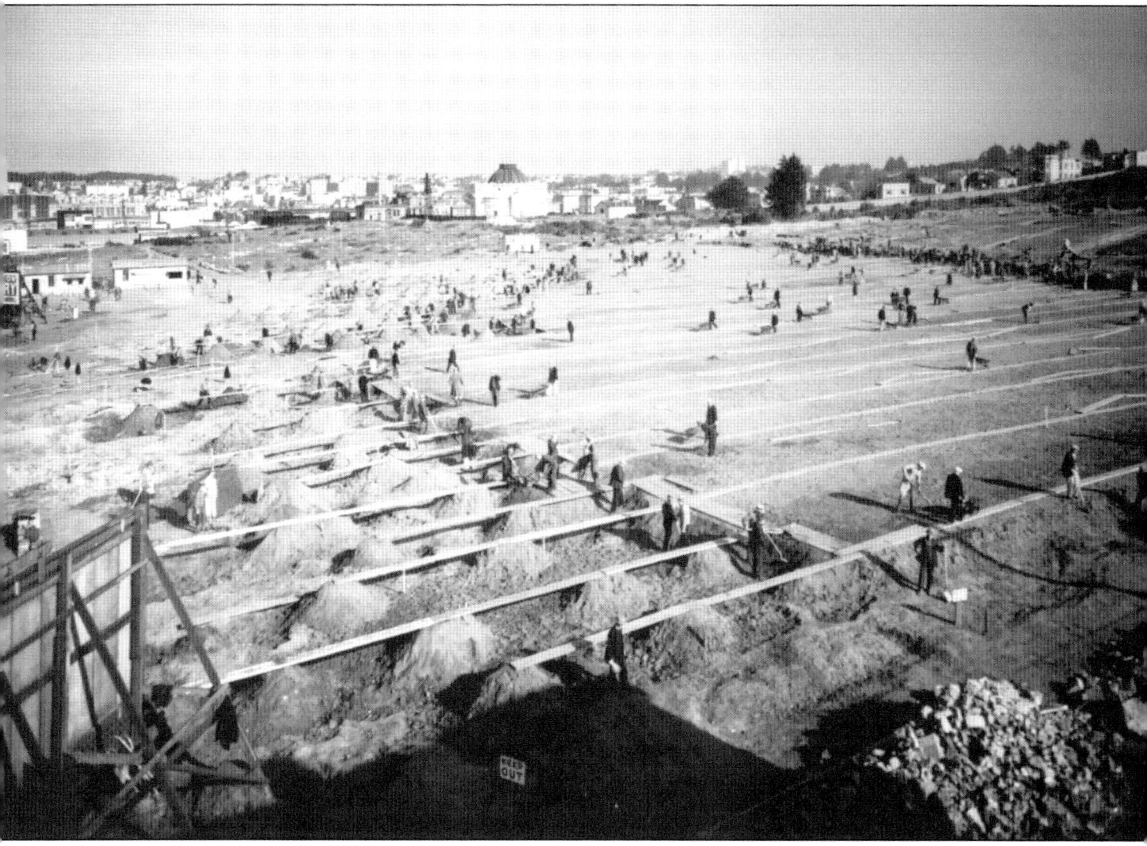

This image was captured during moving day at the Odd Fellows Cemetery. The cemetery began emptying in 1929. This photograph was taken on December 26, 1933, in the area that would someday become Rossi Park, and shows men working to remove bodies. This image includes the only part of the cemetery still standing today, the Columbarium (center). (Courtesy of a private collection.)

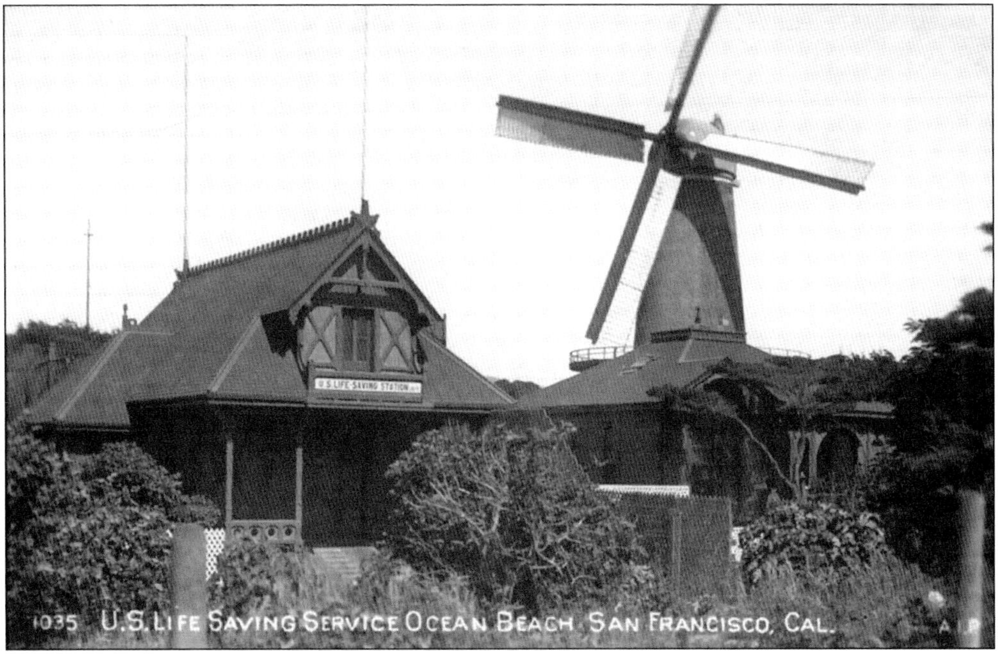

The US Life Saving Station was built in 1879 and appears here at its original Ocean Beach location. When the building was sold at auction, the only bidder for the house, who actually worked for the Coast Guard, paid $75 for it in 1923. The building did not go far; it moved from Golden Gate Park to nearby Cabrillo Street and Forty-Seventh Avenue. (Courtesy of the Dennis O'Rorke collection.)

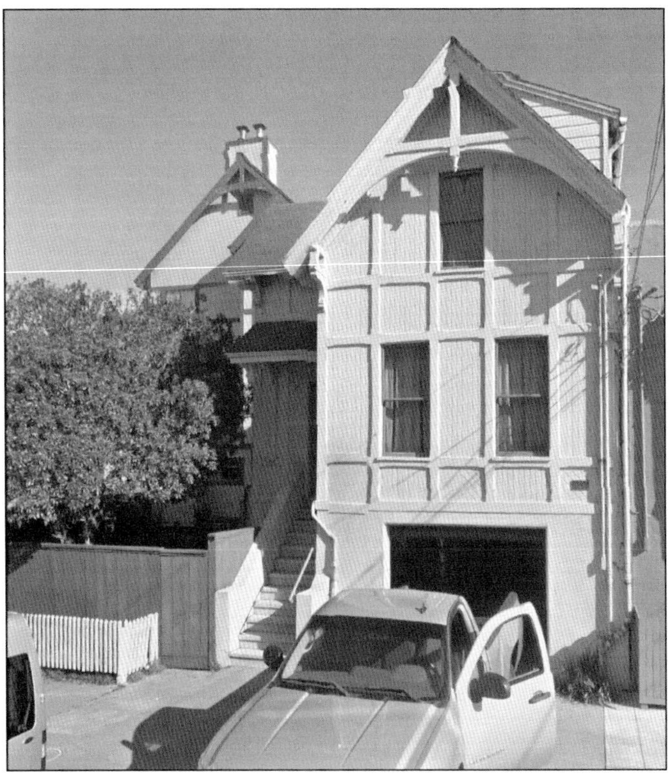

This is the US Life Saving Station in its present incarnation as a private San Francisco home. The house was moved in 1923, and the buyer's relative, who was a contractor, raised it over a garage. While its architecture remains distinctive, to the uninformed eye, it looks like just another San Francisco row house, smack up against the next. (Courtesy of a private collection.)

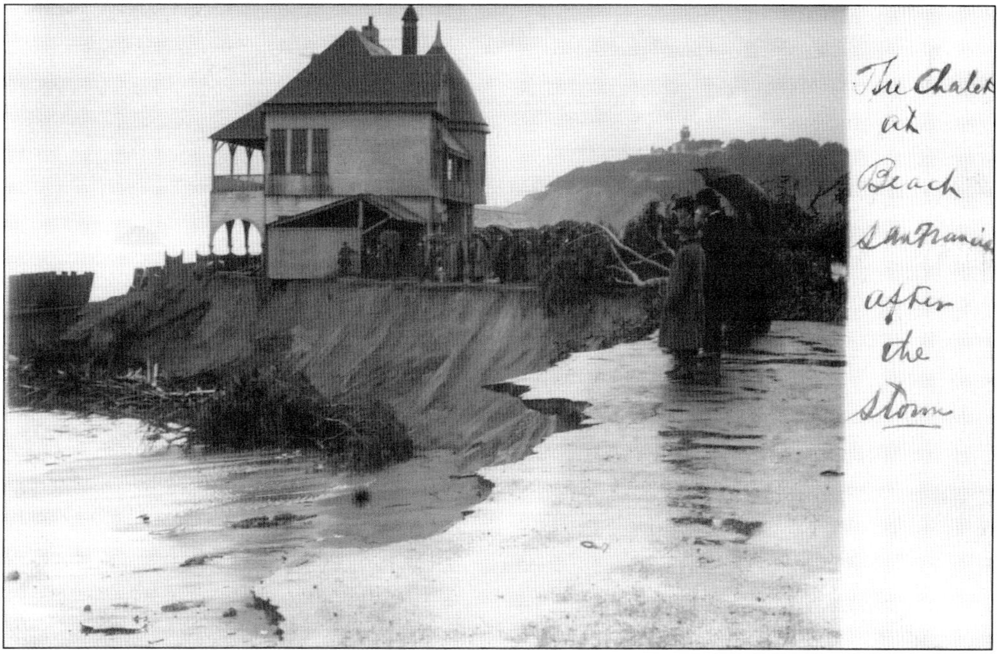

Today's visitors to Ocean Beach will see a restaurant across the highway from the beach, proudly billed as The Beach Chalet from 1925. Here is the original chalet, which was built on the sandy beach bluffs directly across from today's modern restaurant. Note the encroaching erosion. In 1891, architect William O. Banks won a park and recreation department bid to construct this building for $8,000, which was erected in 1892. (Courtesy of the Dennis O'Rorke collection.)

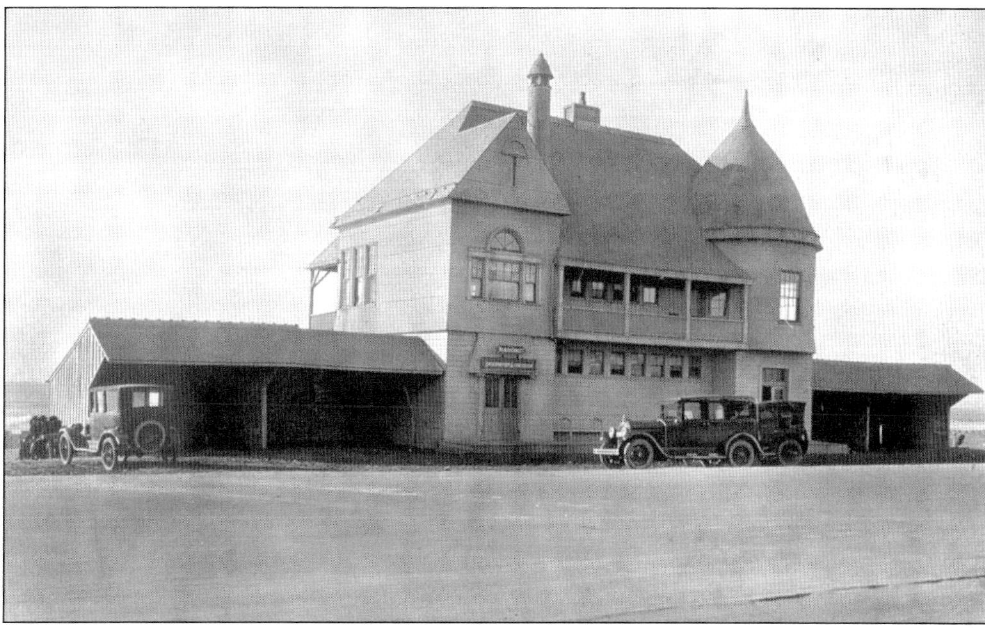

The ocean tides proved a severe threat to the original chalet, despite the construction of a 300-foot breakwater in the early 1900s to protect the chalet and the Great Highway. When storms eroded the wall and encroached upon the chalet, some 100,000 to 200,000 people turned out to witness its possible demise during a pounding winter storm. (Courtesy of a private collection.)

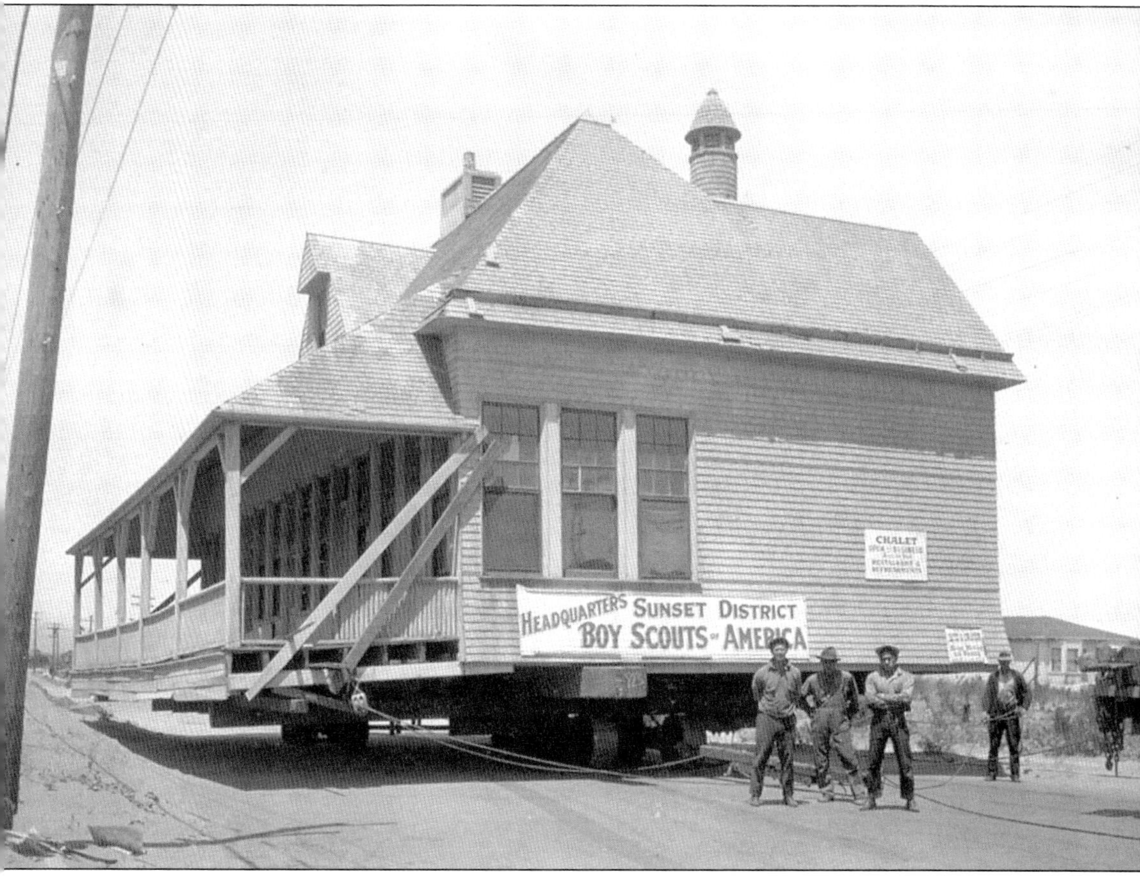

The old chalet building was given to the Boy Scouts on the condition that it would be moved. Parks commissioner Herbert Fleishhacker donated the money to have the building moved, and in the spring of 1925, the first floor of the original Beach Chalet was removed and transported along Irving Street to Twenty-Fourth Avenue. (Courtesy of a private collection.)

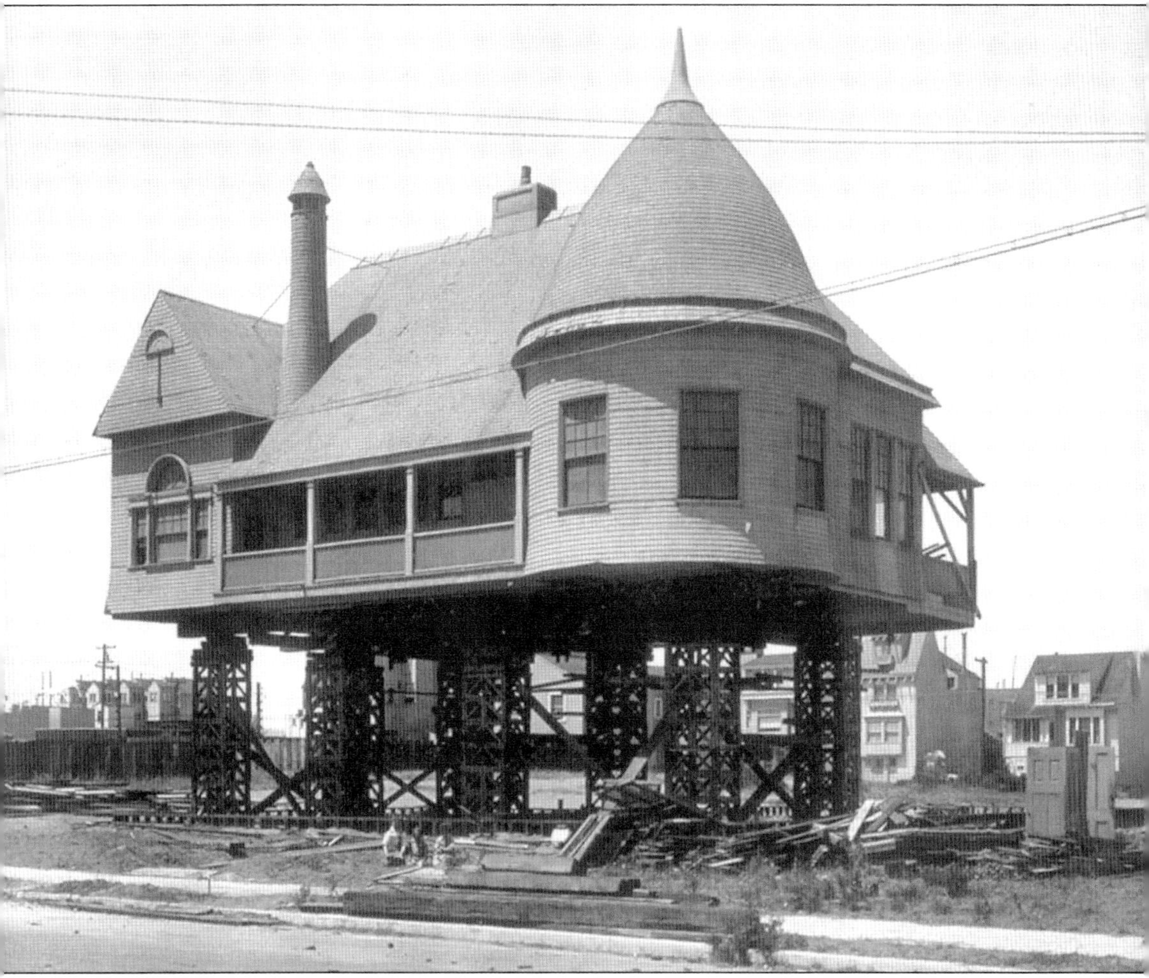

Five lots on Twenty-Fourth Avenue housed the Beach Chalet. Its upper story was supported on cribbing while a foundation and large assembly room were constructed beneath it. For the next 33 years, it hosted Scouts events and numerous community groups. This photograph shows it being renovated in its new Twenty-Fourth Avenue home in 1925. The Scouts sold it to a contractor in 1958, and later, it burned to the ground. (Courtesy of a private collection.)

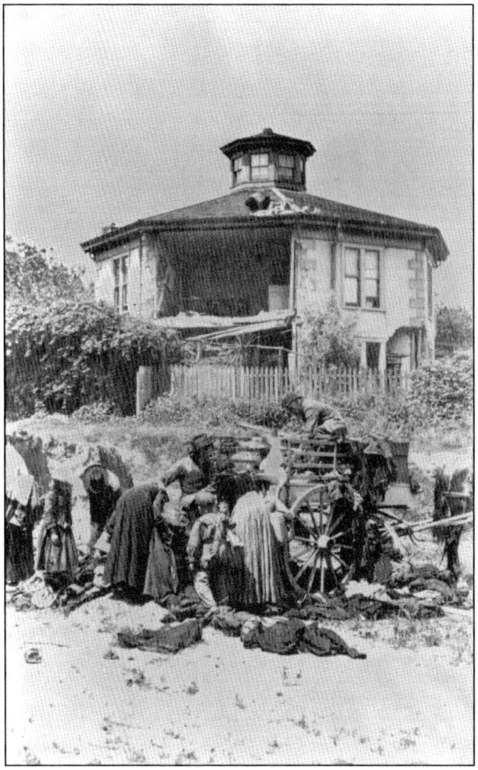

This 1906 photograph, taken by Arnold Genthe, shows the original location of the 1861 McElroy Octagon House, one of five octagon houses in the city, and captures the effects of the 1906 earthquake on the building. It stood vacant and neglected until it was acquired, moved, and restored by the National Society of the Colonial Dames of America. In 1952, PG&E sought bids to tear down the house so the land could be sold. (Courtesy of the Library of Congress.)

The McElroy Octagon House in 1956 is shown in its new location. Two matron members of the National Society of the Colonial Dames of America who lived across the street donated their land for the McElroy Octagon House's new home. Surprisingly, almost nothing was known of its history when the society purchased it. In 1952, it was sold for $1, plus the cost of moving it. The house was rotated before being placed on its new site. Joseph A. Baird took this photograph. (Courtesy of the Library of Congress.)

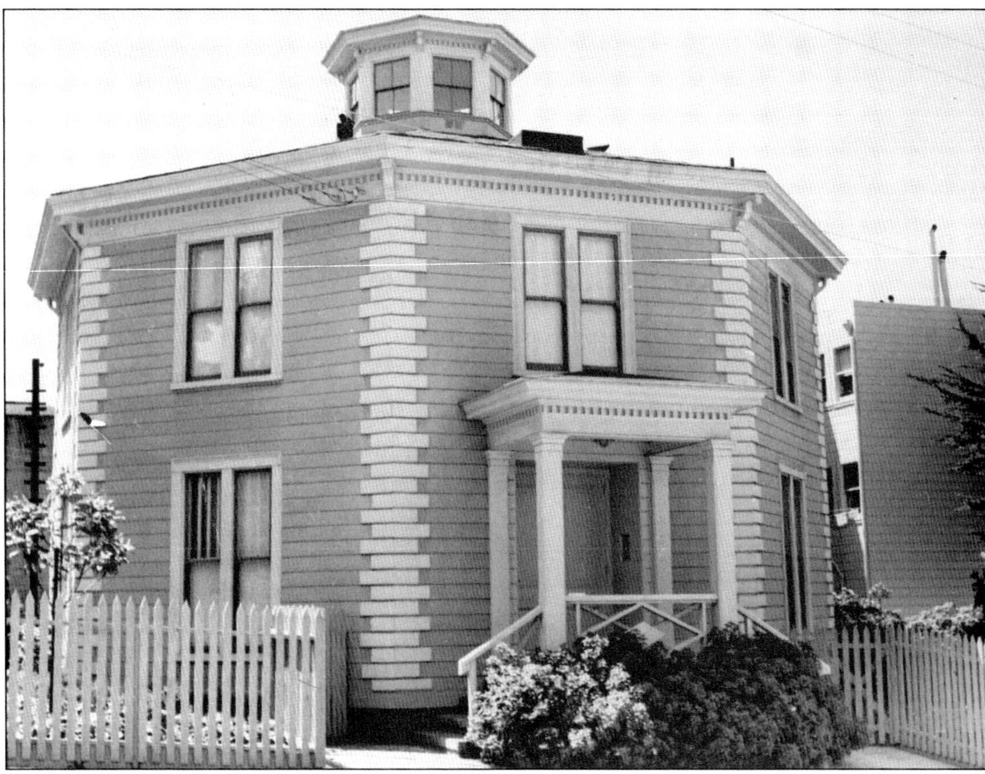

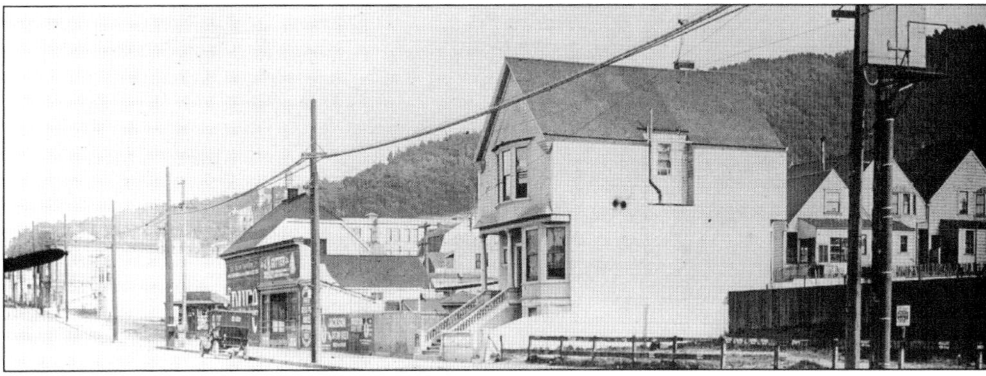

This photograph, probably taken around 1915, shows a house that stood approximately on Irving Street between Ninth and Tenth Avenues. Before 1935, the house was moved to Funston Street between Irving and Judah Streets, where it still stands. There is no other information about this house's moving history. (Courtesy of a private collection.)

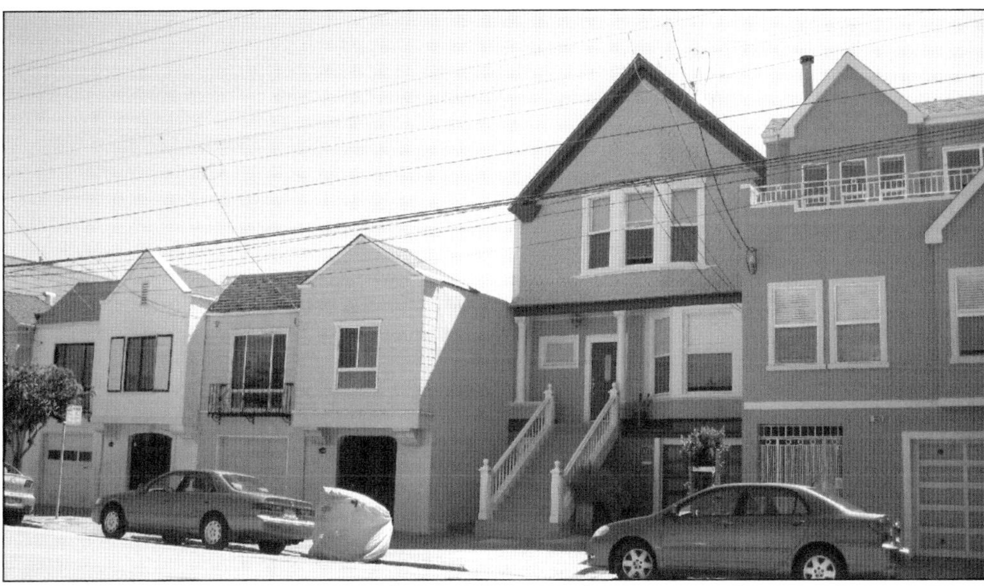

A more modern photograph shows the same house today, at its new home on Funston Street between Irving and Judah Streets. The history of how and why it moved, like so many of the ordinary row houses in San Francisco's neighborhoods, has yet to surface. (Courtesy of the Lorri Ungaretti collection.)

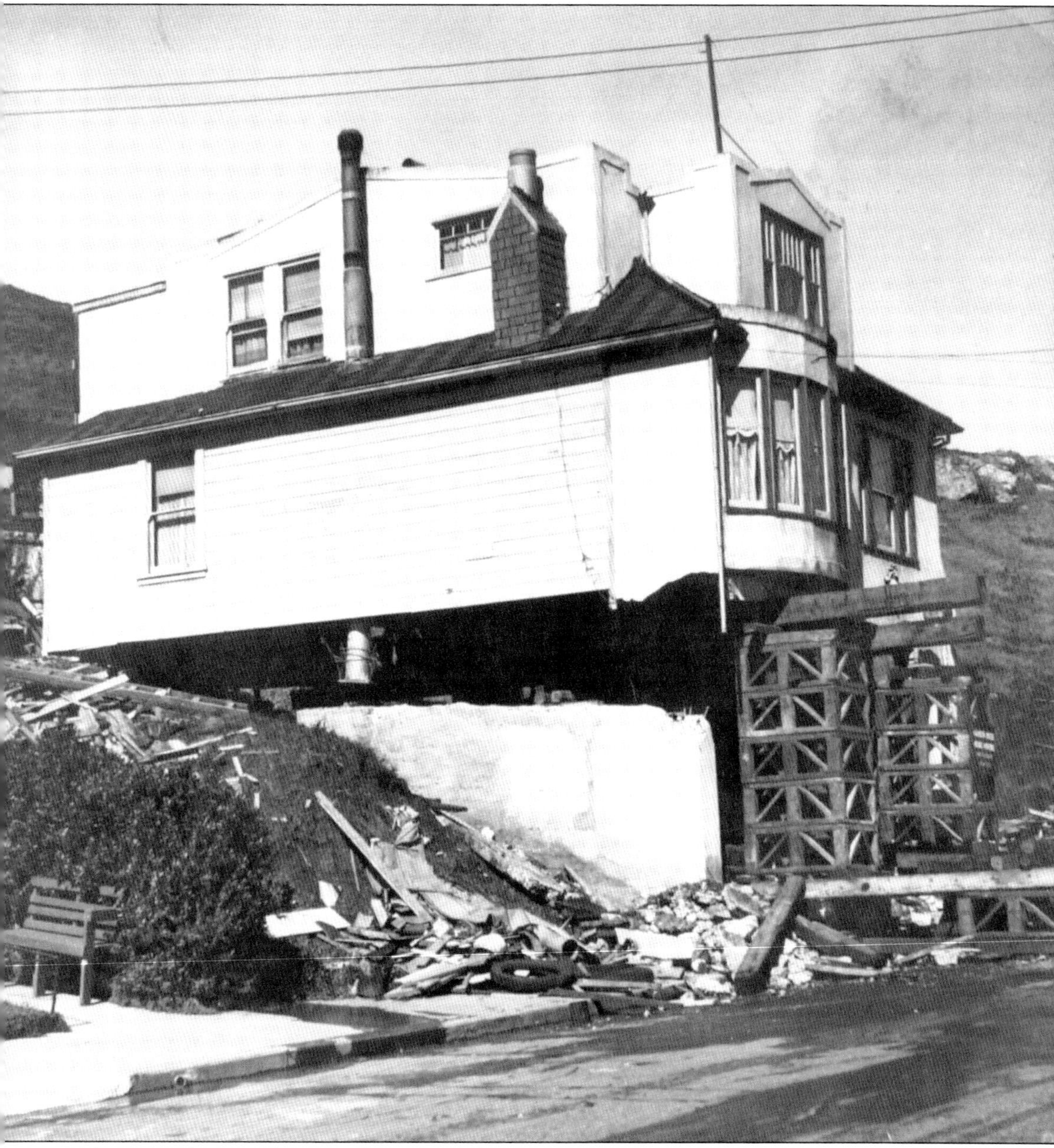

This 1936 photograph sports the title "sliding house on Bernal Heights hill" on the back of the image, but research indicates it may have been located at the top of Folsom Street and was being moved by Hanson Brothers to allow for the completion of the construction of Bernal Heights Boulevard, which was built between 1931 and 1936 to circle Bernal Hill. (Courtesy of the History Center, San Francisco Public Library.)

Five

Movers and Shakers
Building Moves of the 1940s–1960s

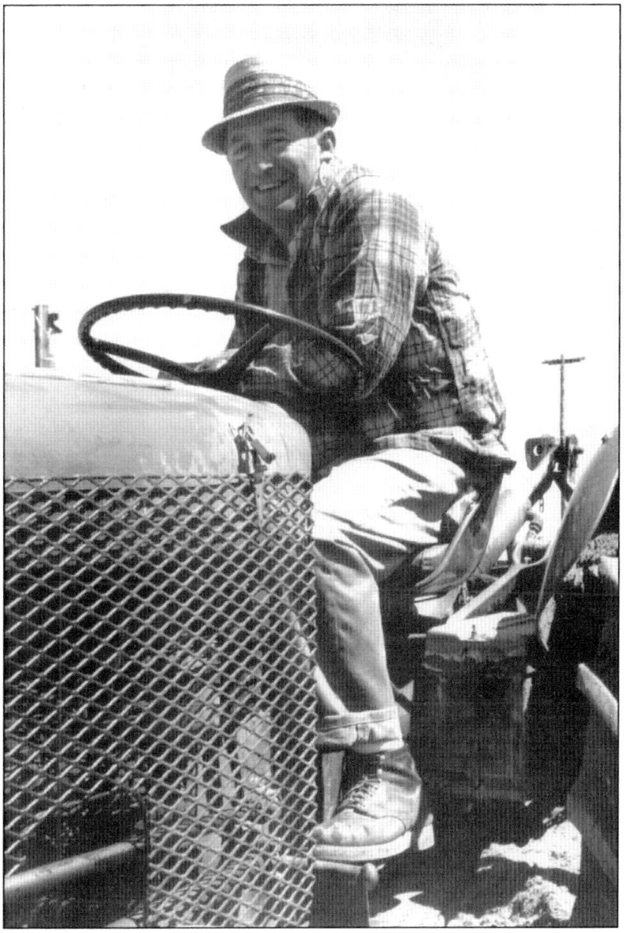

Joseph Caruso, a hardworking Italian American contractor with a big family and a big heart, saw opportunity when the Bay Area Rapid Transit (BART) system employed eminent domain in the 1960s to inform people that their houses had to be moved or destroyed to make way for progress. His journey from contractor to house mover centered on obtaining cheap houses at auction for $300 to $500, moving them onto his vacant lots, and renting them. Joseph Caruso's small local Portola District business would change the lives of everyone he touched. Sweeny Street and Gaven Street vacant lots hosted groups of his buildings (as many as nine in one row), with his construction expertise lending to their move, reconstruction, rental, and eventual sale. His willingness to tell a small child stories about his house-moving business was a direct influence on the creation of this history some 40 years later. (Courtesy of the Caruso family collection.)

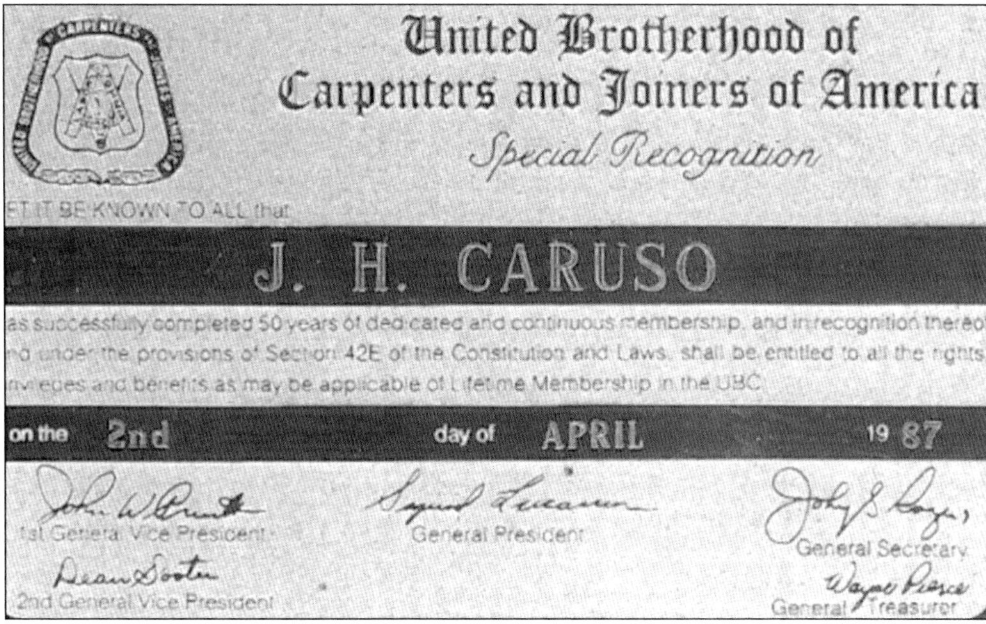

United Brotherhood of
Carpenters and Joiners of America
Special Recognition

ET IT BE KNOWN TO ALL that

J. H. CARUSO

as successfully completed 50 years of dedicated and continuous membership, and in recognition thereof nd under the provisions of Section 42E of the Constitution and Laws, shall be entitled to all the rights, ivileges and benefits as may be applicable of Lifetime Membership in the UBC

on the 2nd day of APRIL 19 87

1st General Vice President | General President | General Secretary

2nd General Vice President | General Treasurer

Joseph Caruso's dedication to his job is recognized in this certificate from the United Brotherhood of Carpenters and Joiners of America. Ten years later, he would receive a pin commending 60 years of achievement. His motivation may have been money, but his side business of moving houses into the neighborhood changed many streets in the Portola District. (Courtesy of the Caruso family collection.)

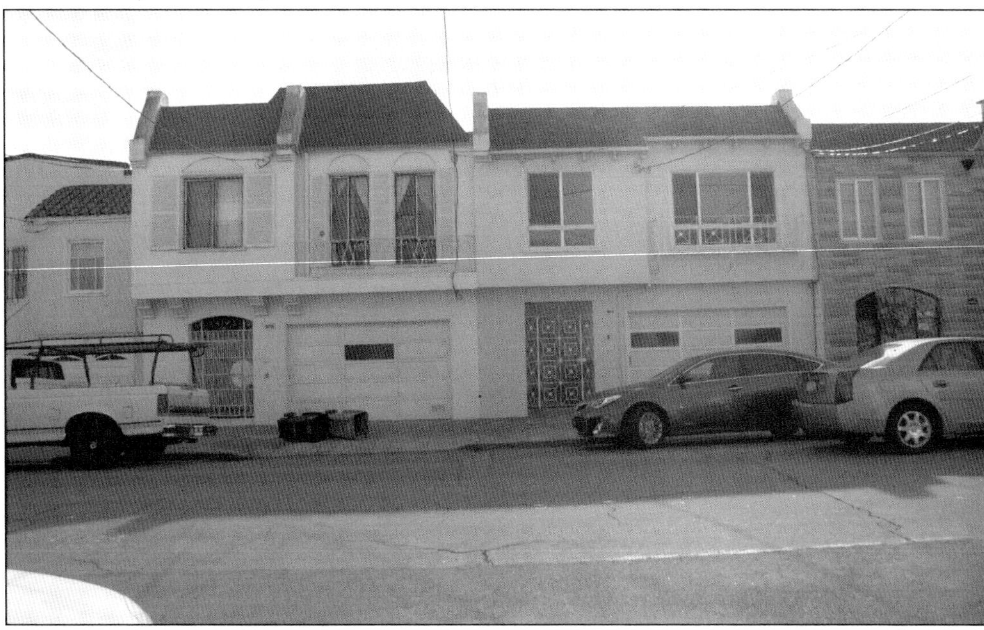

Hanson Movers and Joseph Caruso moved these two row houses (center) from Balboa Park into the Portola District. Caruso's teenage son Anthony's job was to ride atop the building, pushing up street wires as the house crept down Silver Avenue. Power and phone lines were guided over the house by inverted skids on the front of the house. Two-by-fours insulated the men from power lines, most of which were frayed or bare. (Photograph by Beni C. Bacon.)

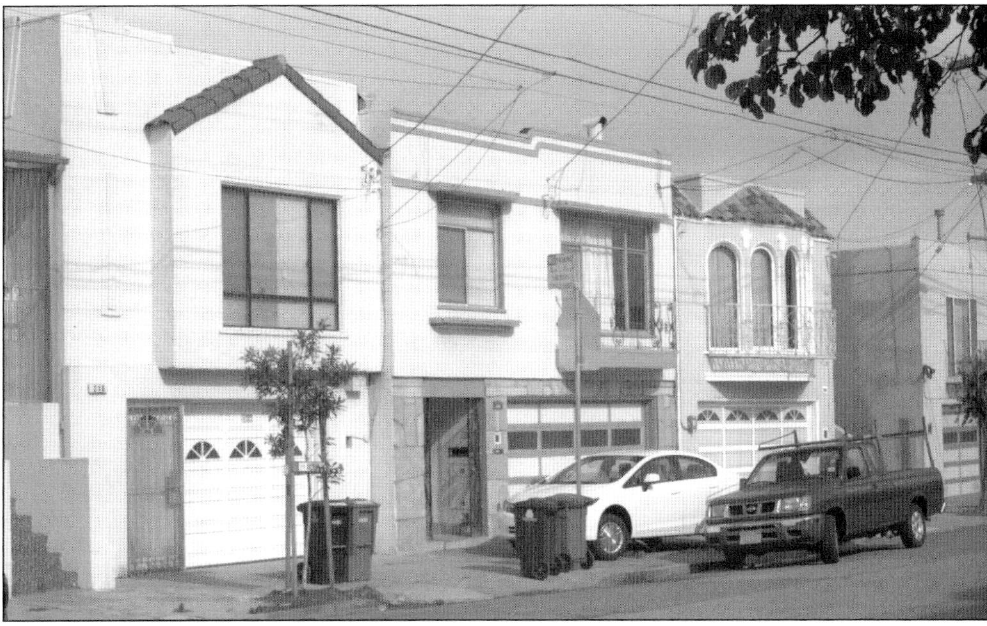

Joseph Caruso's biggest coup was his purchase of a vacant block of land on Gaven Street. It also proved his greatest challenge, as he then had to subdivide the land into lots, all of which had to be 25 feet. The last oversized lot required him to search the city for a wide home that needed moving and would fit on a 33-foot lot; he finally found such a house at Geneva Avenue and Mission Street. (Photograph by Beni C. Bacon.)

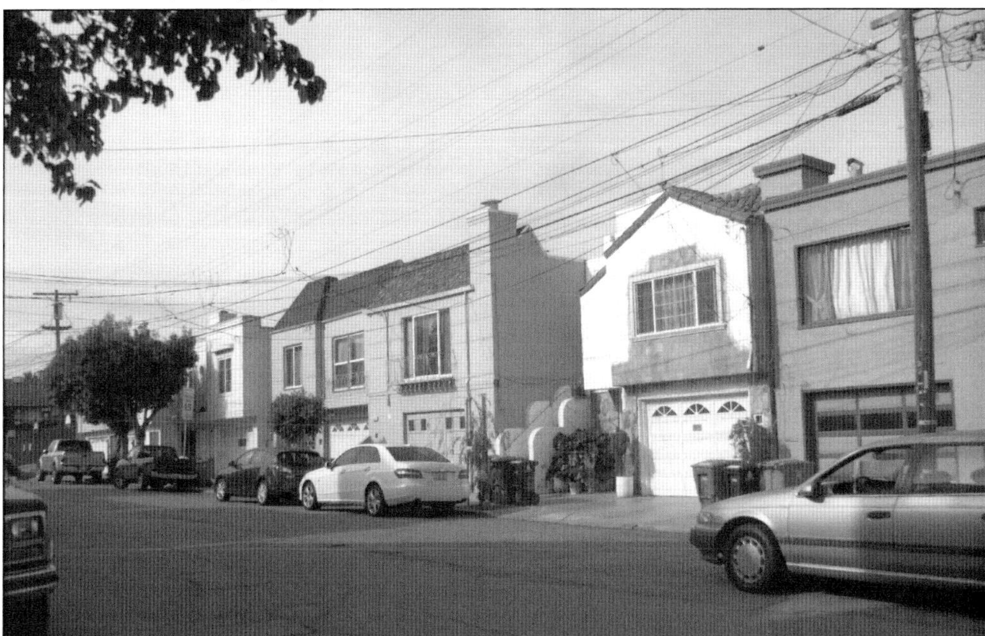

Joseph Caruso moved every house seen in this picture of Gaven Street, one by one. All houses were auctioned due to the BART system's construction. When Joseph Caruso was ready to sell them after years of renting, $2,000 down would allow even struggling renters to own. He had his own payment books and often financed the purchases himself. (Photograph by Beni C. Bacon.)

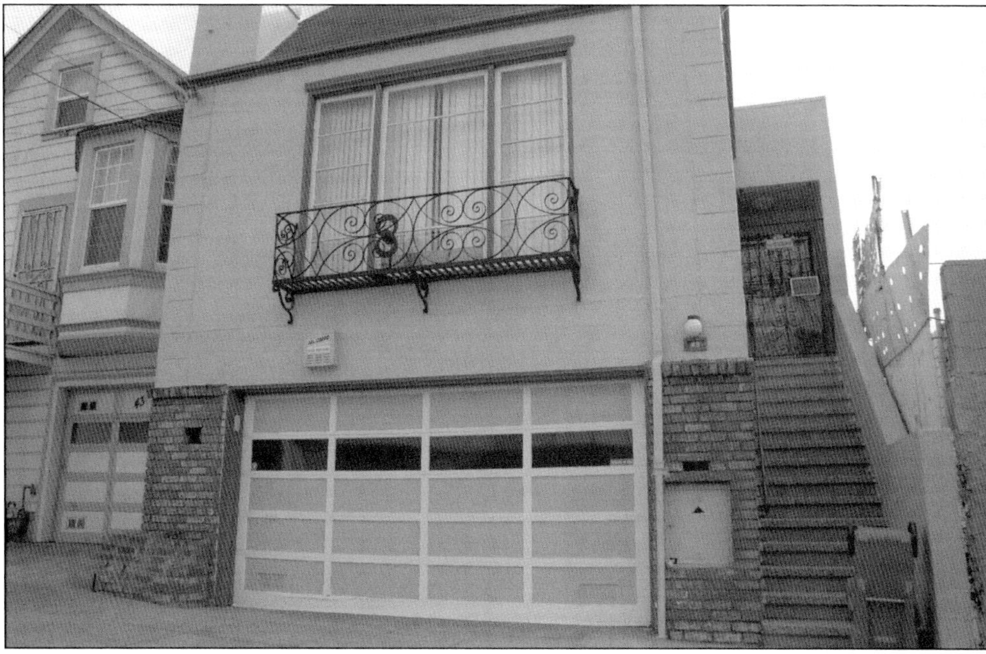

Another of Joseph Caruso's moved houses resides on the first block of Gaven Street. Its brickwork was added on later. When the owner of the building next door blamed Caruso's house-moving activities for causing his home's cracked walls, Joseph Caruso simply bought the disgruntled homeowner's abode to solve the problem. (Photograph by Beni C. Bacon.)

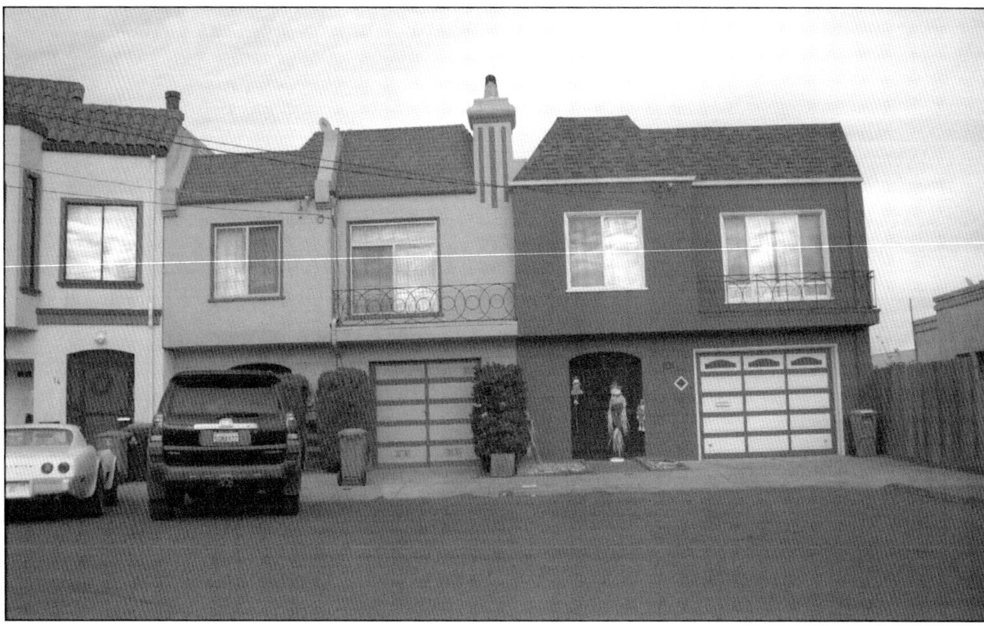

The two houses on Sweeny Street originated on Arco Street, a tiny dead-end side street located several neighborhoods over in Balboa Park. Note that similar houses sport the same tunnel entrances and phony roof fronts (the newer, shallower houses have tile roofs). After the longer homes were moved, taller ones were built in their place, albeit with much smaller yards due to BART, which tunnels underground behind these buildings. (Photograph by Beni C. Bacon.)

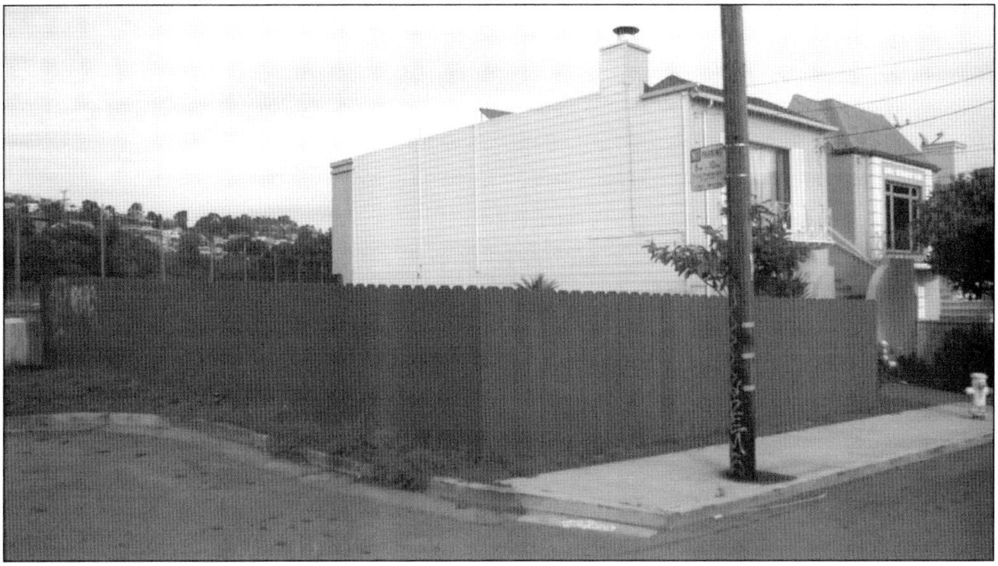

The BART system runs behind this Balboa Park house, which remains next to a vacant lot where one of Joseph Caruso's houses was moved out. Note that despite its expanse, the side of this remaining house has no windows; one clue that it once abutted another building. The house removed would have been just as long as this home—too long for the BART tunnel angling in behind it. (Photograph by Beni C. Bacon.)

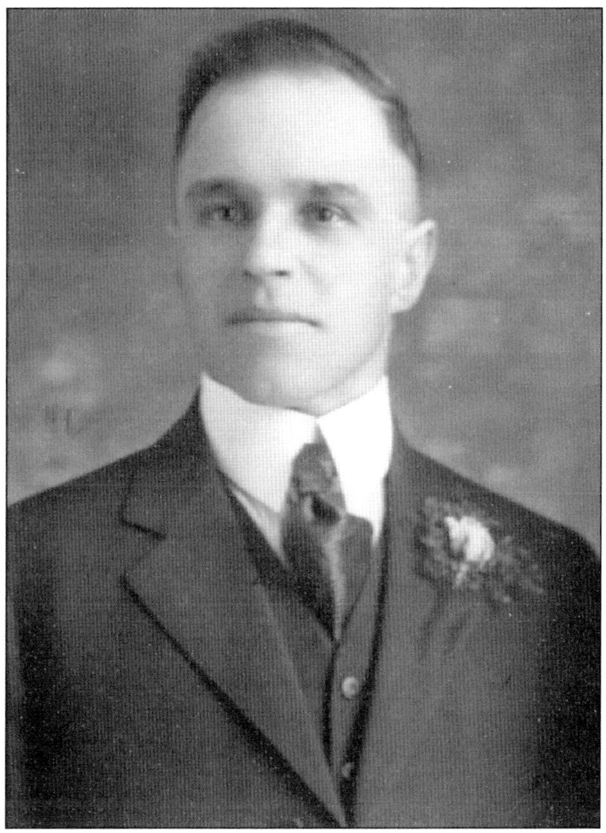

John Kambic was primarily a house builder who constructed a number of homes on San Francisco's Potrero District between 1919 and 1946. Like Joseph Caruso, he saw opportunity in moving and preserving houses. He passed away in 1972, but his legacy lives on in the form of the many houses he moved out of harm's way. This photograph shows him as a young man. (Courtesy of the Donald Kambic collection.)

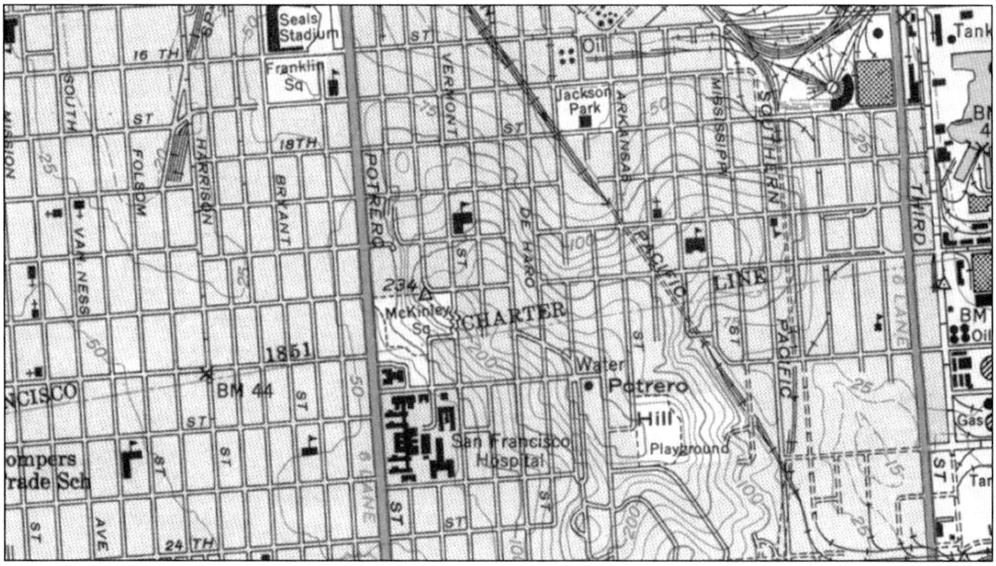

The construction of San Francisco's freeways and transport systems, from Highway 101 to the 280 Freeway and, later, the BART system, ran through neighborhoods and sparked eminent domain battles as homeowners faced the choice of moving their homes or having them purchased and destroyed. This is a pre-freeway 1947 map of the Potrero District. When the 101 Freeway was built, it cut through the neighborhood, seen here at an angle. (Courtesy of a private collection.)

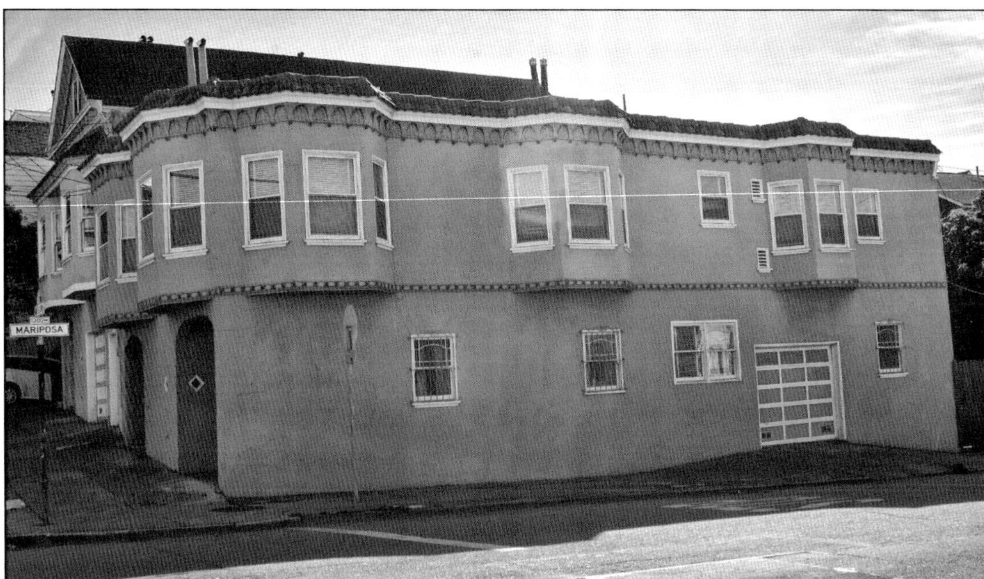

When the 101 Freeway was built through the neighborhood, John Kambic shifted from building houses to moving houses, and he relocated at least 10 houses between 1945 and 1962. This house, which is 25 feet wide at the front and 65 feet long, was moved from San Bruno Avenue to Missouri Street in 1946. (Courtesy of the Mike Shea collection.)

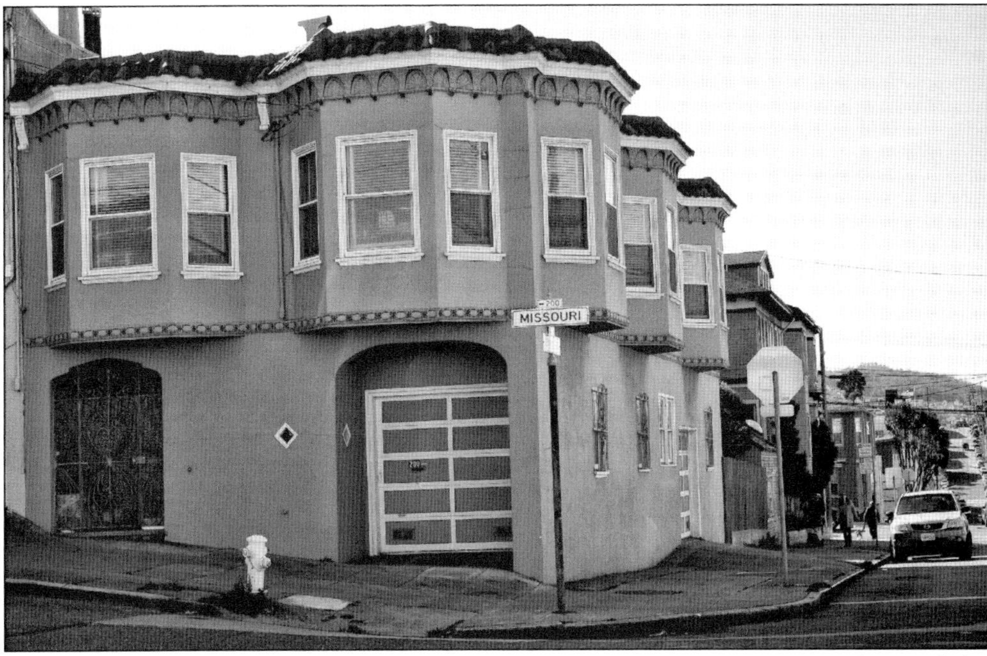

Moving corner-lot houses typically meant larger buildings; however, in some ways, they tended to be easier moves, in that there was more room on one side. At least a corner house did not have to fit between two other houses; although, the building still had to fit precisely on its new lot. (Courtesy of the Mike Shea collection.)

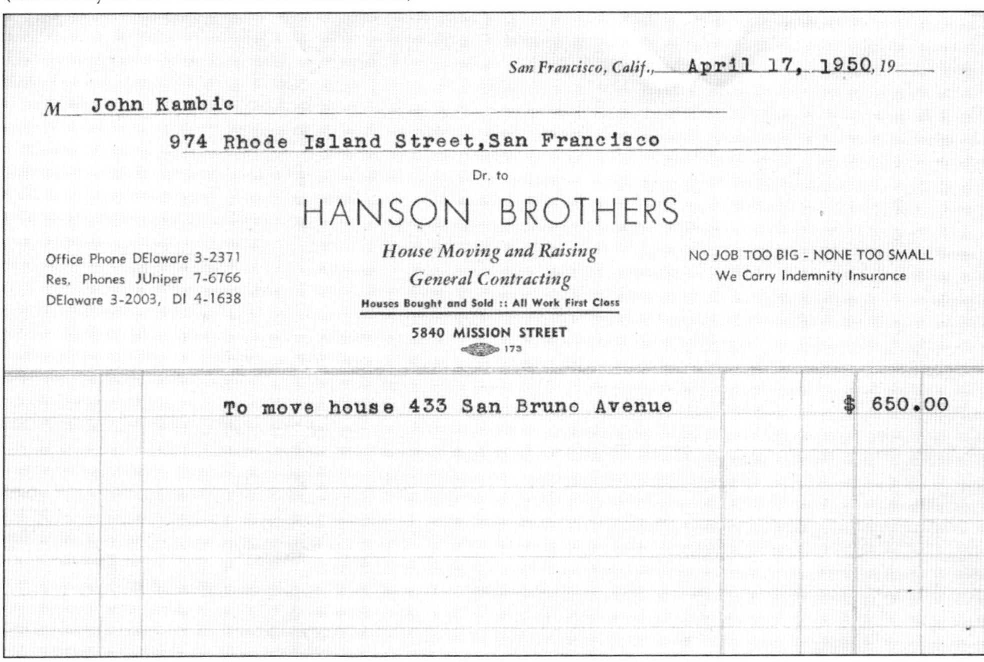

San Francisco, Calif., April 17, 1950, 19

M John Kambic

974 Rhode Island Street, San Francisco

Dr. to

HANSON BROTHERS

House Moving and Raising

General Contracting

Houses Bought and Sold :: All Work First Class

5840 MISSION STREET

Office Phone DElaware 3-2371
Res. Phones JUniper 7-6766
DElaware 3-2003, DI 4-1638

NO JOB TOO BIG - NONE TOO SMALL
We Carry Indemnity Insurance

To move house 433 San Bruno Avenue $ 650.00

While most small contractors did not move the houses they owned or purchased, they did utilize house-moving companies, none of which remain in the city today. John Kambic used Hanson Brothers for all his moves. This Hanson Brothers Moving receipt documents the cost of a typical row house move in 1950. (Courtesy of the Donald Kambic collection.)

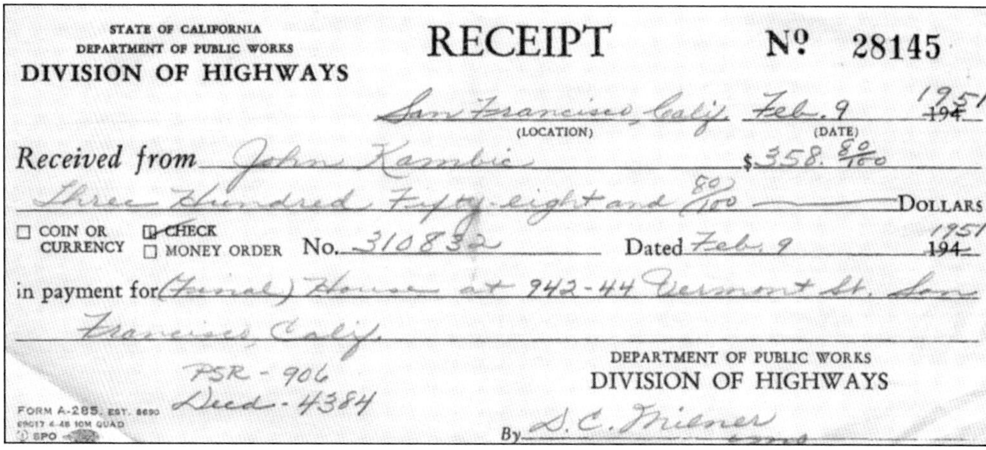

STATE OF CALIFORNIA
DEPARTMENT OF PUBLIC WORKS
DIVISION OF HIGHWAYS

RECEIPT

Nº 28145

San Francisco, Calif. (LOCATION) Feb. 9 1951 (DATE)

Received from John Kambic $358.80/100

Three Hundred Fifty-eight and 80/100 DOLLARS

☐ COIN OR CURRENCY ☒ CHECK ☐ MONEY ORDER No. 310832 Dated Feb. 9 1951

in payment for (Final) House at 942-44 Vermont St. San Francisco Calif.

PSR - 906
Deed - 4384

DEPARTMENT OF PUBLIC WORKS
DIVISION OF HIGHWAYS

By S. C. Milner

FORM A-285. EST. 8690

A paper trail follows the process of buying a house at auction and moving it. This is a 1951 receipt documenting contractor John Kambic's purchase of a Vermont Street house from the Division of Highways. Such houses were typically bid upon at auction and sold for bargain prices because they had to be moved. (Courtesy of the Donald Kambic collection.)

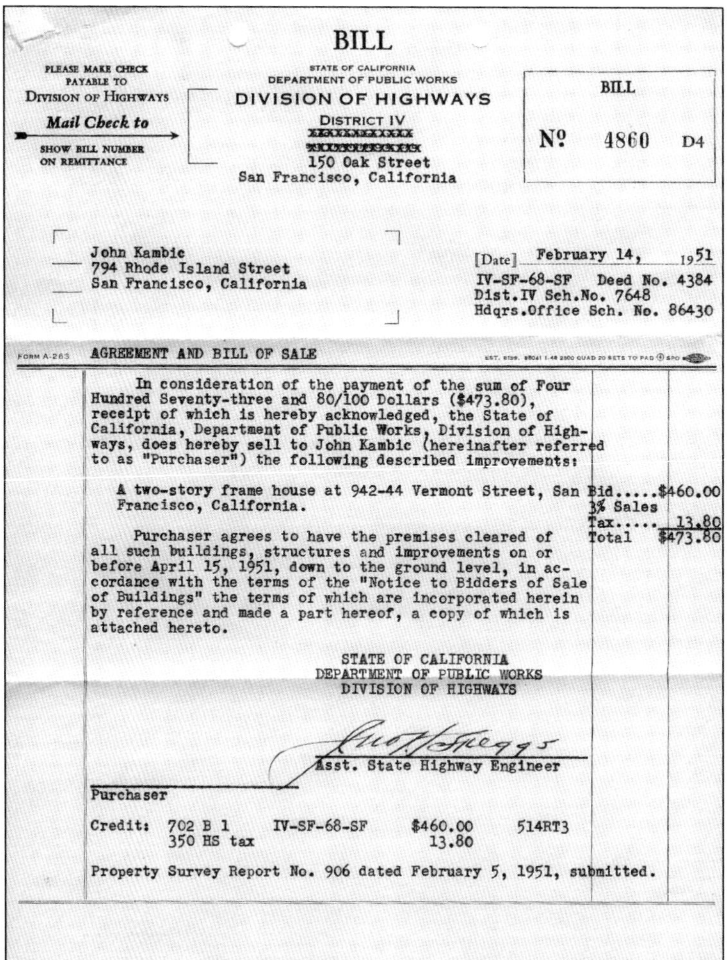

BILL

PLEASE MAKE CHECK PAYABLE TO DIVISION OF HIGHWAYS

Mail Check to

SHOW BILL NUMBER ON REMITTANCE

STATE OF CALIFORNIA
DEPARTMENT OF PUBLIC WORKS
DIVISION OF HIGHWAYS
DISTRICT IV
150 Oak Street
San Francisco, California

BILL
Nº 4860 D4

John Kambic
794 Rhode Island Street
San Francisco, California

[Date] February 14, 1951
IV-SF-68-SF Deed No. 4384
Dist.IV Sch.No. 7648
Hdqrs.Office Sch. No. 86430

FORM A-263 AGREEMENT AND BILL OF SALE

In consideration of the payment of the sum of Four Hundred Seventy-three and 80/100 Dollars ($473.80), receipt of which is hereby acknowledged, the State of California, Department of Public Works, Division of Highways, does hereby sell to John Kambic (hereinafter referred to as "Purchaser") the following described improvements:

A two-story frame house at 942-44 Vermont Street, San Francisco, California.

Bid.....$460.00
3% Sales Tax..... 13.80
Total $473.80

Purchaser agrees to have the premises cleared of all such buildings, structures and improvements on or before April 15, 1951, down to the ground level, in accordance with the terms of the "Notice to Bidders of Sale of Buildings" the terms of which are incorporated herein by reference and made a part hereof, a copy of which is attached hereto.

STATE OF CALIFORNIA
DEPARTMENT OF PUBLIC WORKS
DIVISION OF HIGHWAYS

Asst. State Highway Engineer

Purchaser

Credit: 702 B 1 IV-SF-68-SF $460.00 514RT3
350 HS tax 13.80

Property Survey Report No. 906 dated February 5, 1951, submitted.

Note the date of February 14, 1951, on this bill of sale and the stipulation in the contract that the house had to be moved on or before April 15, 1951, "down to the ground level," in accordance with the bid agreement. With only two months leeway, a buyer had to have both the final destination and moving company in place before buying a building at auction. (Courtesy of the Donald Kambic collection.)

With timelines involved in freeway construction, the city could ill afford to sell buildings to individuals who could not fulfill their end of the sale. A performance bond was required of bidders. Here, the Division of Highways acknowledges payment of a $1,000 performance bond by contractor John Kambic—considerably more than the cost of either purchasing or moving the building. (Courtesy of the Donald Kambic collection.)

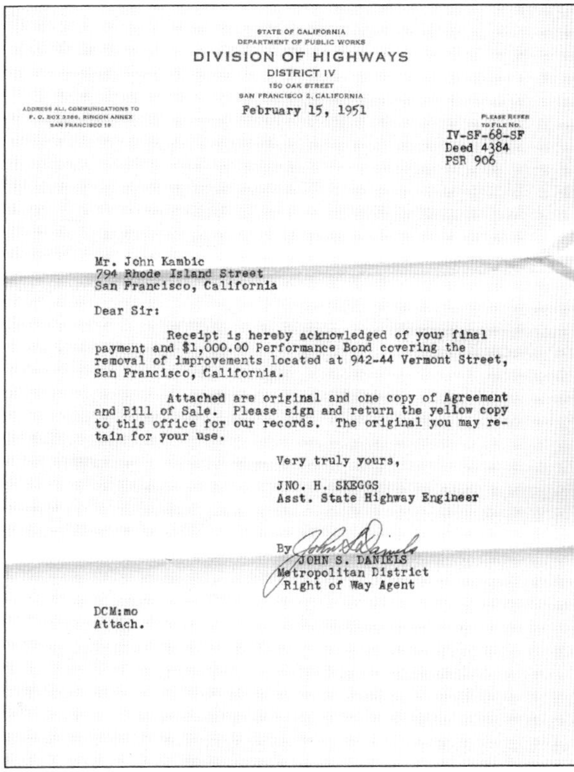

STATE OF CALIFORNIA
DEPARTMENT OF PUBLIC WORKS
DIVISION OF HIGHWAYS
DISTRICT IV
150 OAK STREET
SAN FRANCISCO 2, CALIFORNIA

ADDRESS ALL COMMUNICATIONS TO
P. O. BOX 3366, RINCON ANNEX
SAN FRANCISCO 19

February 15, 1951

PLEASE REFER TO FILE NO.
IV-SF-68-SF
Deed 4384
PSR 906

Mr. John Kambic
794 Rhode Island Street
San Francisco, California

Dear Sir:

Receipt is hereby acknowledged of your final payment and $1,000.00 Performance Bond covering the removal of improvements located at 942-44 Vermont Street, San Francisco, California.

Attached are original and one copy of Agreement and Bill of Sale. Please sign and return the yellow copy to this office for our records. The original you may retain for your use.

Very truly yours,

JNO. H. SKEGGS
Asst. State Highway Engineer

By John S. Daniels
JOHN S. DANIELS
Metropolitan District
Right of Way Agent

DCM:mo
Attach.

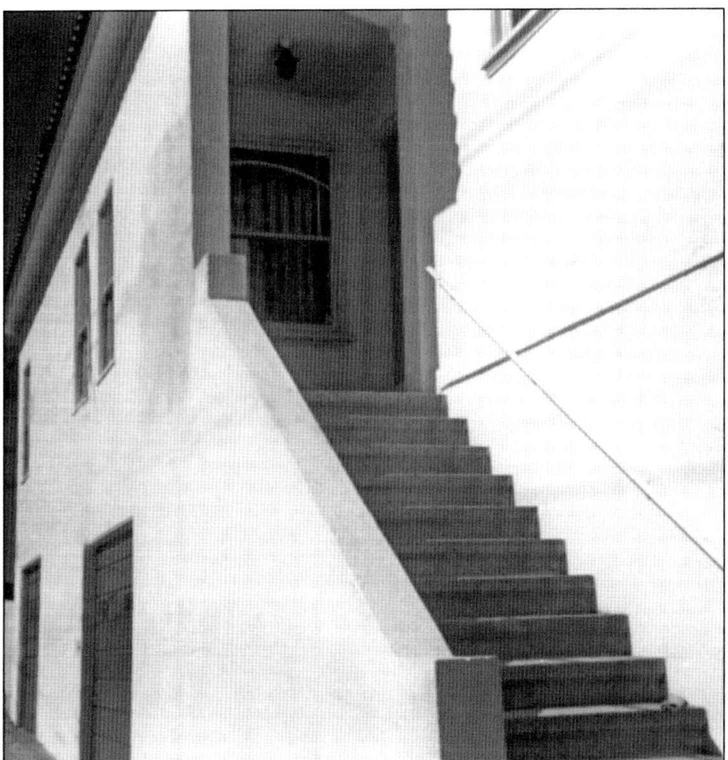

This is another corner-lot house moved by John Kambic. The building, constructed in 1924 on San Bruno Avenue by John Kambic, was moved to Rhode Island Street in 1949. Even though the stairs had to be rebuilt and a new basement constructed, it was still cheaper to buy and move a structure than build one from scratch, especially for contractors who already had the licenses, materials, and knowledge. (Courtesy of the Mike Shea collection.)

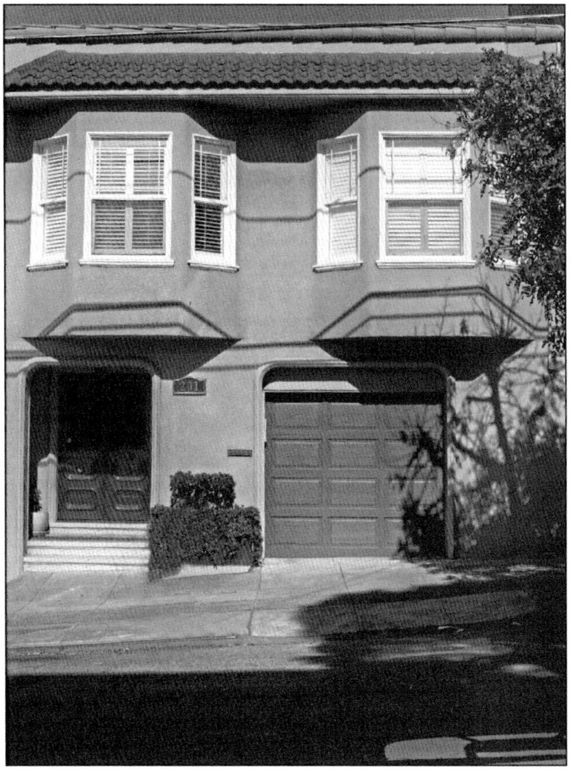

In 1951, this building was moved to Arkansas Street. Its original address is unknown. Note the stucco fronts and similar styles to many of the buildings moved by contractor John Kambic. Such buildings appear in side-by-side rows in many San Francisco neighborhoods. Today, it is impossible to know their origins (or even that they were moved buildings) unless one knows their history. (Courtesy of the Mike Shea collection.)

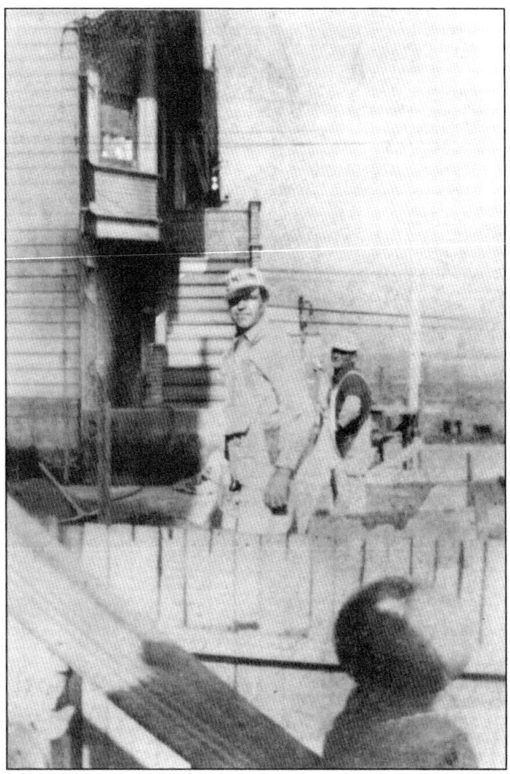

John Kambic is shown building his first house in 1919. Like other small-time contractors who found themselves involved in the house-moving business, John Kambic's efforts preserved buildings and changed neighborhoods. As both a builder and a contractor, Kambic was familiar with city codes, construction, and the permit process, which enhanced his entry into the house-moving business. (Courtesy of the Donald Kambic collection.)

In 1951, this corner building was moved to Rhode Island Street. It was originally constructed in 1910. Its original location is unknown, but John Kambic's bid saved this building and added to Potrero Hill's evolving character. Note that the new corner lot was on a slope, which proved no obstacle to contractor/builder Kambic, who had constructed 14 houses on the steep slopes of Kansas Street. (Courtesy of the Mike Shea collection.)

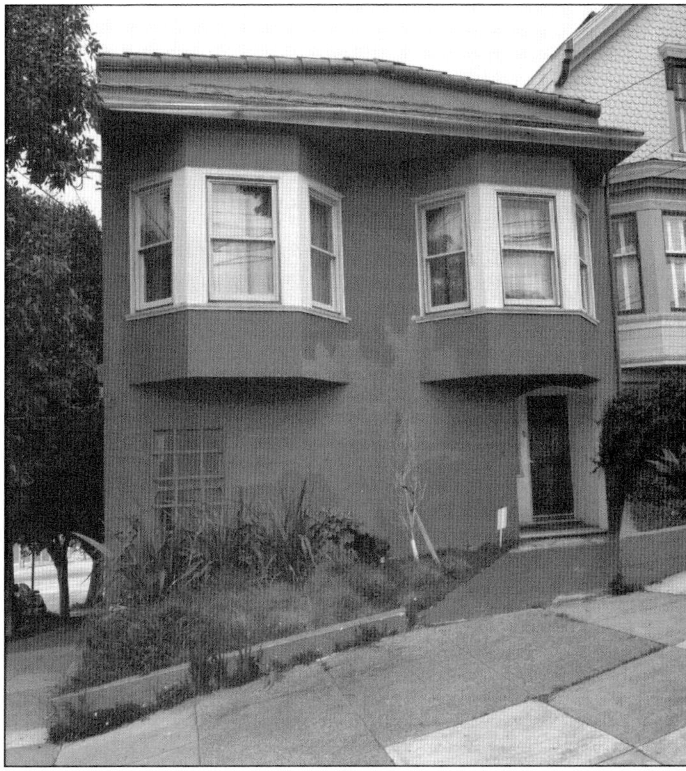

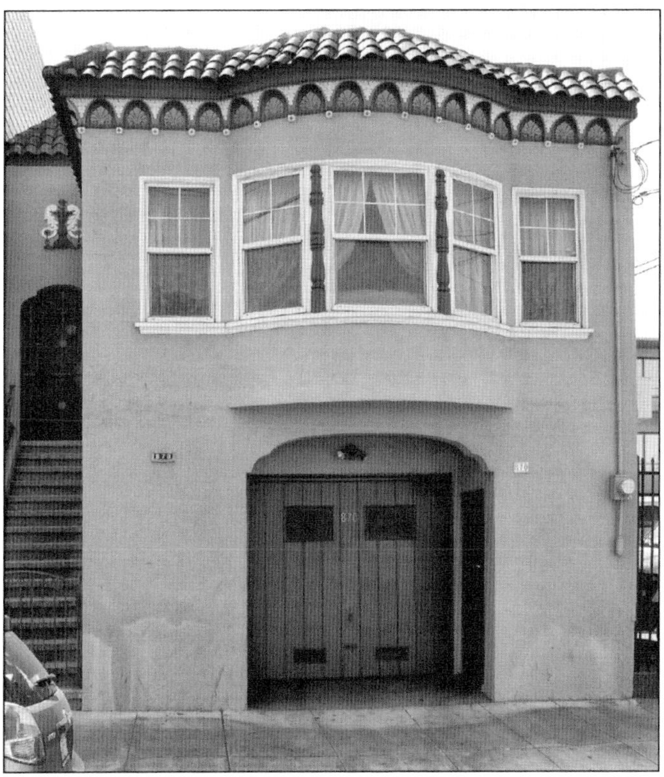

In 1946, John Kambic moved this building to South Van Ness Avenue. He had built it in 1927 on San Bruno Avenue, as a typical San Francisco row house. Its stucco front was one of his building signatures and was also a popular neighborhood style at the time. (Courtesy of the Mike Shea collection.)

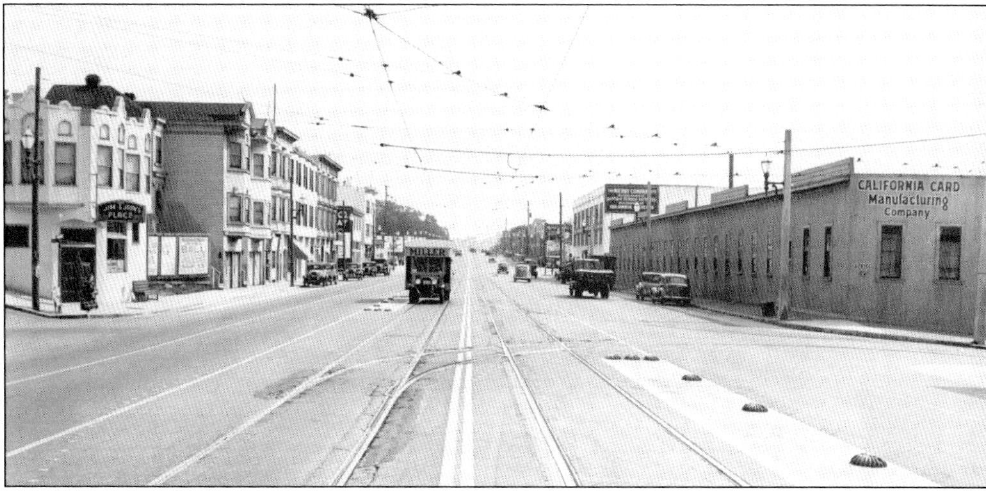

Jim and John's Place, a neighborhood bar, stood on the left side of Potrero Avenue. In 1933, bar owner and manager John Kambic decided to construct a gas station where the bar stood (501 Potrero Avenue) and build a new, larger bar across the street. Kambic saw a golden opportunity to move a building, but not the whole thing. Take a good, close look at the upper second story of Jim and John's Place. (Courtesy of the San Francisco History Center, San Francisco Public Library.)

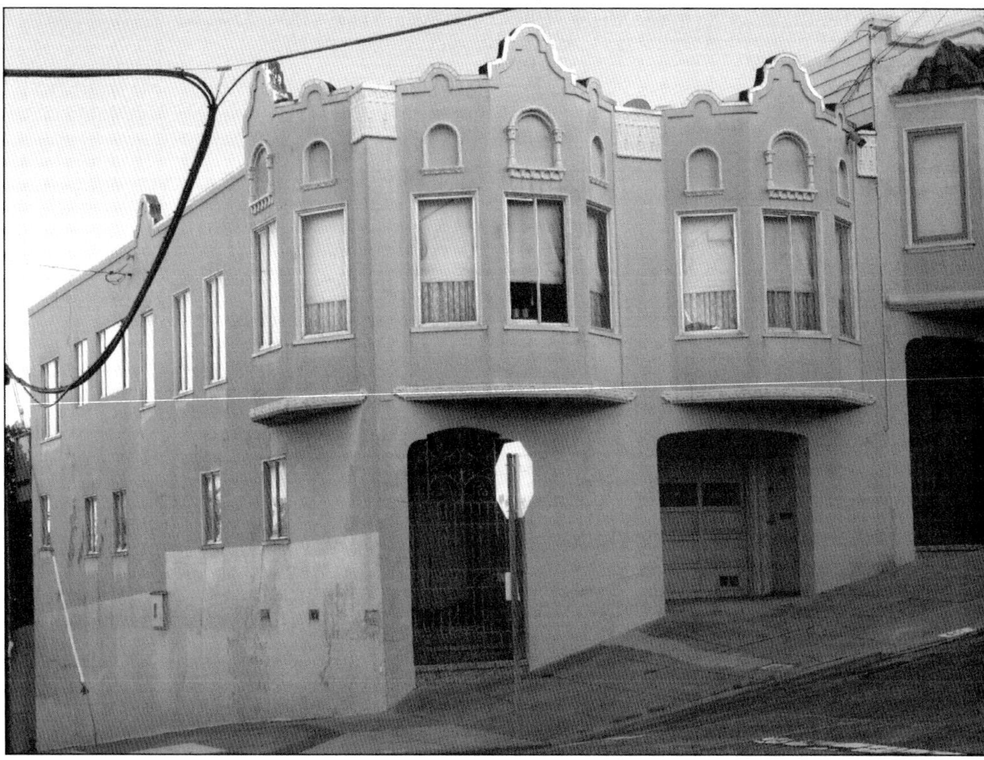

The year 1933 was likely when the upper story of Jim and John's Place moved and became the top floor of a house on Kansas Street. This photograph of the Kansas Street building shows the successful move of an upper floor from one location to another. While San Francisco city records for this address show "year built" as 1933, probably they did not have a category for "moved," especially not "partially moved." (Courtesy of the Mike Shea collection.)

Even after taking careful measurements, Kambic struggled to slide one house between two others on Vermont Street. Apparently some of the siding was warped, which made the fit a little too tight. Using bars of soap, John soaped the sides of the house, making it slippery enough to slide into place and rest on top of the new garage walls and foundation. (Courtesy of the Mike Bowman collection.)

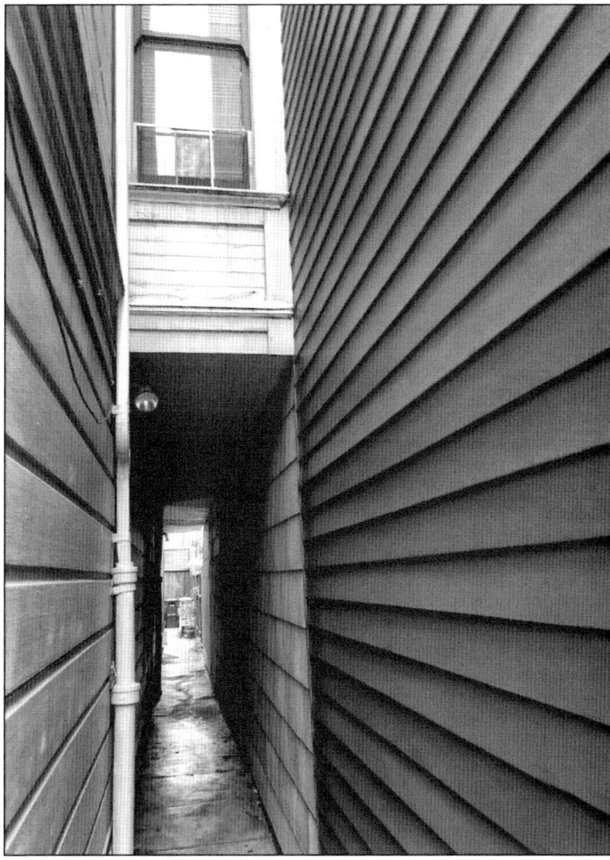

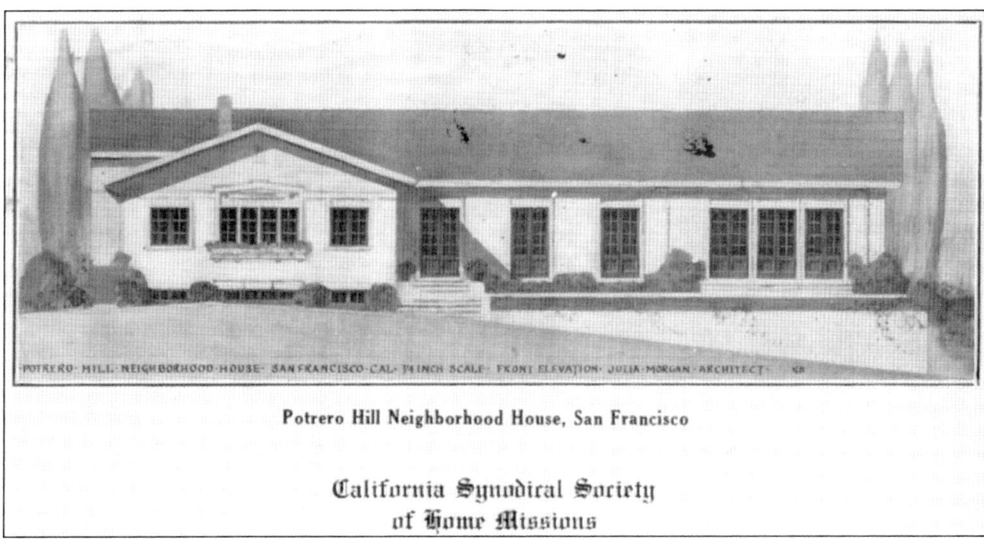

The Potrero Hill Neighborhood House was designed by architect Julia Morgan in 1919, opened in 1922, and was moved to allow for the construction of Southern Heights in 1924. To make way for Diagonal Street, it was situated 90 feet north of its original location to where it stands now, at the corner of DeHaro Street and Southern Heights Avenue. This old drawing shows the building before it was moved. (Courtesy of the Potrero Hill Archives.)

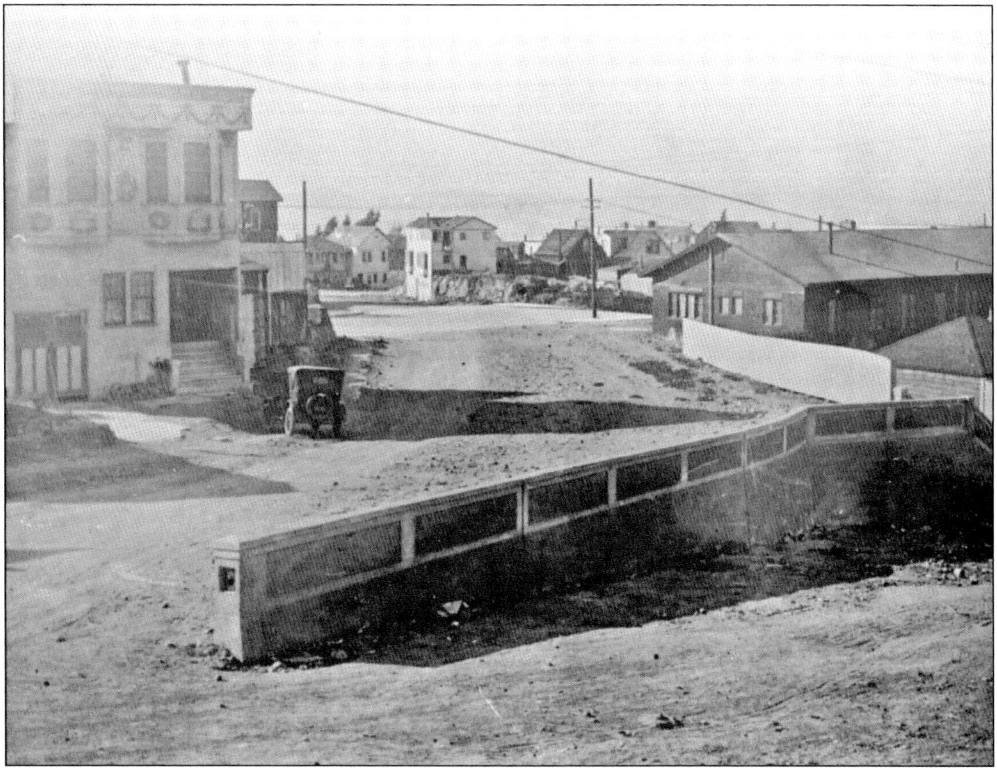

This is a 1924 photograph of the Potrero Hill Neighborhood House just after it was moved. It is the dark building at the right with a pitched roof. It stands in the same spot today, hosting various community groups and sporting a scenic view of San Francisco and the East Bay. (Courtesy of the Potrero Hill Archives.)

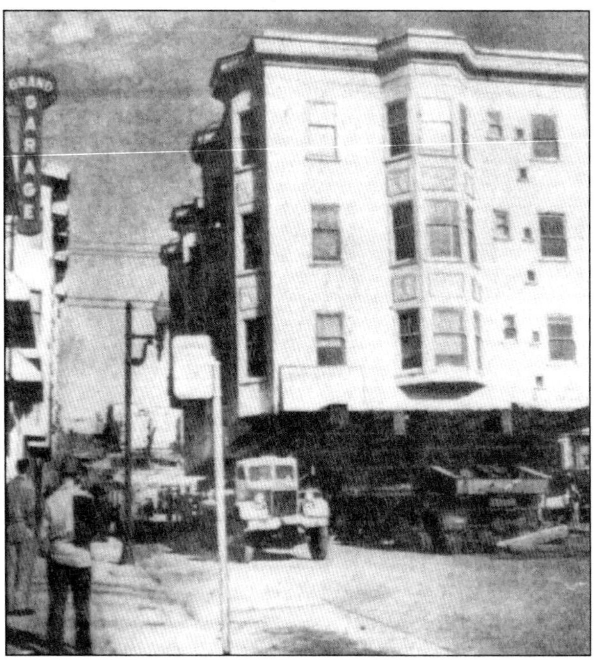

In 1950, this three-story, 400-ton apartment building was relocated to Vallejo Street for the Broadway Tunnel's construction. The 90-foot-long building had to negotiate an eight percent grade. It was set on 120 pneumatic tires and an Army surplus tank carrier, turned on a 60-foot wide street, and backed into a 50-foot wide lot. According to mover Richard Barr Montgomery, one could not stick a piece of tobacco paper between the apartment and the buildings beside it. (Courtesy of the Steve Montgomery collection.)

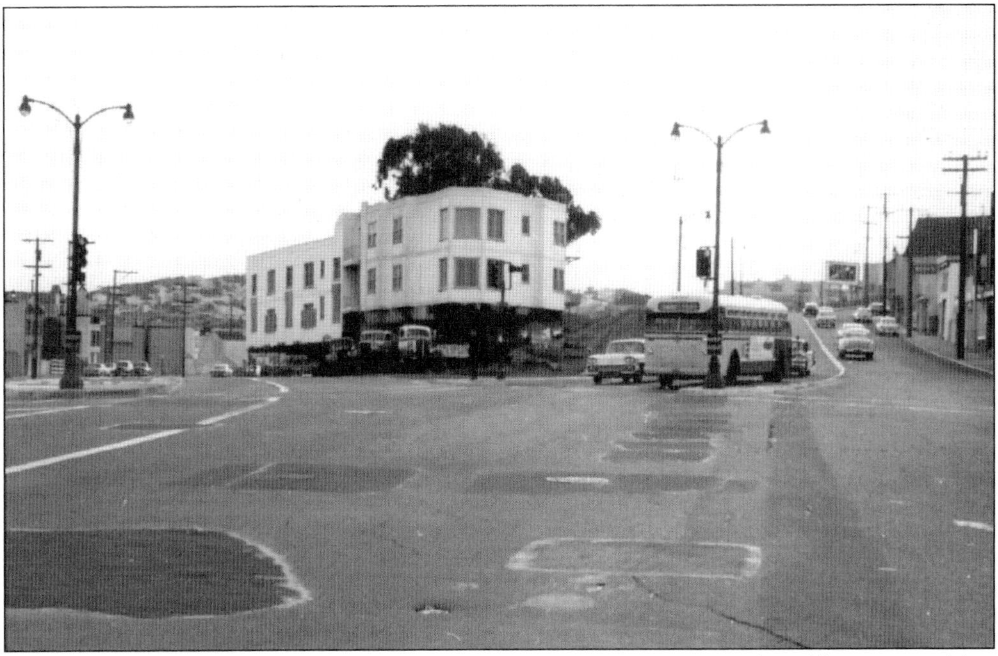

This apartment building was 60 feet wide in back and was constructed to fill its original lot. It was located on San Jose Boulevard and was moved in the late 1950s, when the Bernal Cut was widened. It was the biggest building Hubert Trost ever moved on wheels, traveling two to three blocks to its new home. It was moved in the daytime, down the street and across traffic. (Courtesy of the Hubert Trost collection.)

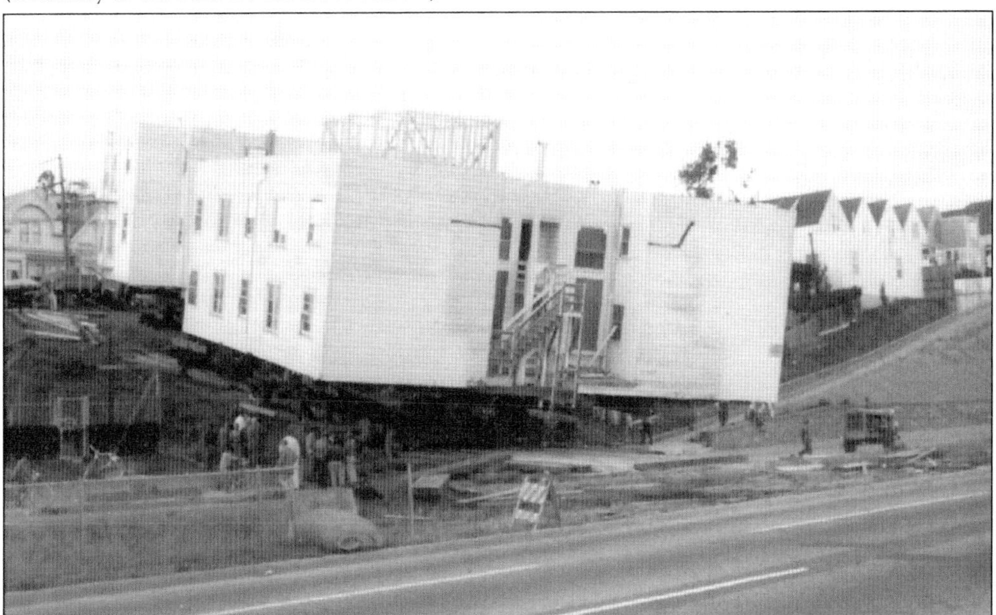

This picture of a huge apartment building in transit proves that even an oversized building can be moved uphill. The building was jacked high in the air when it was leveled off; it is seen here at an angle. Trost Movers would have to back it uphill to get it placed properly. Note the spectators, who are sensibly standing well behind it. (Courtesy of the Hubert Trost collection.)

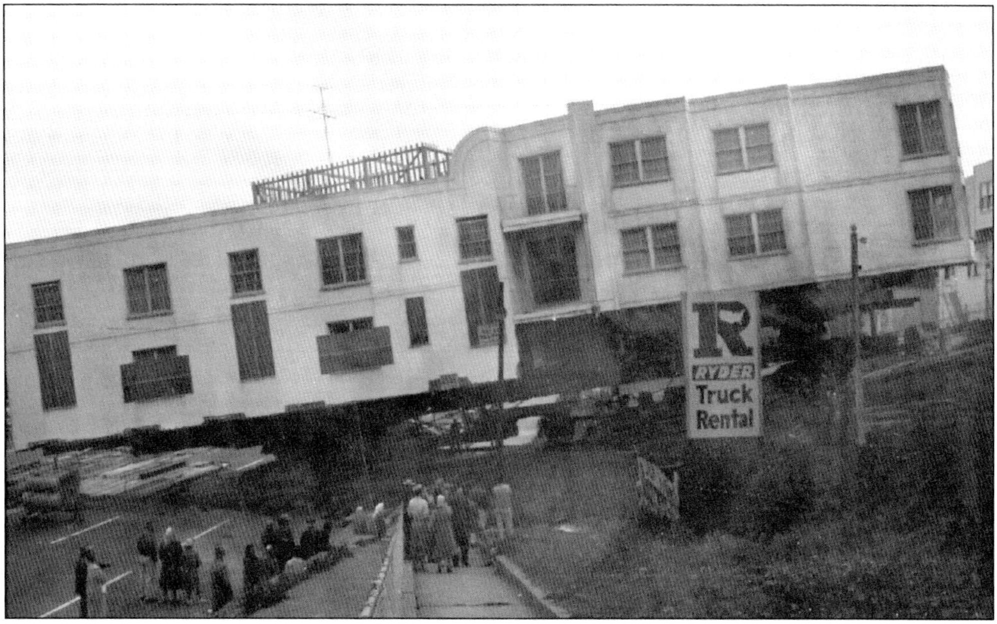

One of the remarkable aspects of this particular move was Trost's challenge of fitting a 110-foot-long apartment building into a sloping lot. Even when viewed from across the street, the venture looks challenging, requiring movers to back the entire building up as well as into an uneven lot. Even today, some longtime residents recall seeing this; it is one of the most amazing moves in San Francisco's modern building-moving history. (Courtesy of the Hubert Trost collection.)

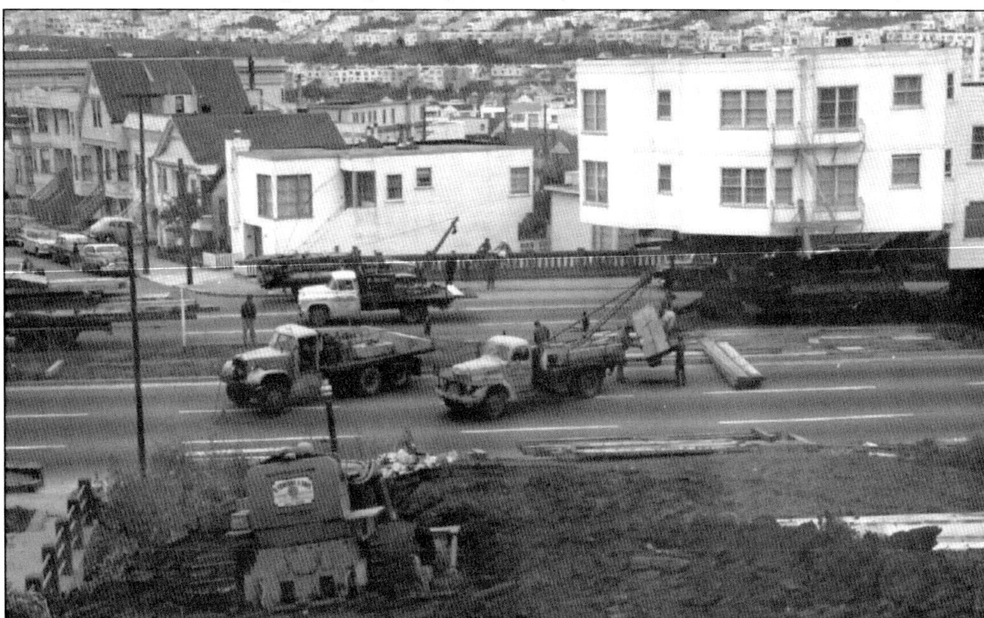
This image, shot from across the street, provides a better idea of the number of vehicles involved in moving such a massive structure. Blocks were placed behind every truck wheel so that if a cable broke, it would still stop. A beam was placed across the back tires and wedges were driven under them any time the trucks had to stop. (Courtesy of the Hubert Trost collection.)

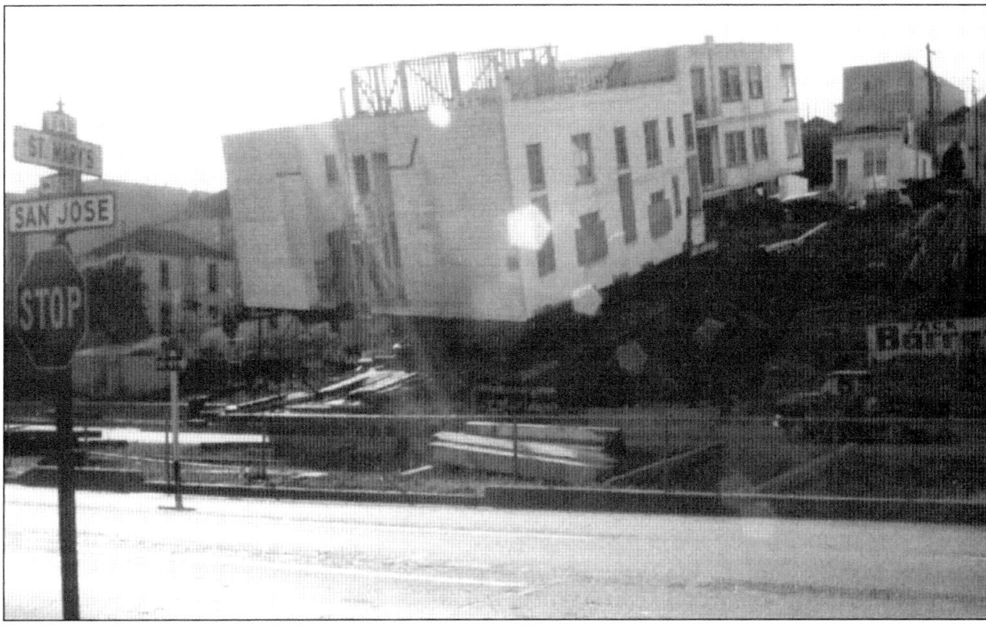

Perseverance pays off! The building has been pulled entirely onto the lot. The apartment had to be jacked high in the air before it would clear its new foundation. The back end was 60 feet wide. In the 1950s, there were no "pumpers" pouring cement after the building arrived, as is done in modern times. Today, this building has several stories beneath it, which includes parking. (Courtesy of the Hubert Trost collection.)

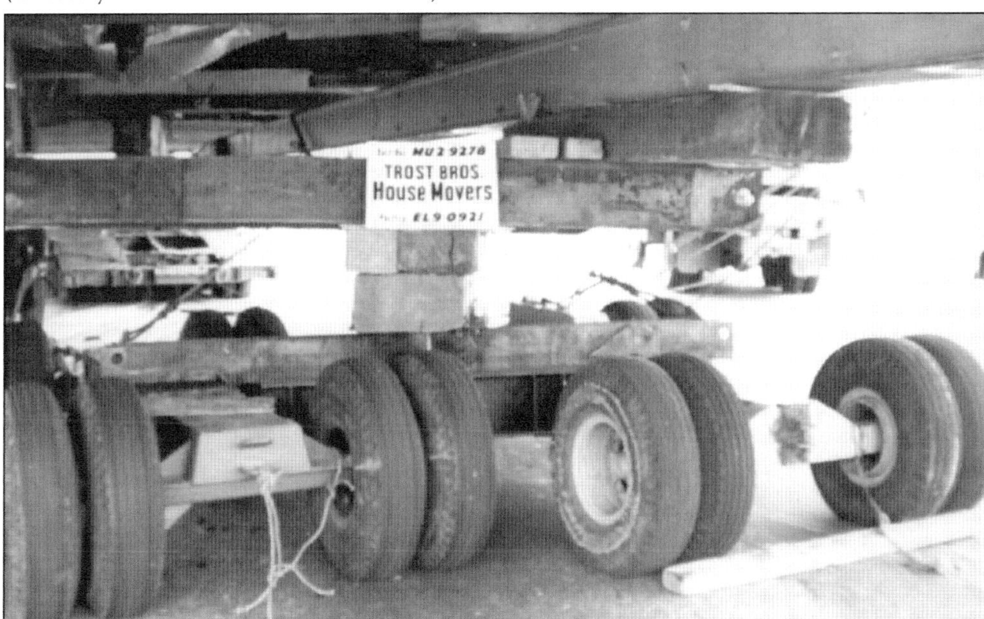

This close-up shot of part of a mover's truck shows how many tires were on the back axel of the vehicle, alone. Note the block under the back tires. Whenever the structure stopped moving, all the wheels were blocked to assure that the truck stayed in place. As a result of his many precautions, Hubert Trost never experienced a runaway house. (Courtesy of the Hubert Trost collection.)

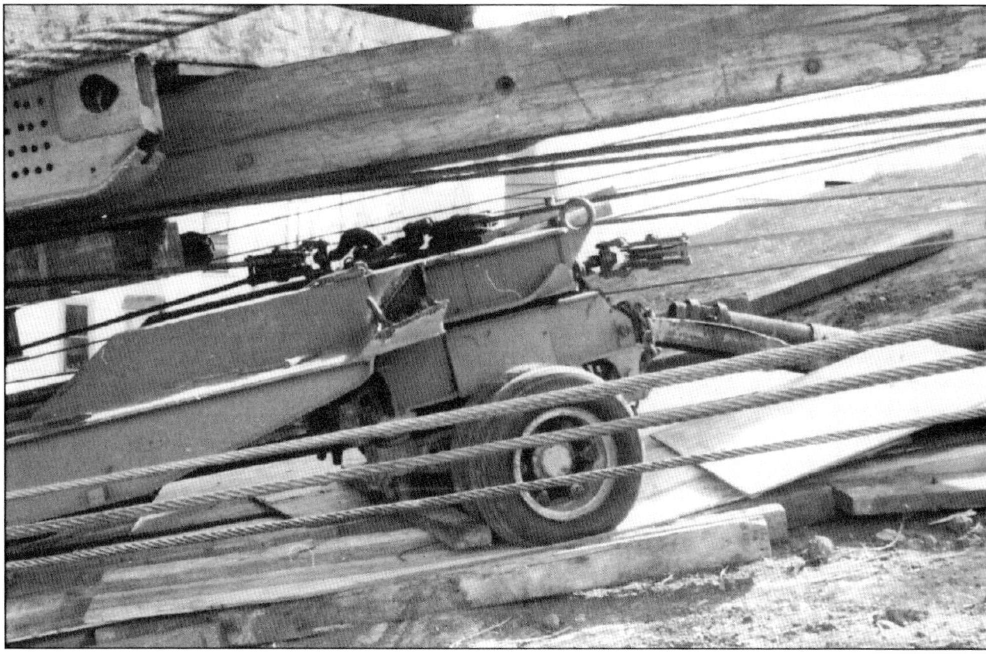

Many cables were used under the building to pull the structure during the course of its move. Trost Movers broke cables twice during this move, so redundancy in placing extra cables was a key to avoiding disaster. The same cables were also used to pull the building up the hill. Trost's trucks all had winch cable systems. (Courtesy of the Hubert Trost collection.)

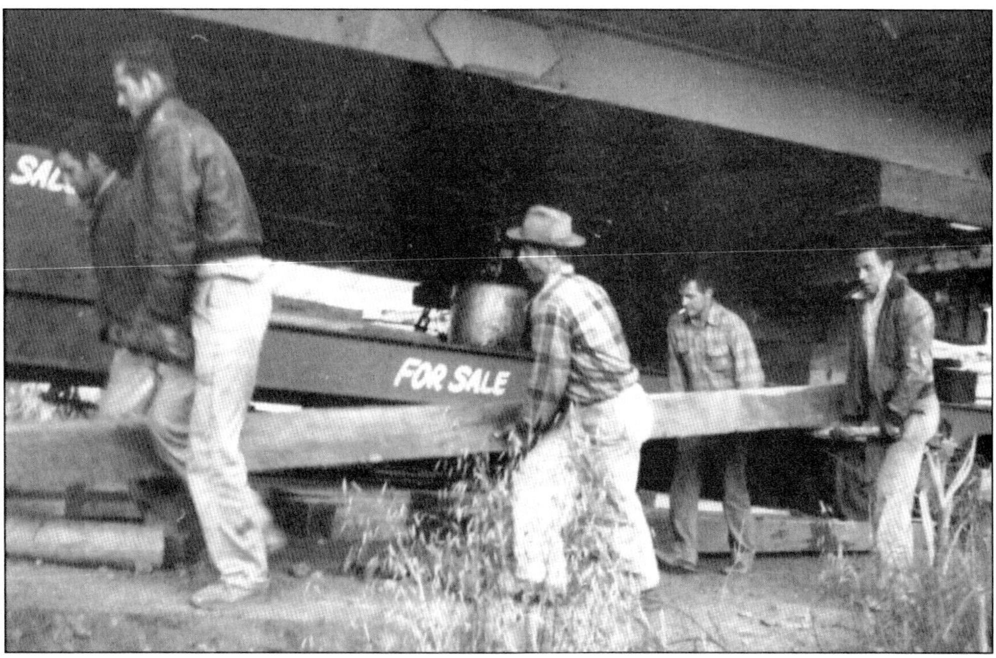

Lumber plays a big role in moving houses, from building cribbing and creating tracks to bracing and wedging truck wheels and serving as skids to help buildings slide during the move. Trost's workers carry lumber to lay down track, with plywood over it, to make the building's move smoother. (Courtesy of the Hubert Trost collection.)

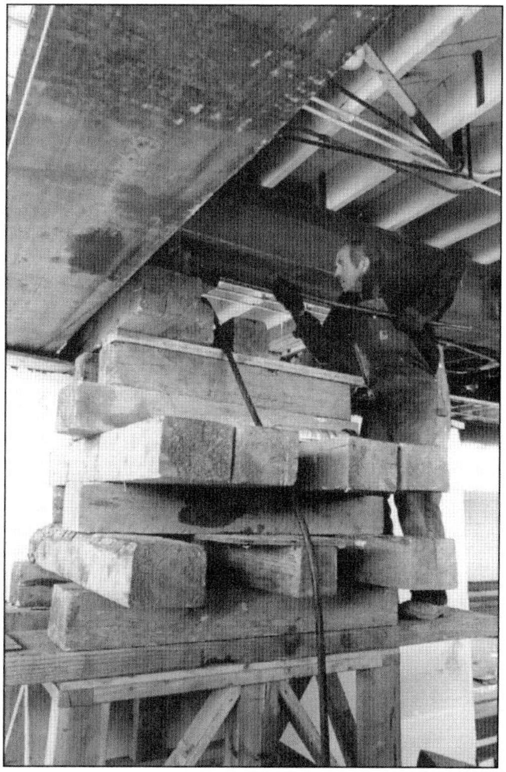

Cribbing is a reliable method of supporting a structure. Buildings need to be raised both before and after moving. Before a move, the structure must be high enough to slide low bed trucks underneath. Once the building arrives at its destination, it has to be high enough to slide over a foundation. The worker here knows that cribbing will keep the structure stable as he works underneath it. (Courtesy of the Hubert Trost collection.)

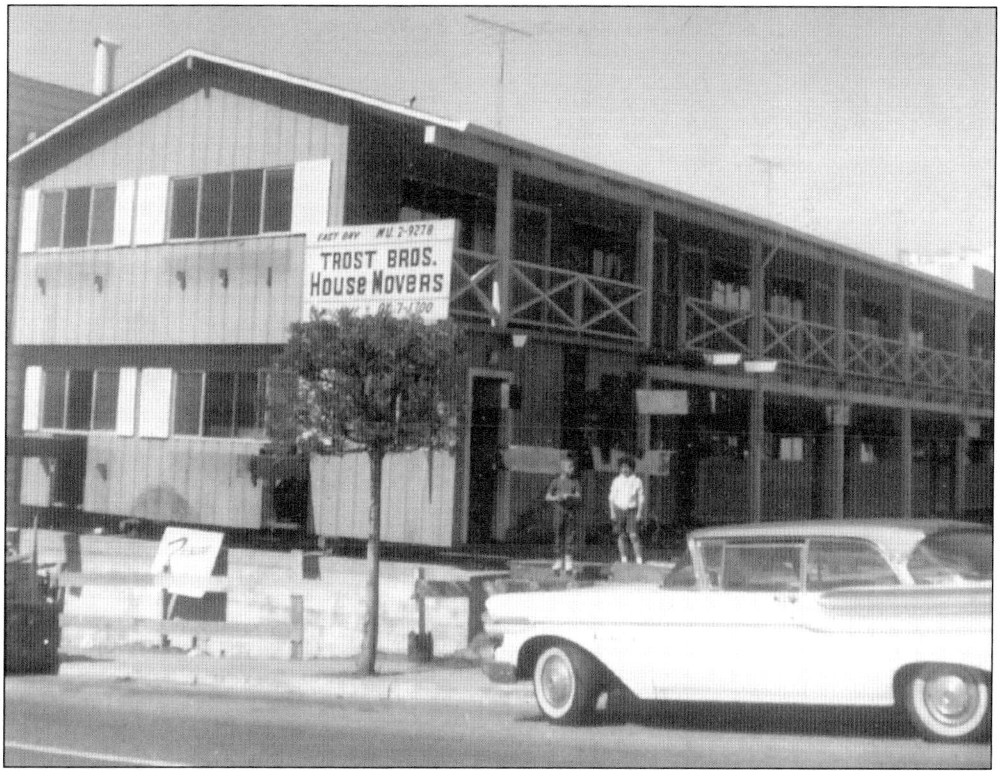

Not all moves conducted by Hubert Trost involved moves over city streets. A different kind of job involved the Lombard Street Cable Car Motel, which needed to be moved sideways so that another unit could be constructed on the same lot. Building moves that avoided city streets still involved much work. (Courtesy of the Hubert Trost collection.)

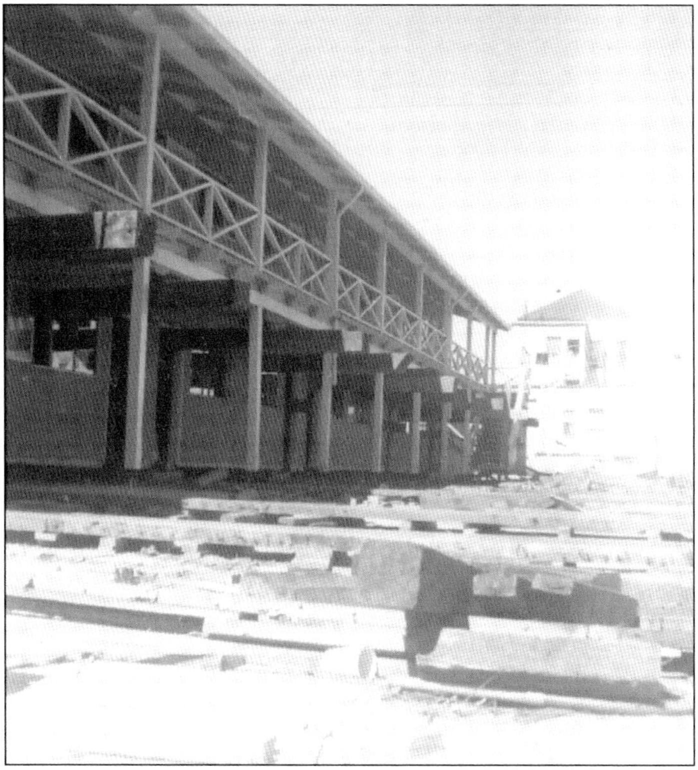

Eighty percent of most building moves use the same basic principles and procedures. Here, the long Cable Car Motel is being raised up in the early stages of preparing for its move. The grading work and lot preparations beside it were required before it could move sideways on the lot. (Courtesy of the Hubert Trost collection.)

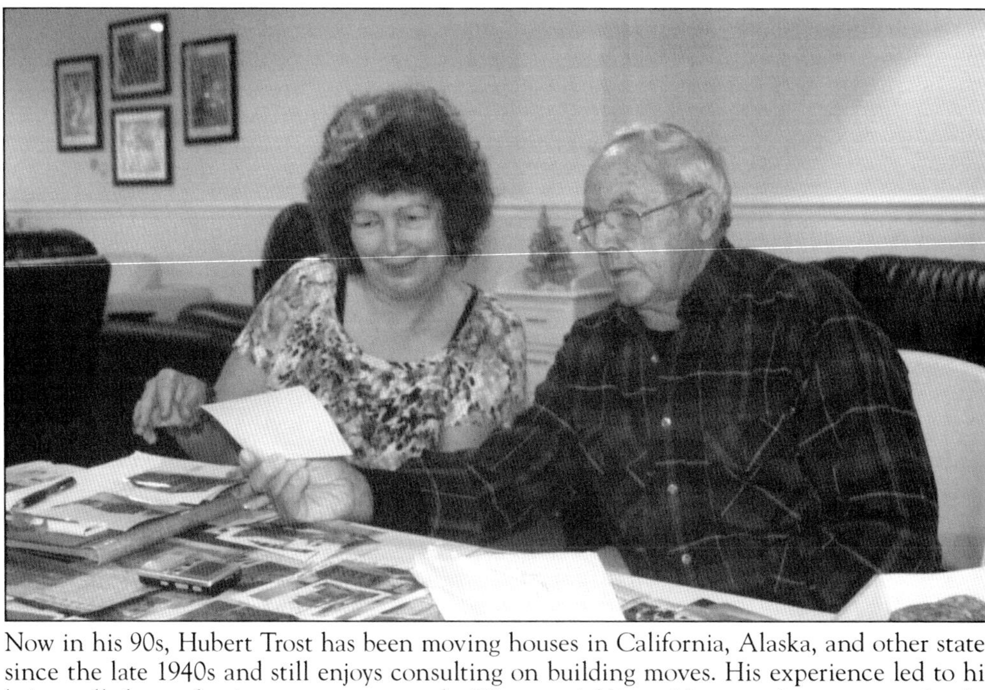

Now in his 90s, Hubert Trost has been moving houses in California, Alaska, and other states since the late 1940s and still enjoys consulting on building moves. His experience led to his being called out of retirement to oversee the Western Addition Victorian house moves. In this photograph, the author reviews Trost's vast collection of photographs documenting his historic building moves while listening to his stories. (Photograph by Beni C. Bacon.)

In 1962, architect Norman Gilroy rejected the notion that San Francisco's historic buildings should be sacrificed in the name of progress. 1818 Broadway, a mansion that Willis Polk designed for Dr. Francis Moffitt in 1914, was slated to be razed for an apartment complex. Its owners agreed to sell Gilroy the mansion (shown here at its original locale) if he moved it off the site. (Courtesy of the Norman Gilroy collection.)

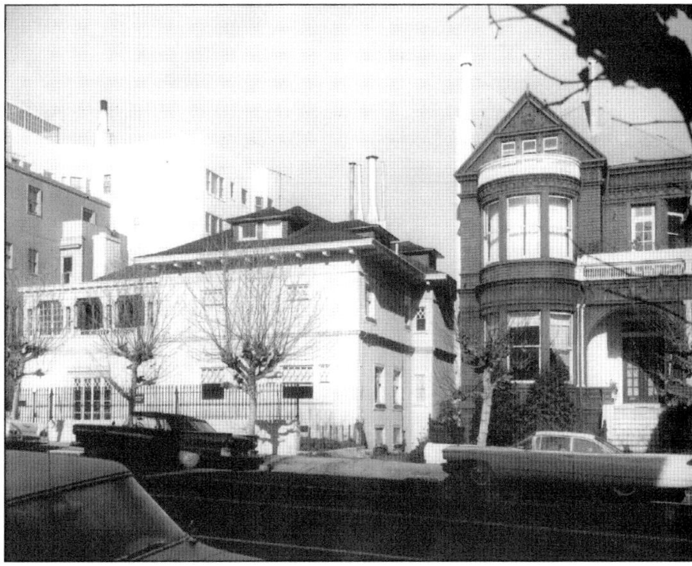

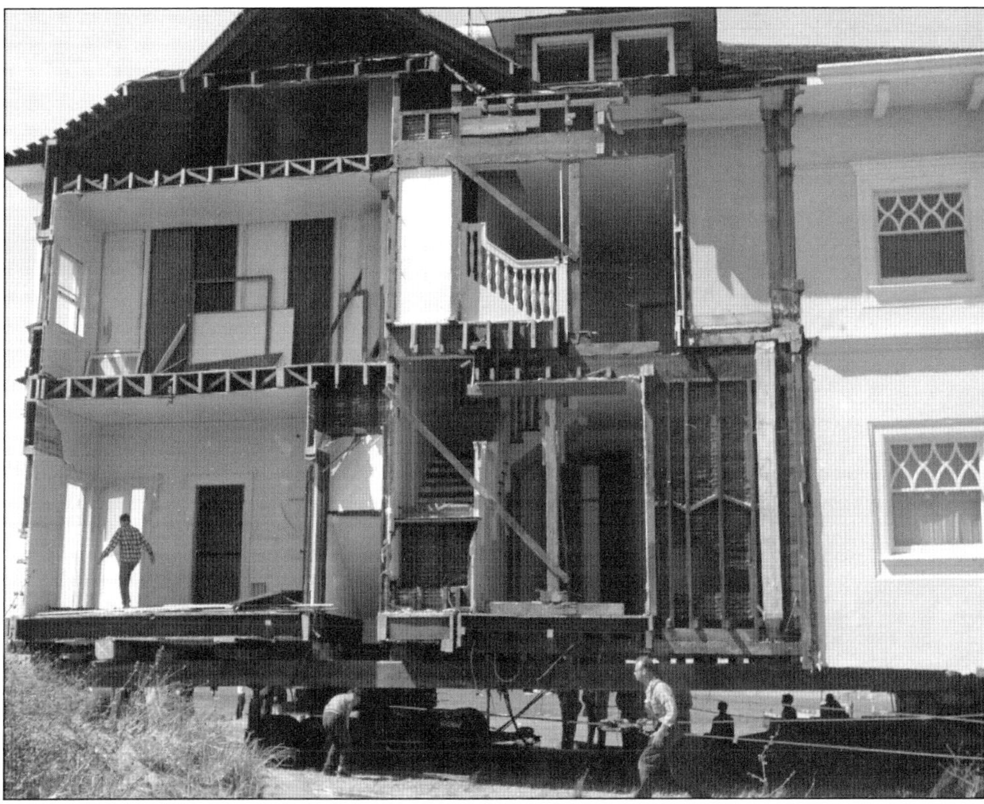

After several months of negotiating for financing and for building and transportation permits at both ends of the move, Moffitt Mansion was ready to journey to the property of some partners on Belvedere Island, which was 15 land and sea miles away across the bay. Using a chainsaw, workers literally sliced the 15-room mansion into two neat sections, each 30 feet high, 35 by 40 feet on plan, and weighing 85–100 tons. (Photograph by J.R. Wilson, courtesy of the Norman Gilroy collection.)

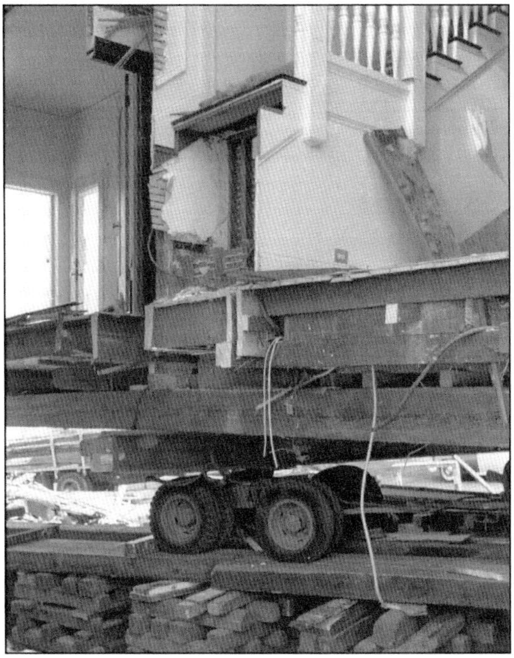

This half of a house is ready to go! Ayen Movers claims this was the "largest and most complicated moving job ever attempted in San Francisco." It required 30-foot-vertical street clearances, navigating a 2.5-mile route through a congested area, and an elevation drop of 185 feet. Completed at night to avoid disrupting traffic, the move required lowering live transit and power lines at several major street intersections to allow the sections to pass. (Photograph by J.R. Wilson, courtesy of the Norman Gilroy collection.)

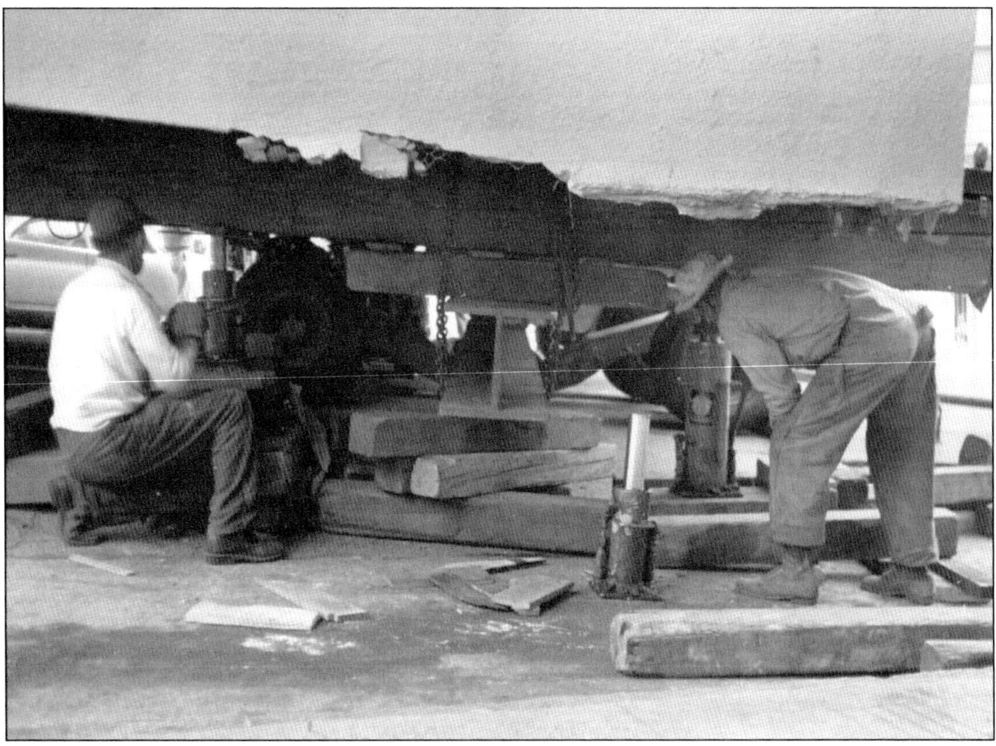

"If you hear this particular whistle, don't think: just run," the foreman warned. As the first house section moved onto the steep Franklin Street hill, its full weight suddenly canted onto its front dolly. With a scream like a train whistle, the impact tore a one-inch steel box beam in two, knocking a two-foot hole in the street. Movers scattered like rabbits. Here, workers jack the house up at 3:30 a.m. (Photograph by J.R. Wilson, courtesy of the Norman Gilroy collection.)

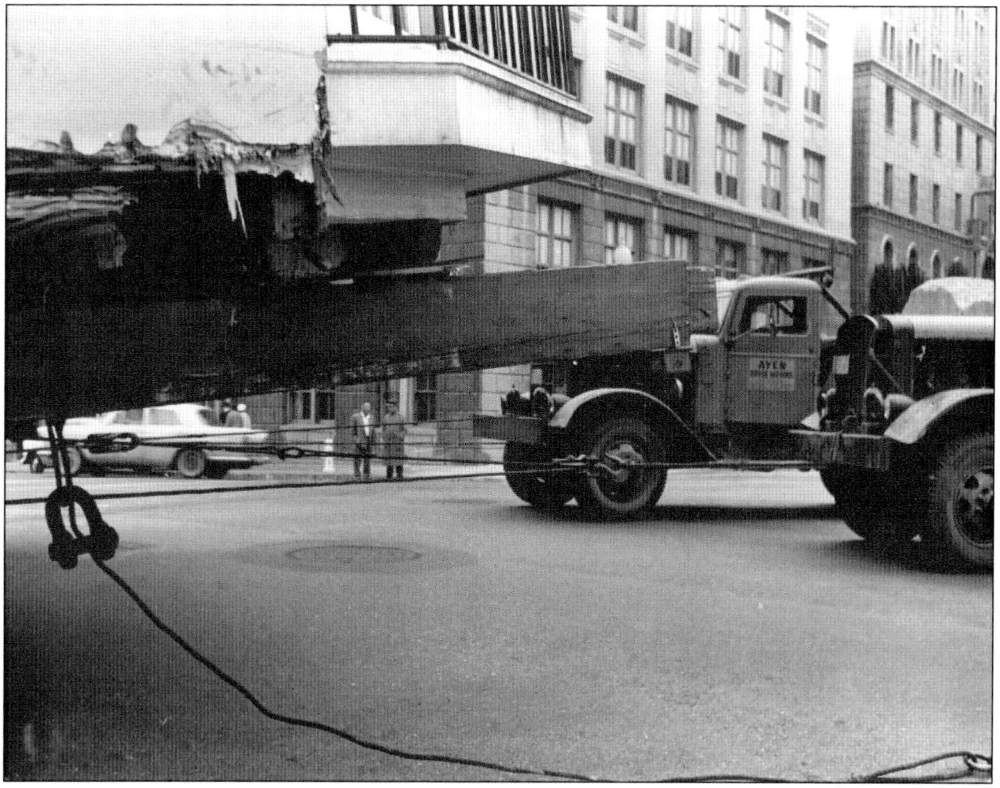

Facing a 6:00 a.m. deadline to raise the Muni Transit lines or incur significant penalties, Ayen Movers' solution was a "bull wagon" driven by a jaunty volunteer. With 85 tons of house hovering behind him, he piloted his load down seven steep blocks of Franklin Street, playing chicken with cars at every intersection. The photograph shows the section loaded onto an Ayen truck. It made it with just minutes to spare. (Photograph by J.R. Wilson, courtesy of the Norman Gilroy collection.)

It must have been quite a sight for San Francisco residents to wake up that morning and see two halves of a gigantic mansion rolling along one of the city's busiest streets, just outside their windows. This photograph shows the two sections on the move, with a curious bystander walking alongside observing the cutaway half of the building. (Photograph by J.R. Wilson, courtesy of the Norman Gilroy collection.)

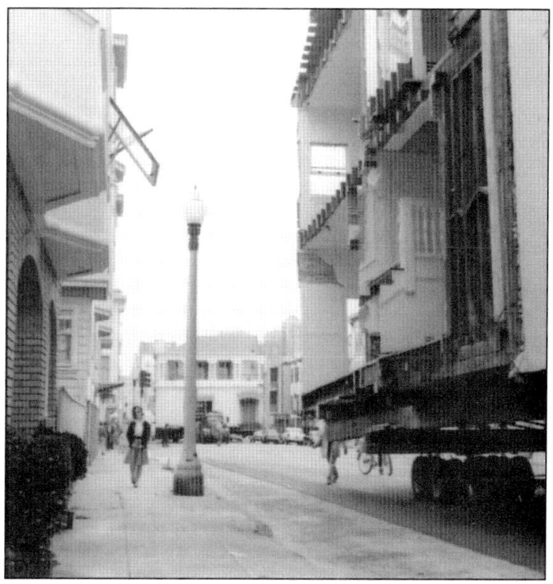

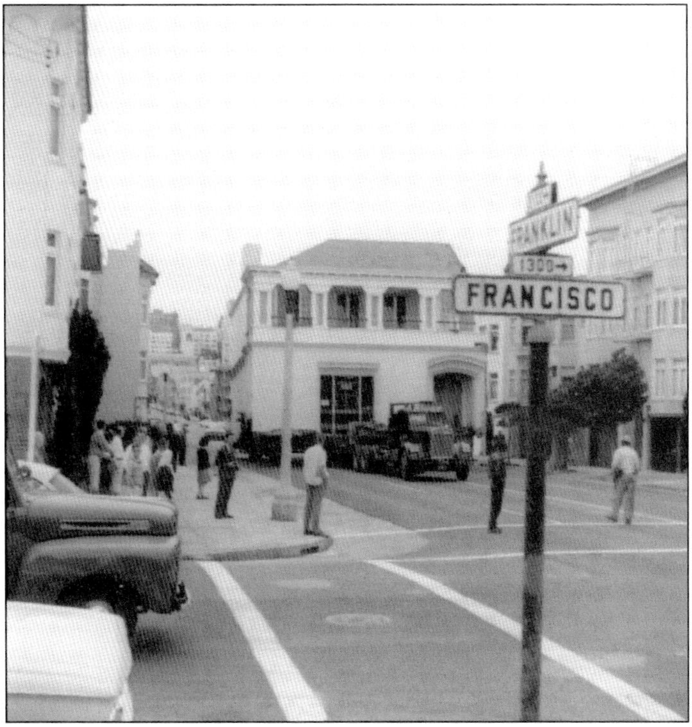

The Moffitt Mansion is shown passing Franklin and Francisco Streets and nearing the place on the Marina Green where it would await transfer to the barge that would take it to its new home. The move was completed by about 9:00 a.m. on moving day, June 25, 1962. (Photograph by J.R. Wilson, courtesy of the Norman Gilroy collection.)

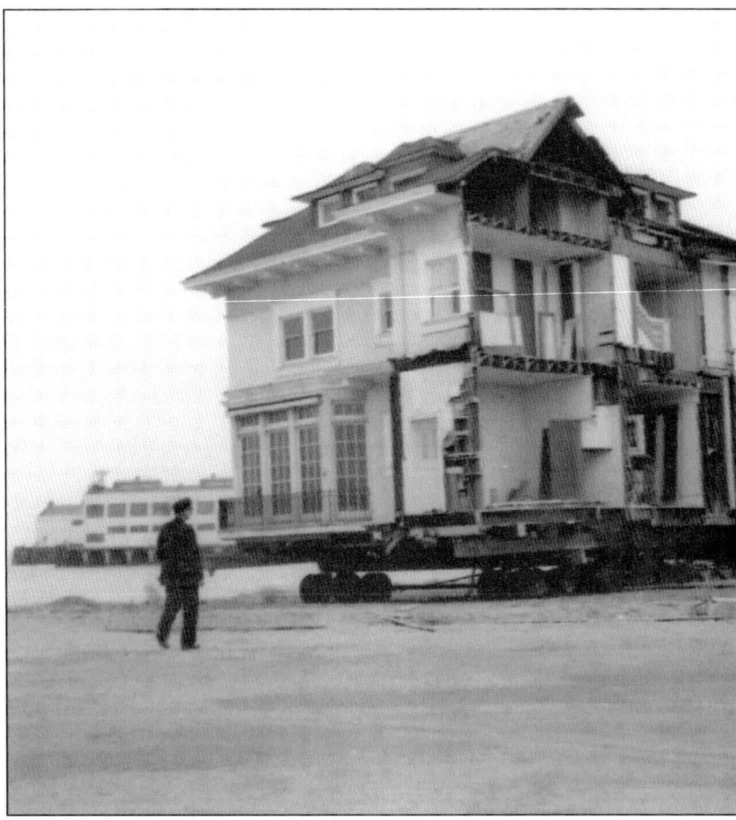

While it waited for the right conditions of tide and weather, the "house on the move" became the subject of much speculation in San Francisco. Even Herb Caen contributed columns and dedicated poetry to the house. But a sad note came when vandals made off with marble fireplaces, carved pilasters, and anything else they could lay hands on. A Pinkerton guard, hired to provide 24/7 security, is shown in the picture. (Photograph by J.R. Wilson, courtesy of the Norman Gilroy collection.)

The time spent waiting for the right weather condition was not wasted. This photograph shows the two sections being weatherproofed for their sea journey. Meanwhile, temporary tracks and a ramp were being built to slide the building halves over the seawall onto the barge for transport. In this photograph, the sections of the building have been raised, ready for loading, while a sign indicates their imminent move to Belvedere, across the water. (Photograph by J.R. Wilson, courtesy of the Norman Gilroy collection.)

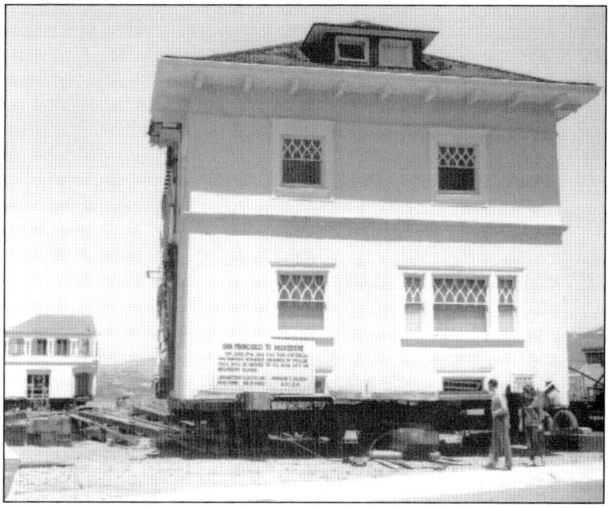

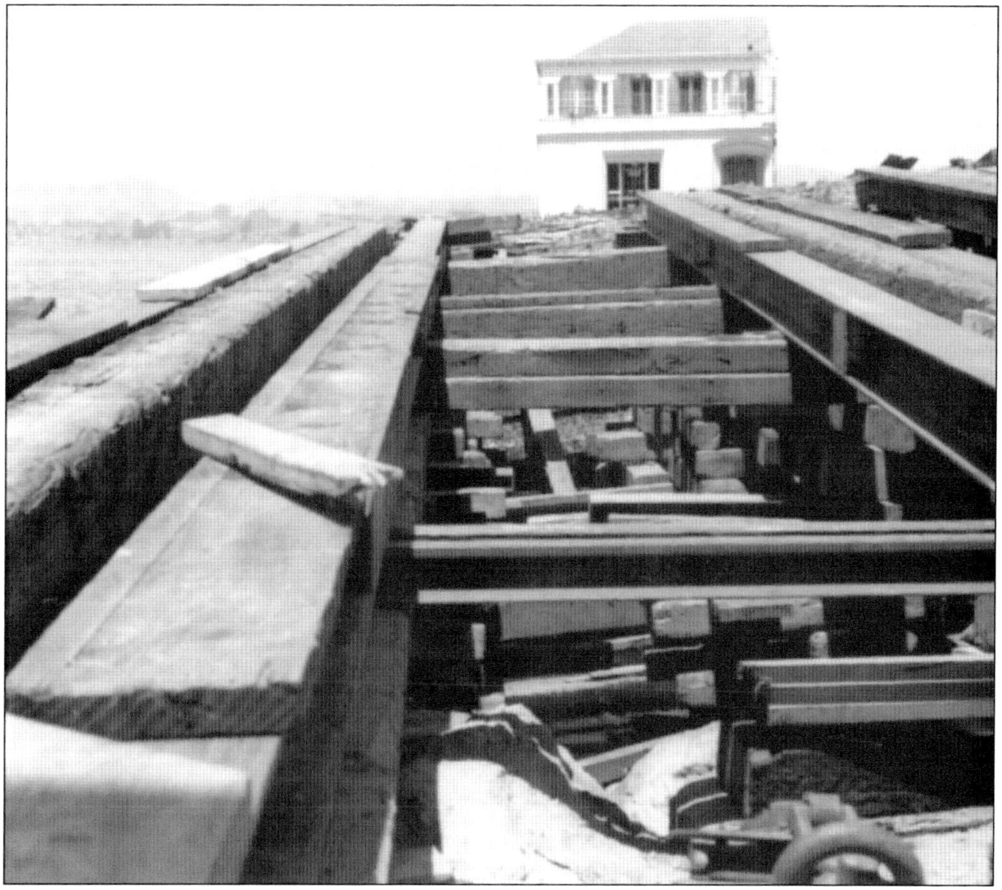

A close-up shot of the track to the barge shows the amount of work and detail that went into building the ramp to slide the buildings from land to barge. A similar ramp for unloading was later built on the other side of the bay. With one of the halves of the Moffitt Mansion in the distance, it is easy to appreciate the immense size and scope of the project. (Photograph by J.R. Wilson, courtesy of the Norman Gilroy collection.)

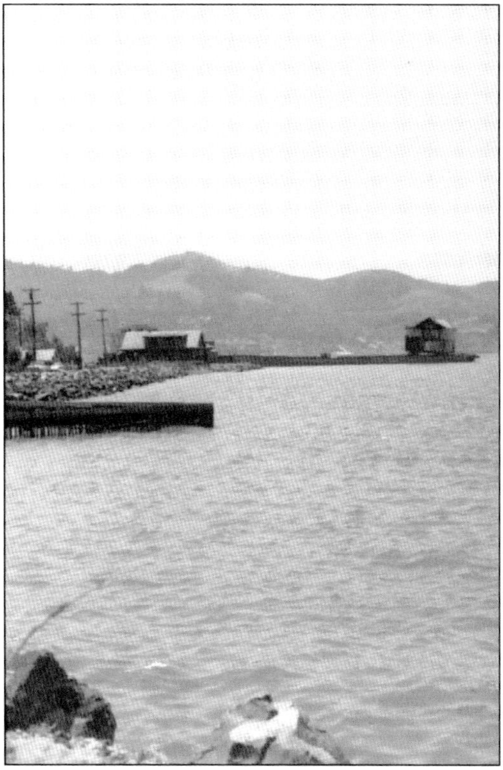

In this shot, the house and barge, with its tug captained by Master Mariner John Seaborne, is approaching the shoreline of Belvedere Island. The trip had taken one full day, battling the wind and tides in the Golden Gate all the way. The follow-up positioning and siting work was left to the Ayen house movers, and contractors were hired to restore and reconstruct the residence and landscape its grounds. (Photograph by J.R. Wilson, courtesy of the Norman Gilroy collection.)

On West Shore Road, the sections were lowered into place on newly poured concrete foundations. This view shows the house after the halves were rejoined. Amazingly, the gap between the sections was exactly the width of the first chainsaw cut made on Broadway. The original Polk drawings, found walled up in the house, guided the restoration, and damaged pilasters and moldings were replaced with plaster casts and high-quality modern-day hand carving. (Photograph by J.R. Wilson, courtesy of the Norman Gilroy collection.)

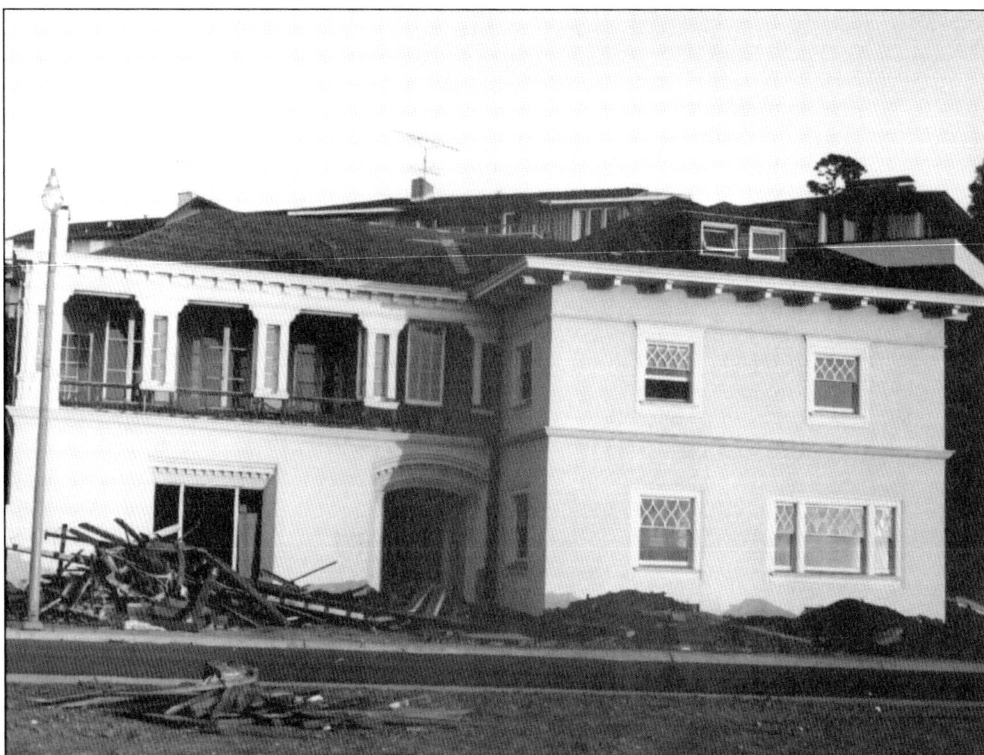

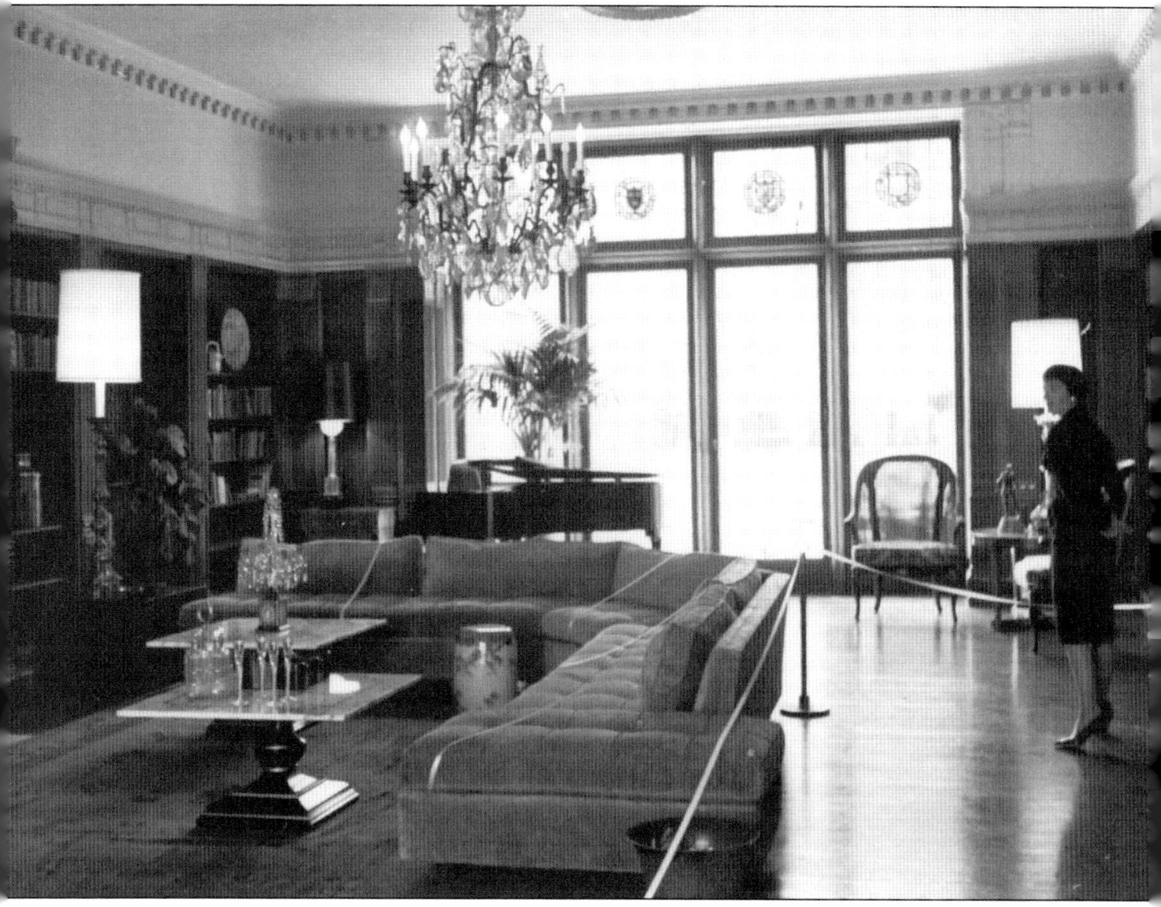

This interior shot captures just one room of the residence's restored glory. The Moffitt Mansion move is testimony to how an idealistic gamble by a single architect inspired others to preserve important buildings for posterity. Without Norman Gilroy's vision and determination to convince city officials that historic houses could still be moved and preserved, the later rescue and restoration of many of the Painted Lady Victorians in the Western Addition might never have happened. (Photograph by J.R. Wilson, courtesy of the Norman Gilroy collection.)

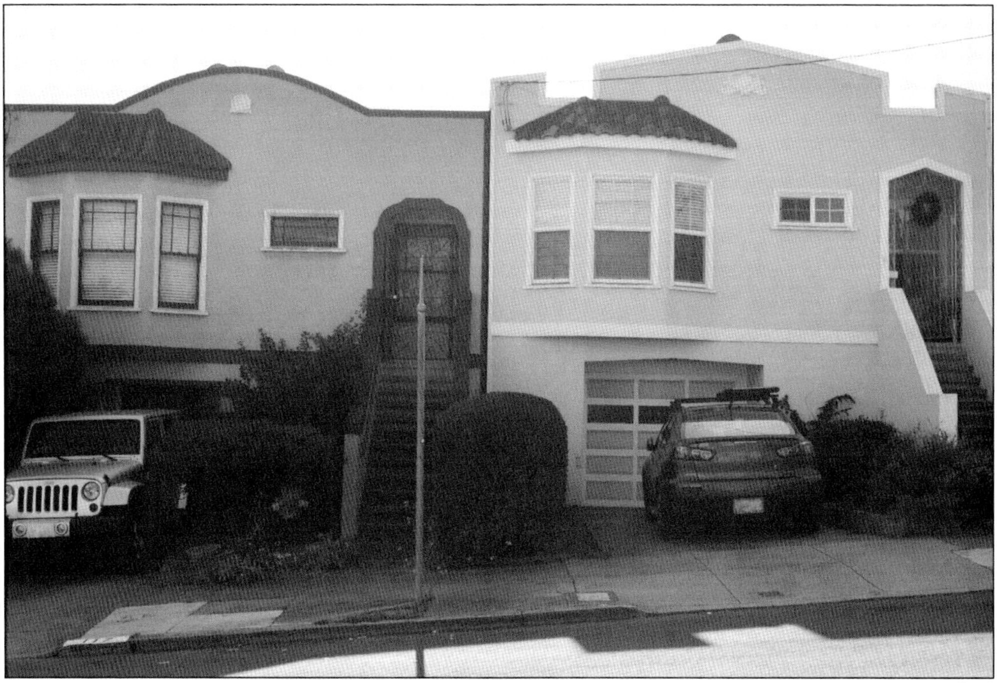

A Mediterranean-style home, built in 1926, once stood adjacent to these in the Sunnyside. Condemned by the California Highway Department to make way for Interstate 280, it was put up for auction in 1960. A young couple won the house with their $1,500 bid (about $11,650 today). They purchased an empty lot in Glen Park for $3,000, then moved the house 1.1 miles for $3,000 more. (Courtesy of the Evelyn Rose collection.)

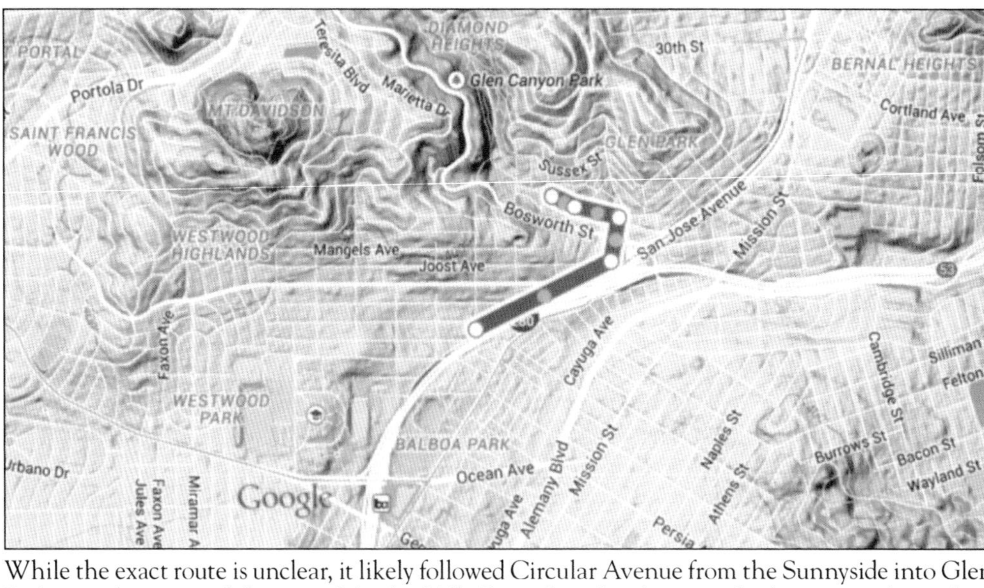

While the exact route is unclear, it likely followed Circular Avenue from the Sunnyside into Glen Park in order to avoid the steep Martha Hill. From Circular Avenue, the house may have then moved up Diamond Avenue to Chenery Street. The move took almost the whole day because of the size of the house, as well as because electrical wires had to be disconnected as they made their way along the route. (Courtesy of Evelyn Rose and Google Maps.)

At the top of the hill, the mover uncovered a manhole, inserted a large steel pole into it, attached cables to pole and house, then hoisted the house uphill at an 11 percent tilt. The front stairs broke and were later replaced for free. Because the street is narrow, the house had to be backed in with its front angled into the setback yard of a house across the street. (Courtesy of the Evelyn Rose collection.)

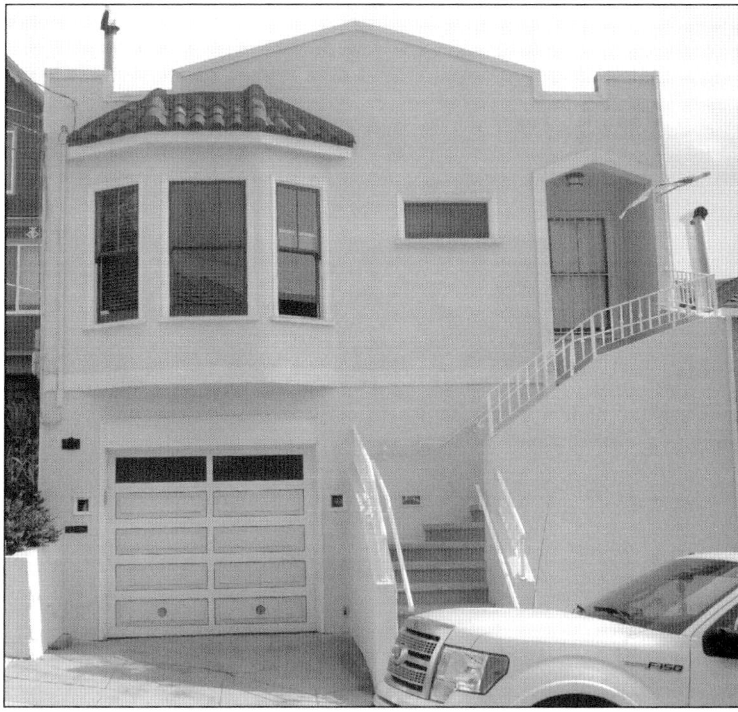

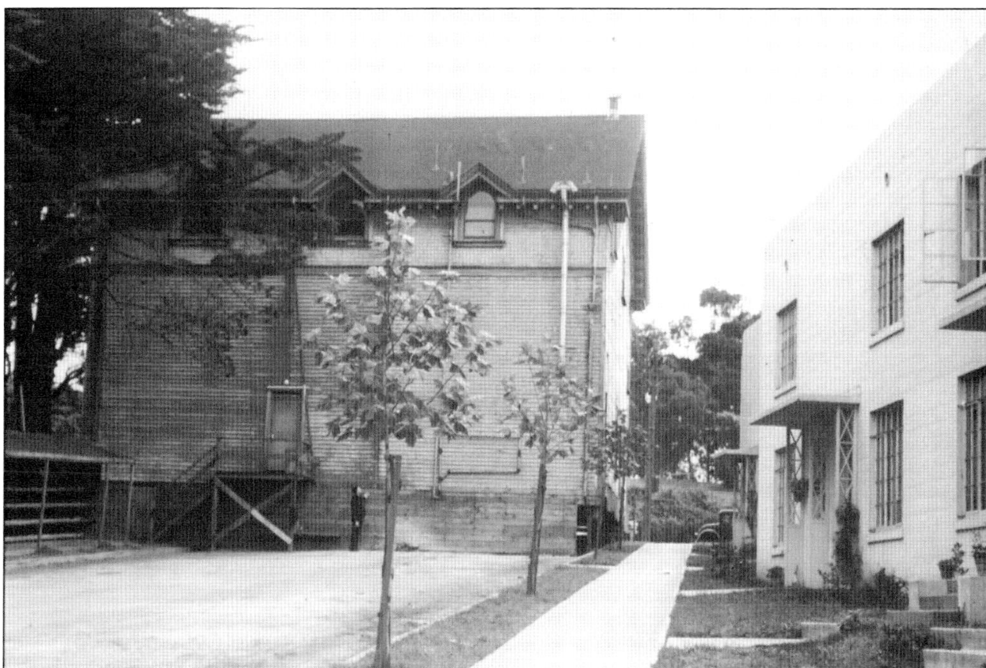

Pictured in 1940 is the old Engine No. 32 Fire Station in Bernal Heights (at Appleton and Elsie Streets) in the middle of the street. Jacked up on stilts, dilapidated and worn, it abuts the well-built Holly Courts, at right. On the left is a shed built for the fire hose; there was no room for it inside. The old firehouse was moved to make way for the Holly Park Housing Project. (Courtesy of the History Center, San Francisco Public Library.)

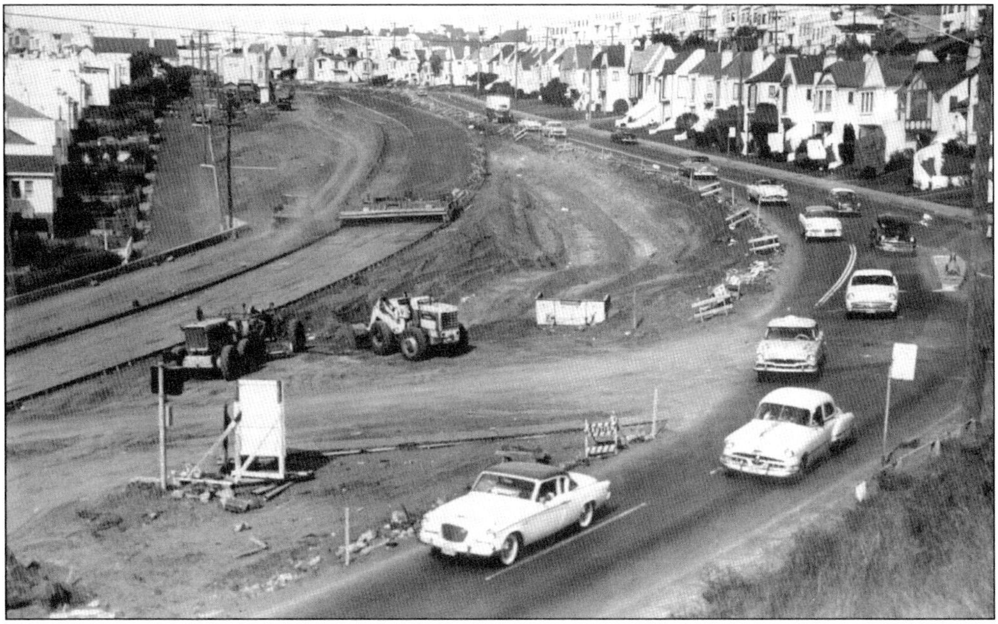

This 1958 photograph depicts the widening of Portola Drive in the last five months of the project. It was taken from Miraloma Drive. The long scar in the center of the picture once contained houses, which were moved out to permit the expansion project. The plans called for two 12-foot traffic lanes on each side of the center strip. (Photograph by Eddie Murphy, courtesy of the San Francisco History Center, San Francisco Public Library.)

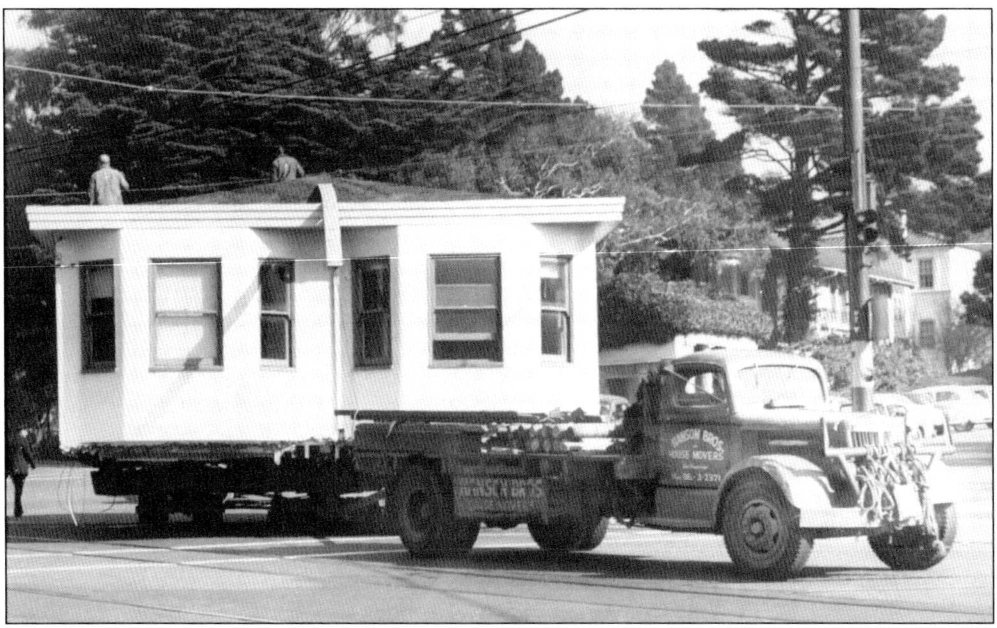

The Portola Drive construction project required the removal of houses before it could begin. A truck and trailer are shown hauling a house away from the 1200 block of Portola Drive in November 1955 to make way for the street's widening. The house will roll past St. Francis Circle on its way to a Daly City site. This house was among first homes to be moved from Portola Drive. (Courtesy of the San Francisco History Center, San Francisco Public Library.)

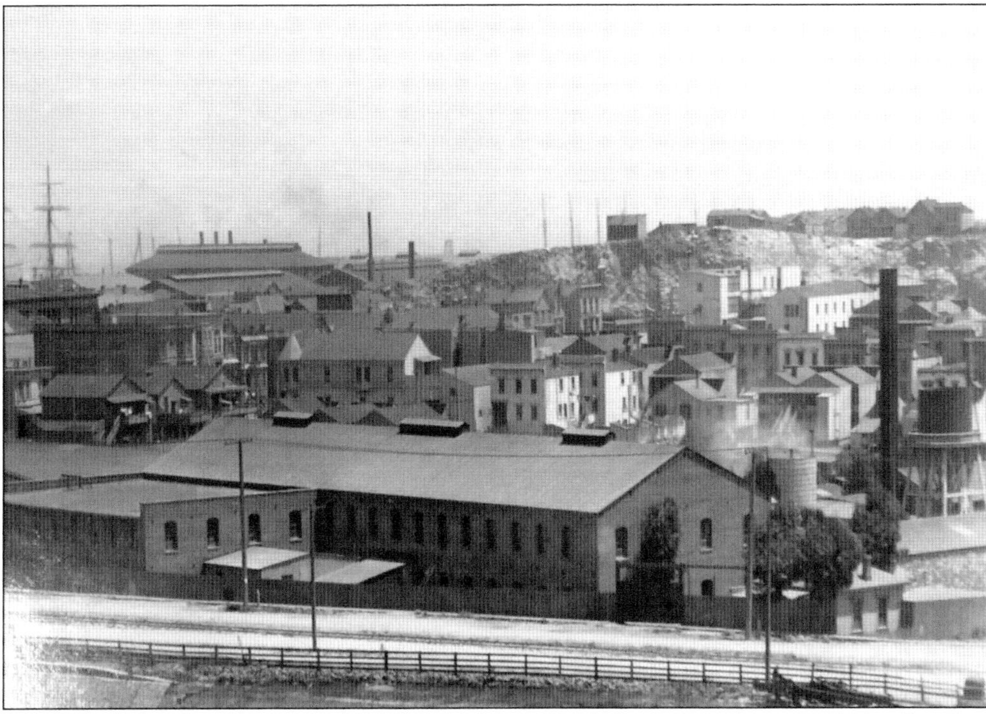

The Tubbs Cordage Company Office Building is a small frame structure now located in San Francisco Maritime National Historical Park. This 1890 structure was originally located at the Tubbs Cordage Factory at 611–613 Front Street. This image of its original (and first) location shows the Tubbs office at far right of the group of industrial buildings in the middle of the photograph. (Courtesy of the San Francisco Maritime National Historic Park and Potrero Hill Archives Project.)

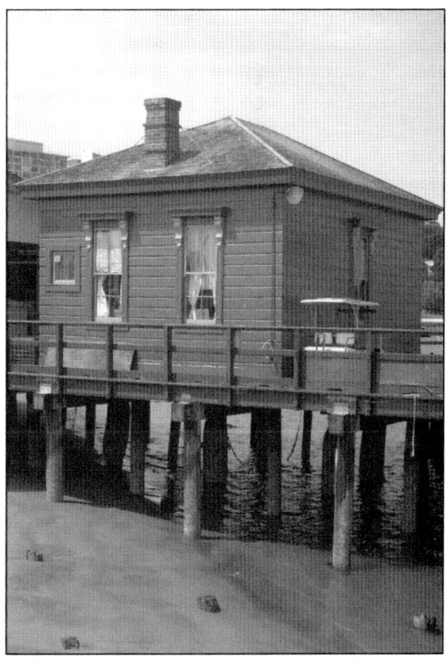

The Tubbs Cordage Company Office Building moved to the Hyde Street Pier for display and preservation in 1963 when the company closed; however, it made a second emergency move in 1990 to its current location, which rests on landfill, when the pier supporting it became unstable. This photograph is of its current location. The choice was made to move and preserve a tiny office because it represents San Francisco's last link to an early commercial maritime endeavor—rope-making. (Courtesy of the Alvis E. Hendley collection.)

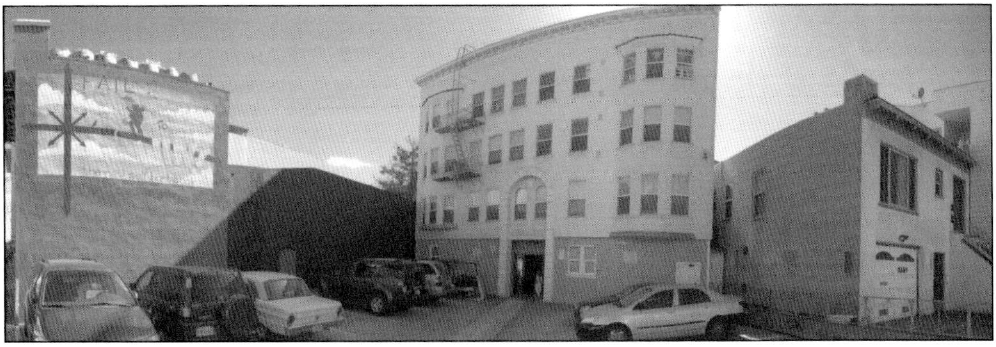

The angled building at Mission and Army Streets moved onto its lot from across the street when Army Street was widened in the early 1940s. When it was moved, it was swung around 180 degrees so that the old south portion (facing Army Street) became the new north segment. Even in the 1940s, parking was scarce. The moved building was set back on its lot, likely to create parking spaces. (Courtesy of Burrito Justice.)

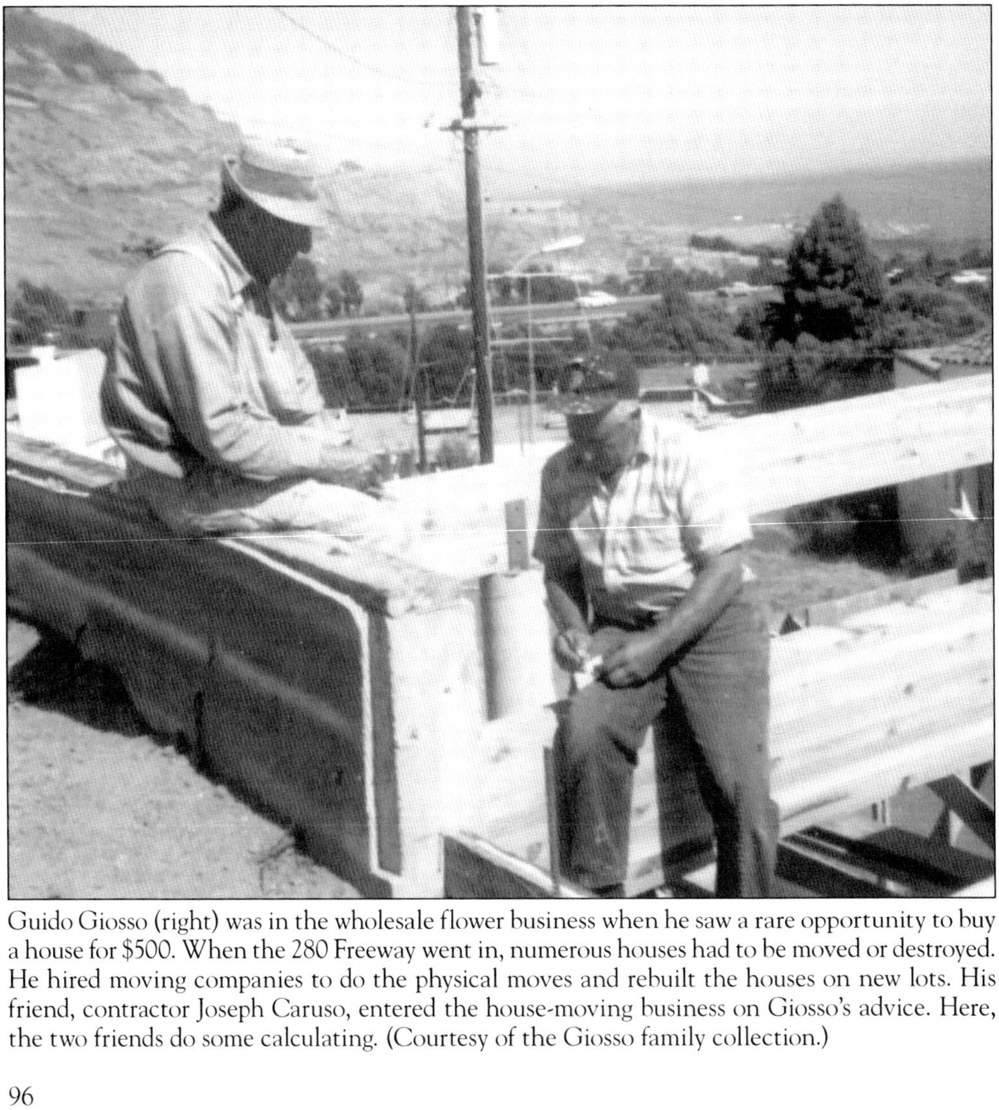

Guido Giosso (right) was in the wholesale flower business when he saw a rare opportunity to buy a house for $500. When the 280 Freeway went in, numerous houses had to be moved or destroyed. He hired moving companies to do the physical moves and rebuilt the houses on new lots. His friend, contractor Joseph Caruso, entered the house-moving business on Giosso's advice. Here, the two friends do some calculating. (Courtesy of the Giosso family collection.)

Three workers stand on framework that will eventually hold a moved house. Guido Giosso moved over 60 houses in the Oceanview, Crocker-Amazon, and Portola Districts. Nearly all were due to the 280 Freeway's construction. At one point, he had seven to eight houses on stilts. The family knew that once the freeway was finished, the golden opportunity for making money on moving houses would vanish—and it did. (Courtesy of the Giosso family collection.)

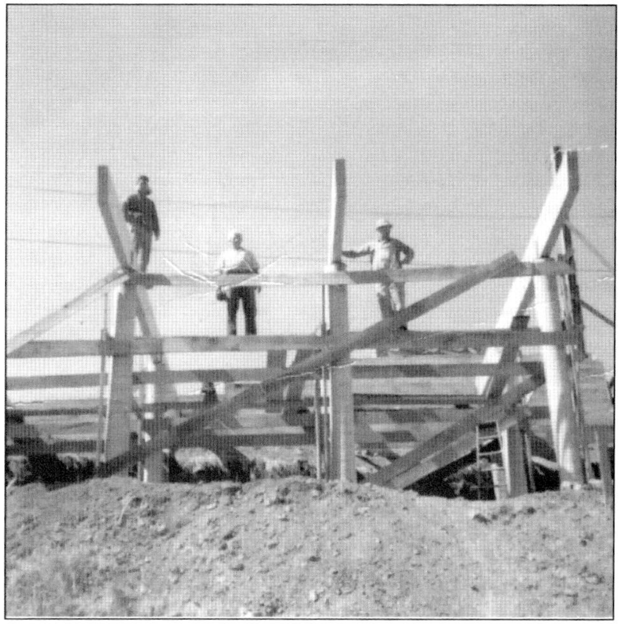

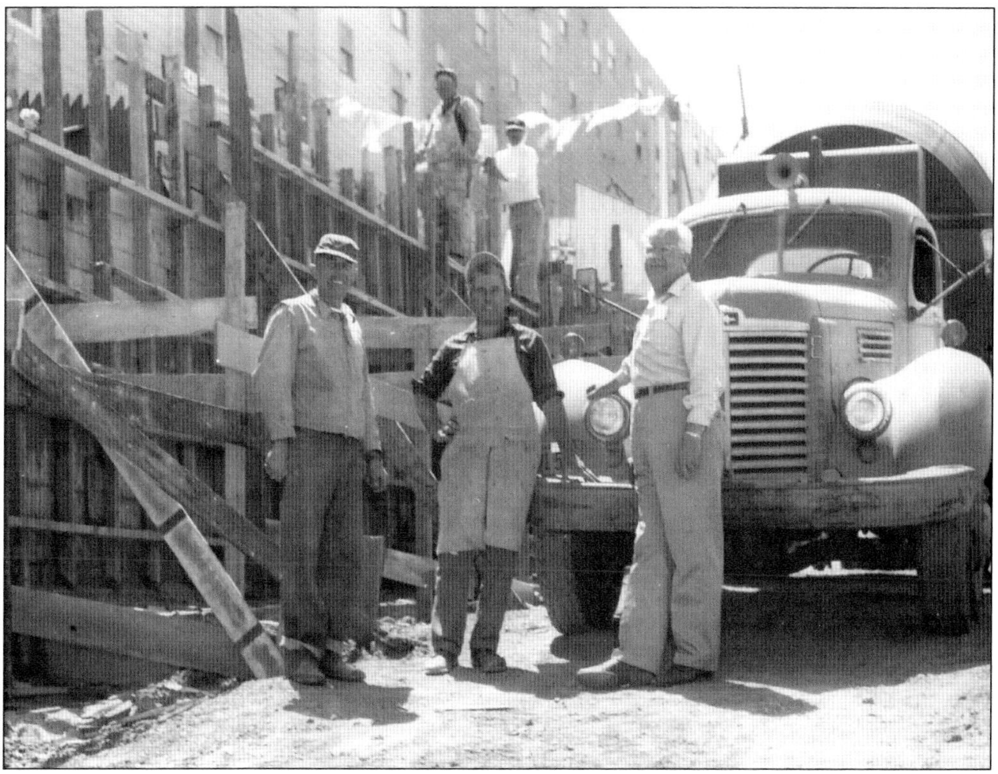

From left to right, an unidentified worker, Guido Giosso, and Lou Jolly stand in front of a house moving to Brussels Street. A 12-foot-high wall had to be built before the house was moved into the Brussels Street lot. Four other moved houses were below it, bought over a period of two- to three-month increments. Entire blocks were often put together from auctioned, moved houses. (Courtesy of the Giosso family collection.)

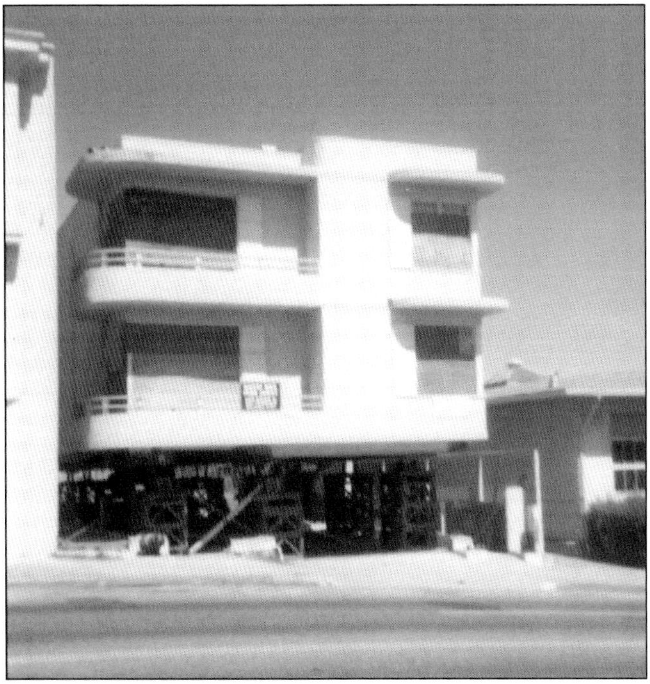

While Guido Giosso's primary business came from auctioned houses from the 280 Freeway project, he also moved other buildings. This two-unit flat was originally on Twenty-Second Avenue and Cabrillo Street. It had to be moved to make way for a new school. It is now on Forty-Eighth Avenue but is still a two-unit flat. It moved in 1968. (Courtesy of the Giosso family collection.)

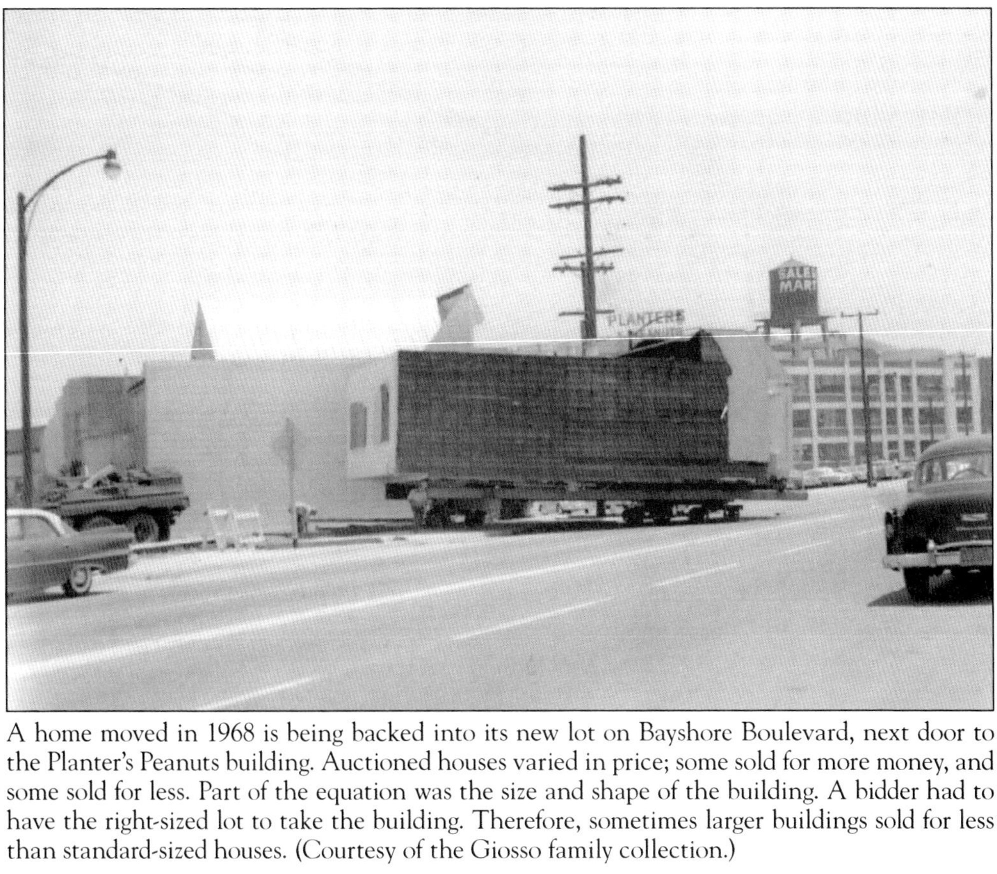

A home moved in 1968 is being backed into its new lot on Bayshore Boulevard, next door to the Planter's Peanuts building. Auctioned houses varied in price; some sold for more money, and some sold for less. Part of the equation was the size and shape of the building. A bidder had to have the right-sized lot to take the building. Therefore, sometimes larger buildings sold for less than standard-sized houses. (Courtesy of the Giosso family collection.)

This house had to be turned and raised up 10 feet before it was properly situated on its lot. It was moved from the nearby city of Colma to a vacant lot near the Bayside Motel in the neighborhood known as Little Hollywood. Some of the houses that had to make way for the 280 Freeway were beautiful homes that were only 10 to 15 years old. (Courtesy of the Giosso family collection.)

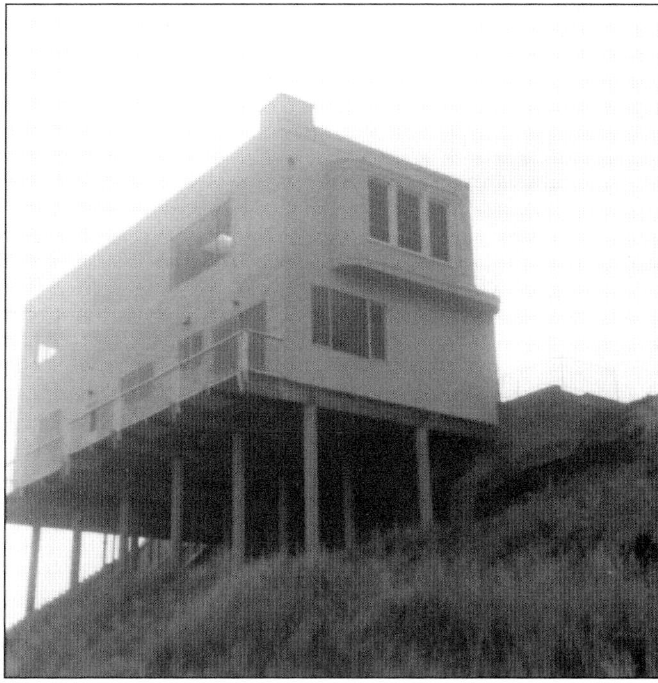

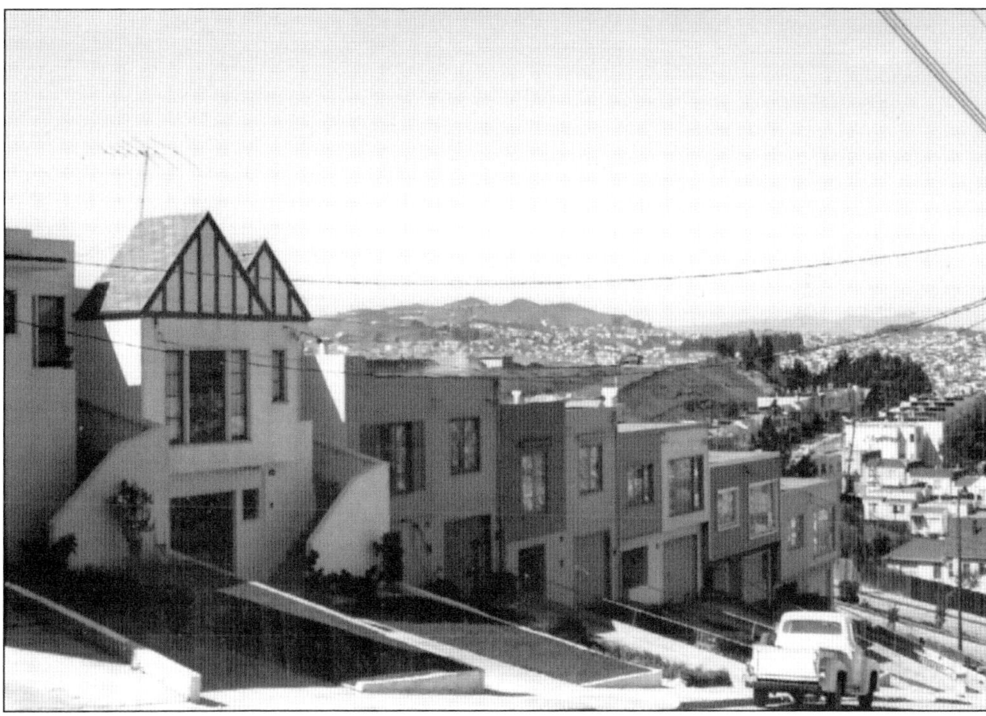

This looks like a typical San Francisco hill of row houses, but they were not originally built that way. Five of the houses in this photograph were moved onto their lots and were purchased at auction over a period of months. The 280 Freeway created new neighborhoods, even as it destroyed others, thanks to the efforts of entrepreneurs who saw opportunities in bargain houses. (Courtesy of the Giosso family collection.)

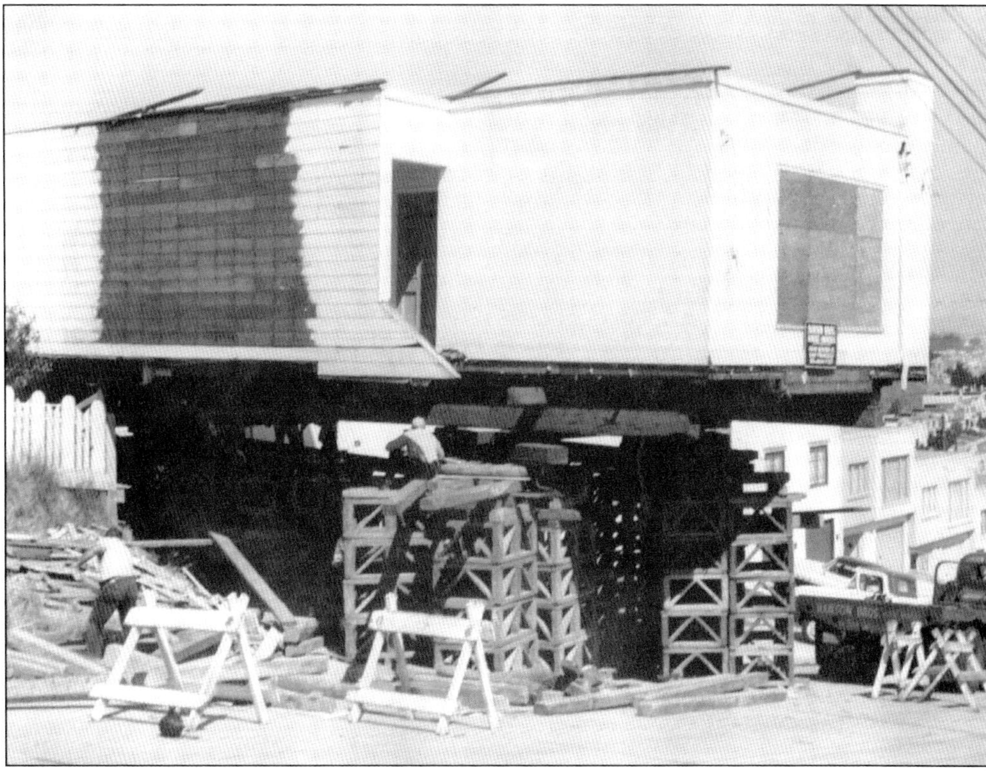

A moved house is raised on cribbing, on its new lot and in position. The house is placed six inches higher on cribbing, which allows the bottom to be built underneath before it is dropped into place as the top floor of the structure. A retaining wall had to be built around this Brussels Street house. (Courtesy of the Giosso family collection.)

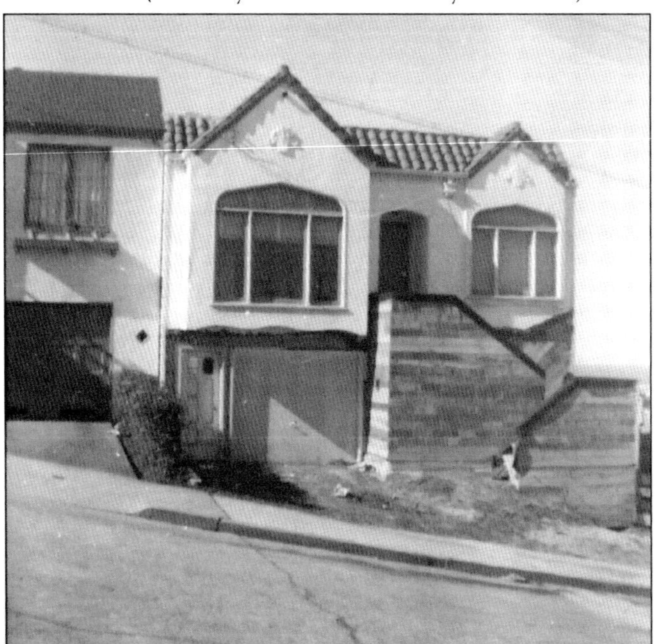

Guido Giosso and his family and workers stripped this house and tore the bottom off in preparation for moving. Once it was moved, it was left raised as they rebuilt its foundation. In this photograph, the differences between old top and new bottom can clearly be seen. When stucco is applied, the house will look as though it were built as one unit. (Courtesy of the Giosso family collection.)

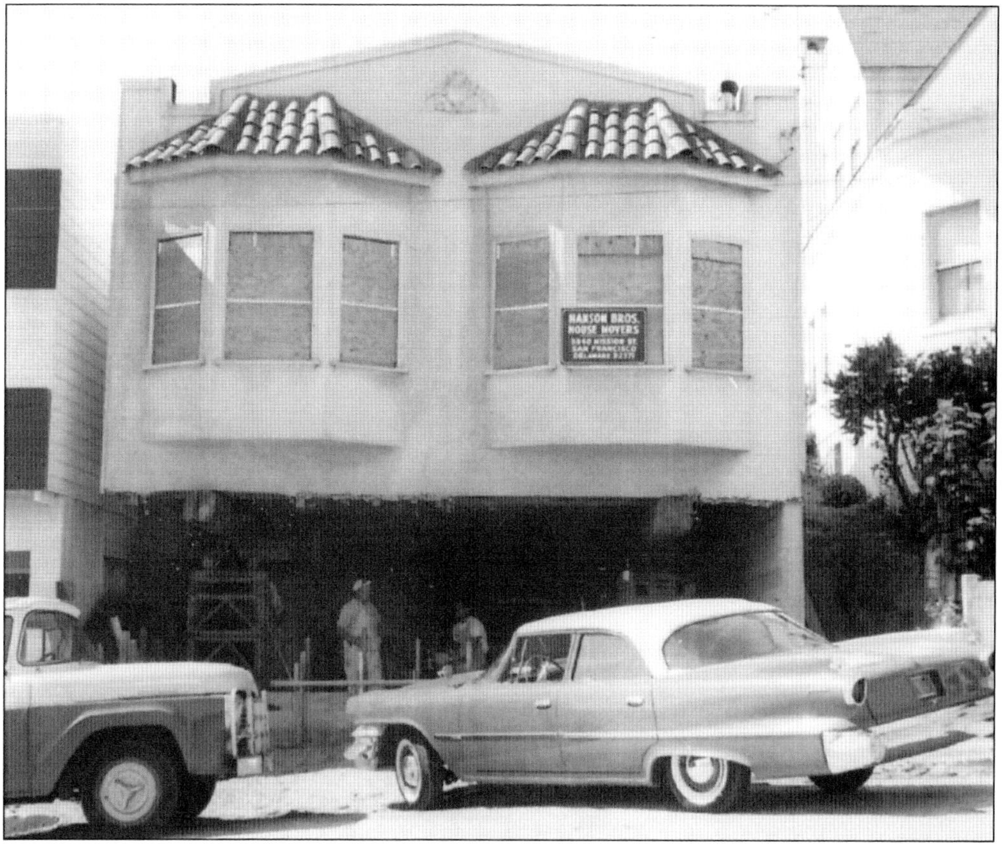

Building out the bottom of the house involves leaving enough extra clearance to allow it to be lowered into place when ready. The Hanson Brothers Moving sign is displayed in the window, indicating that this building was moved by the company. Workers under the house are building the new garage. (Courtesy of the Giosso family collection.)

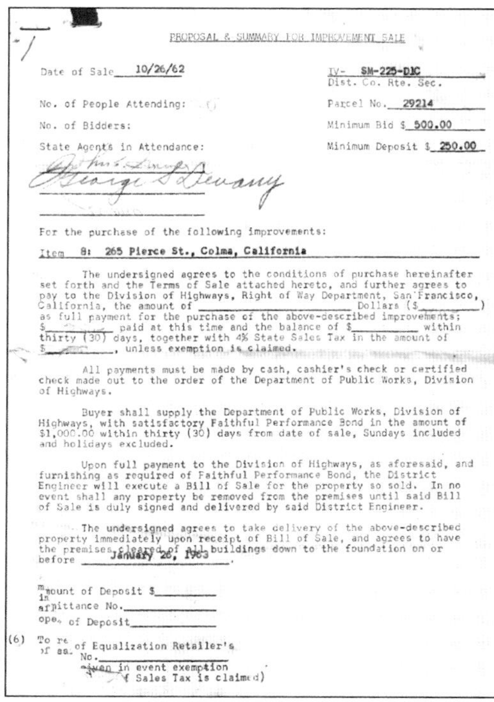

PROPOSAL & SUMMARY FOR IMPROVEMENT SALE

Date of Sale 10/26/62

IV- SM-225-DJC
Dist. Co. Rte. Sec.

No. of People Attending:

Parcel No. 29214

No. of Bidders:

Minimum Bid $ 500.00

State Agents in Attendance:

Minimum Deposit $ 250.00

George S Devany

For the purchase of the following improvements:

Item 8: 265 Pierce St., Colma, California

The undersigned agrees to the conditions of purchase hereinafter set forth and the Terms of Sale attached hereto, and further agrees to pay to the Division of Highways, Right of Way Department, San Francisco, California, the amount of ________ Dollars ($______) as full payment for the purchase of the above-described improvements; $______ paid at this time and the balance of $______ within thirty (30) days, together with 4% State Sales Tax in the amount of $______, unless exemption is claimed.

All payments must be made by cash, cashier's check or certified check made out to the order of the Department of Public Works, Division of Highways.

Buyer shall supply the Department of Public Works, Division of Highways, with satisfactory Faithful Performance Bond in the amount of $1,000.00 within thirty (30) days from date of sale, Sundays included and holidays excluded.

Upon full payment to the Division of Highways, as aforesaid, and furnishing as required of Faithful Performance Bond, the District Engineer will execute a Bill of Sale for the property so sold. In no event shall any property be removed from the premises until said Bill of Sale is duly signed and delivered by said District Engineer.

The undersigned agrees to take delivery of the above-described property immediately upon receipt of Bill of Sale, and agrees to have the premises cleared of all buildings down to the foundation on or before January 26, 1963.

mount of Deposit $______
ittance No.______
ope of Deposit______

(6) To re... of Equalization Retailer's No.______ ...iven in event exemption ...f Sales Tax is claimed)

The terms of sale for winning a Division of Highways auction bid for a building were very specific. This three-page contract documents what can and cannot be done with such a structure. When the Giosso family members won this Colma building, they had to pay cash and supply a $1,000 performance bond before a bill of sale could be issued. (Courtesy of the Giosso family collection.)

TERMS OF SALE (at the site)

Prospective bidders will be furnished a Bid Proposal form at the sites. All bids to be considered must be made upon said Bid Proposal to be furnished and submitted to State's representative at time of sale and prior to close of sale. Bidders or their duly authorized representatives are required to be personally present at the time of sale.

Immediately upon conclusion of sale State's representative shall publicly announce highest amount bid.

A deposit of cash, cashier's check or certified check, for the amount of the deposit as shown on Notice to Bidders of Sale of Buildings will be required to be made at the time of opening of bids.

Successful bidder agrees:

(1) To pay the balance due in cash, cashier's check or certified check within thirty (30) days, Sundays included and holidays excluded.

(2) To supply a satisfactory Faithful Performance Surety Bond in the amount of $1,000.00 on each item, within thirty (30) days from date of sale, Sundays included and holidays excluded. The Performance Bond shall be one issued by a reputable Bonding Company on their own standard form.

(3) If the successful bidder fails to pay the balance due or furnish the Department with a Faithful Performance Bond, the successful bidder will forfeit all his rights hereunder, including monies in the amount of the deposit, and thereupon title to said improvements shall revert to State to dispose of as it sees fit, without recourse by purchaser.

(4) To not remove any property until full payment is made, bond is furnished and contract is accepted by State by issuing a Bill of Sale.

(5) To remove the improvements within the specified time and within ten (10) days after removal of improvements, remove all combustible materials and other rubbish including shrubbery and trees which have been cut or uprooted to facilitate moving operations leaving only concrete foundations, retaining walls and flatwork on the premises, provided, however, that all mudsills, steel tie bolts and reinforcing steel protruding from said remaining concrete foundations shall be removed, bent over, or sheared at all exposed surfaces of the concrete foundations; and in the event there are basement or hazardous holes exposed by the removal of the improvements, upon completion of moving operations, the purchaser shall construct a temporary barricade fence around the basements of other hazards to the satisfaction of the Division of Highways, for the purpose of protecting pedestrians and animals; and in all other respects purchaser shall leave the premises in a reasonably safe condition or State shall have the right to complete lot cleaning operations at Buyer's expense. In the event any utiltiy service lines to other improvements are disconnected, destroyed or otherwise impaired in any way by reason of the removal of said improvements, purchaser at his own cost and expense shall provide such other improvements adequate, substitute utility service lines in lieu of those affected. Purchaser will repair all sidewalks broken during removal operations.

(6) To relocate all buildings purchased as units and shall not demolish any of said buildings for salvage of materials.

Page two of the contract outlines further terms of sale, which include forfeiting all rights if payments were not made in 30 days and agreeing to relocate the buildings as units. It was not permissible to demolish the building for salvage of materials under the auction terms, and buyers had to repair sidewalks or any utility lines broken during the move. (Courtesy of the Giosso family collection.)

(7) Purchaser shall have only the right to remove the improvements as specified and shall enjoy no other rights upon the premises. Before removing any trees, purchaser will contact the Division of Highways.

(8) Upon acceptance of the contract by State, if purchaser defaults in any of his obligations thereunder, the purchaser will forfeit all his rights hereunder, including any or all monies paid on account of the purchase price, as liquidated damages for his failure to perform, and State may demolish or remove the improvements and Purchaser will reimburse State for costs of said demolition, removal and site clearance.

The successful bidder may either remove the improvements himself or cause it to be done by other. While no State Contractor's License is required to purchase these improvements and to cause them to be removed by others, the person or company who performs the work of removing the building must be a licensed State Contractor under Chapter 9, Division 3, of the Business and Professions Code, unless the total net renumeration received by the successful bidder, including cash and value of the removed improvements, is less than $100.00.

The State of California makes no guarantee that any buildings sold will be movable or that permits will be granted to place them in any specific location. The purchaser of the building or buildings assumes all risk and responsibility in the moving operations, including any loss by reason of vandalism after acceptance by State of the deposit as above provided.

Purchaser should secure all necessary permits and certificates required in connection with the removal of any building, and should comply with all pertinent local ordinances.

The State reserves the right to reject any and all bids.

State of California
Division of Highways
150 Oak Street
San Francisco, California

FIRST CLASS MAIL

Purchasers could not move trees on the lot without contacting the Division of Highways for permission. No state contractor's license was required of the buyer to purchase or move the buildings, but the actual move had to be made by a licensed state contractor. The division made no guarantees that the structures were actually moveable or that permits would be issued for specific destinations. (Courtesy of the Giosso family collection.)

Six

Redevelopment
Relocating the Western Addition

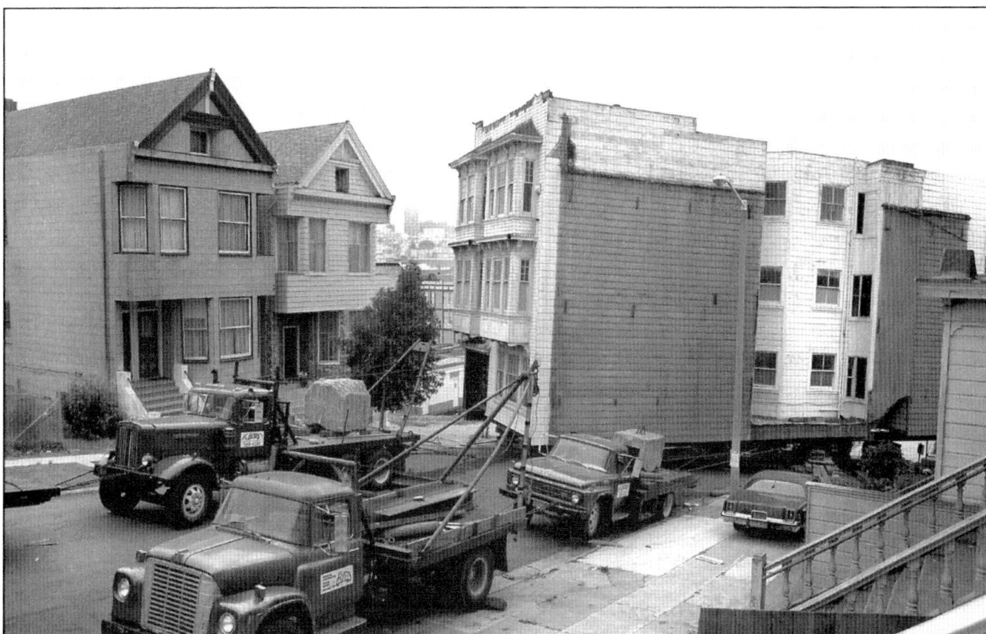

The story of the Western Addition Victorian house moves is one replete with social and political struggle. The Western Addition had long been viewed as a dangerous slum, but by declaring the neighborhood "blighted," the city became eligible for federal funds to tear down the old Victorians and replace them with new structures. Members of the community tried to save their neighborhood, but by the end of the 1970s, approximately 2,500 Victorians had been torn down, 883 businesses had closed, and 20,000 to 30,000 residents had been displaced. In all, 12 homes were relocated in what may have been the largest house moving project in San Francisco history. In this photograph, trucks laboriously pull the structure up the street to its new location, which could be many blocks away. Most traveled about one mile to their new resting place. Weight blocks had to be put on this particular building to keep it from rolling down the hill. Now at Ellis and Divisadero Streets, it was formerly located at 3875–3879 Sacramento Street. (Courtesy of the David Glass collection.)

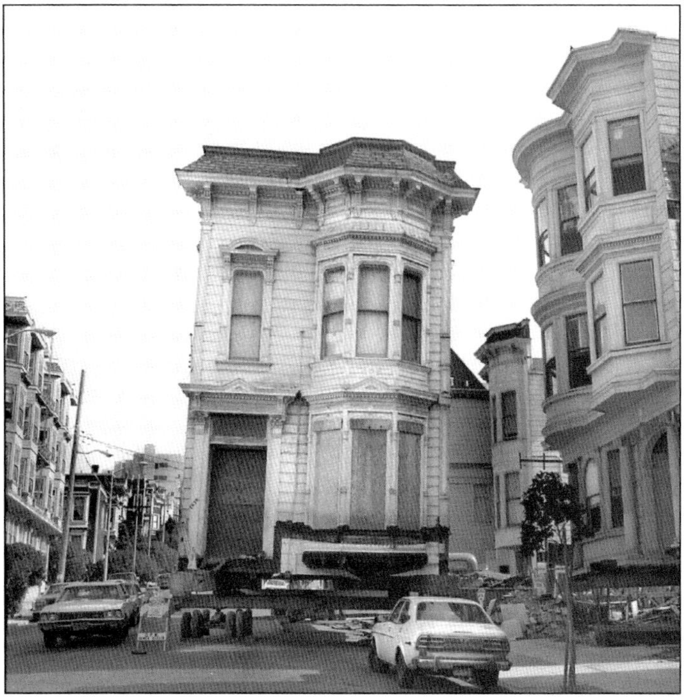

This Buchanan Street Victorian, moved in 1977, was parked at the curb for several days, awaiting moving trucks. The houses were moved in groups, at night, but they had to be "staged" to move in these groups, which sometimes meant that the houses rested in the street until it was their turn. (Courtesy of the David Glass collection.)

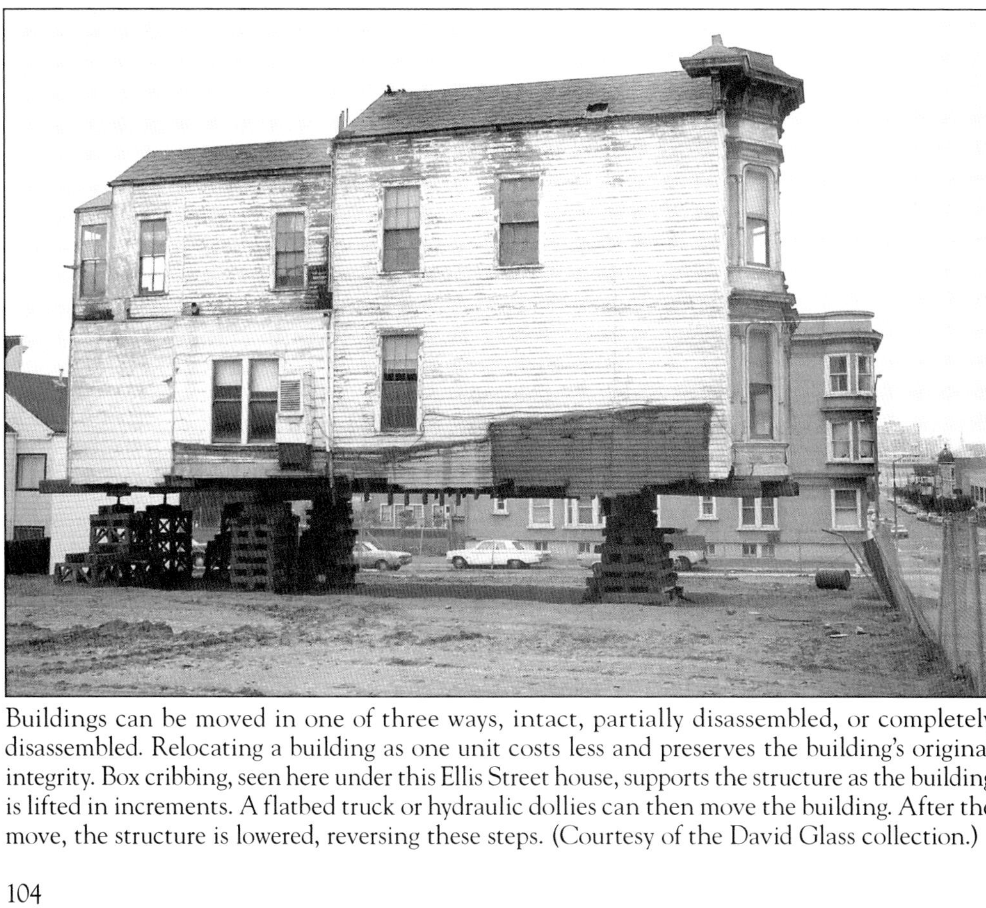

Buildings can be moved in one of three ways, intact, partially disassembled, or completely disassembled. Relocating a building as one unit costs less and preserves the building's original integrity. Box cribbing, seen here under this Ellis Street house, supports the structure as the building is lifted in increments. A flatbed truck or hydraulic dollies can then move the building. After the move, the structure is lowered, reversing these steps. (Courtesy of the David Glass collection.)

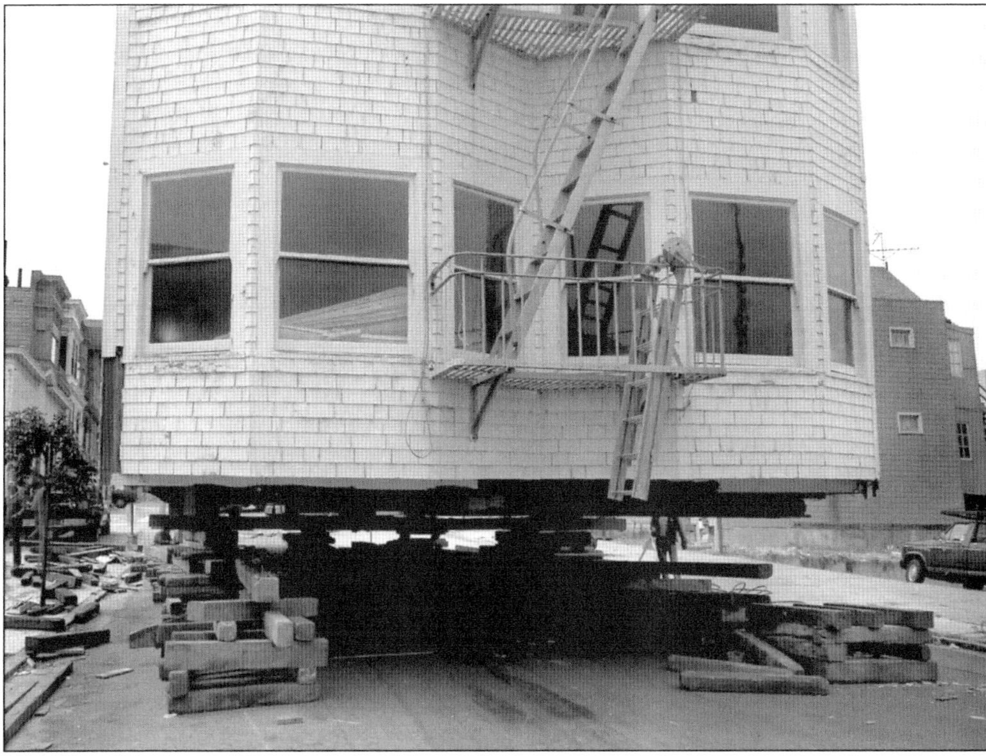

This close-up view of the Divisadero and Ellis Streets house displays the importance of cribbing in the moving operation. The house mover expressions "lift an inch, crib an inch" and "pack as you jack" are common reminders to operators of the importance of cribbing in securing and protecting a building before and after its move. (Courtesy of the David Glass collection.)

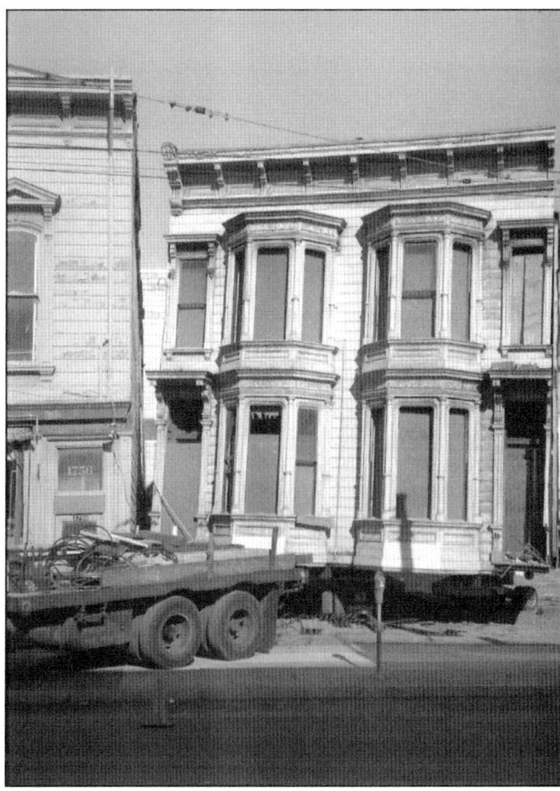

One of the challenges involved in moving a building in a high-density city such as San Francisco is to angle it out of position in its old location and slip it into its new location. This photograph illustrates some of the problems. Note the parking meter in front and the building right next door. This photograph was shot on the 1700 block of Fillmore Street. (Courtesy of the David Glass collection.)

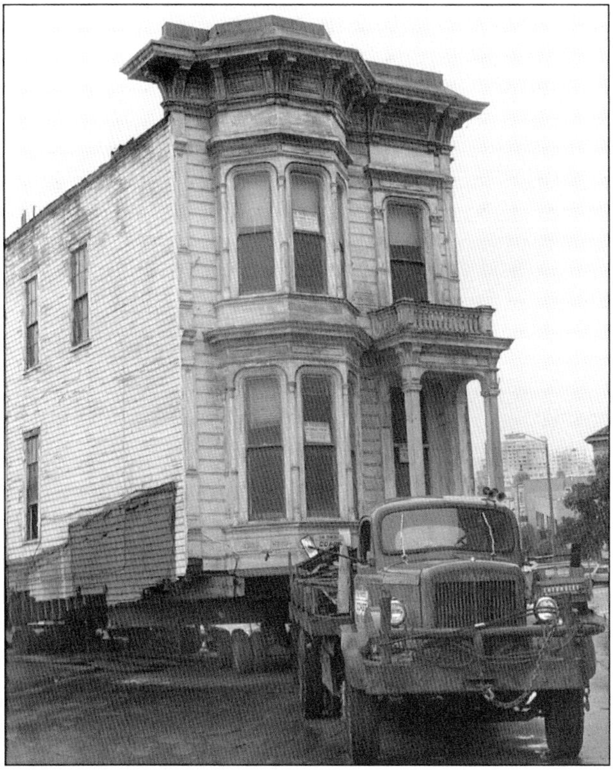

How can a truck transport a house weighing tons? Here, a Victorian building is raised and placed on rollers so that a truck can tow it up the street. In the early days, the horse/capstan method was used to move buildings. Mechanical steam donkeys evolved into flatbed trucks as the preferred moving machine of choice. (Courtesy of the David Glass collection.)

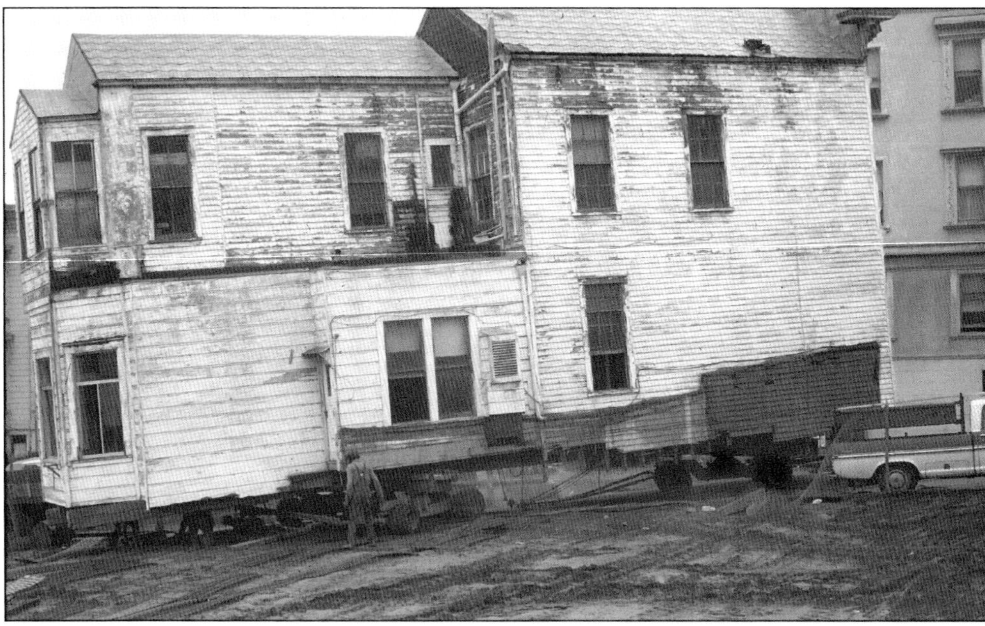

Jacks, trailers, and human attention were all required to move these large historic structures. Here, a laborer monitors the placement of support and transport equipment on a Western Addition house. This remains the largest mass-building-moving project in San Francisco's history, even though the number of houses saved from destruction was miniscule in comparison to those that were torn down. (Courtesy of the David Glass collection.)

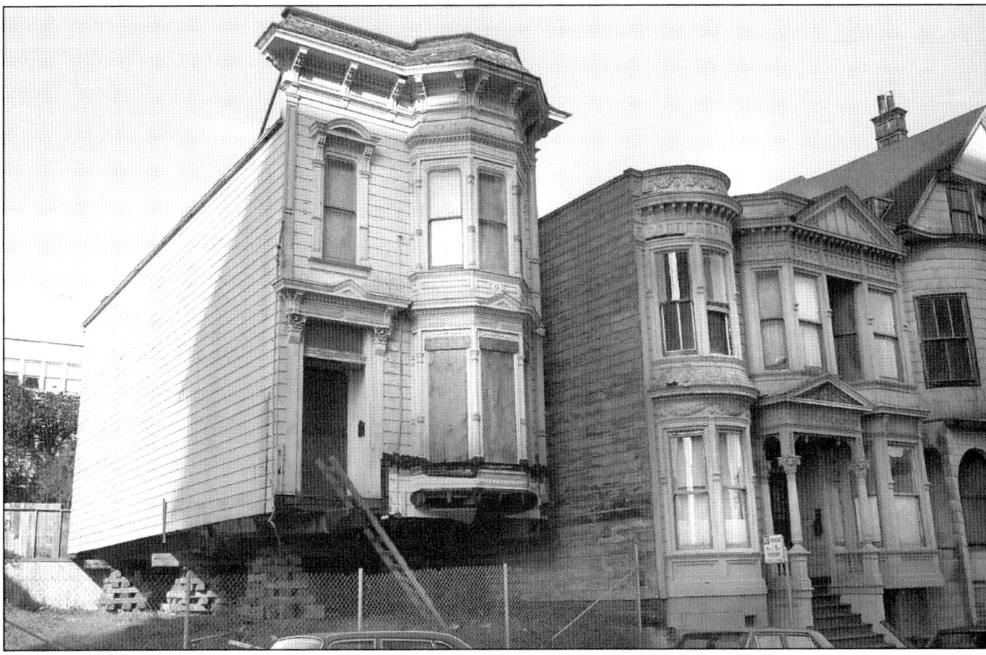

All windows on this Post Street house have been boarded up in preparation for its relocation. Other photographs show some homes being moved without boarding up doors and windows. Some of the Victorians had to be shoehorned into place, as in a Turk Street move where the dimensions were miscalculated. The three inches of siding had to be shaved off by a carpenter knowledgeable about Victorian homes, while standing on a 40-foot ladder. (Courtesy of the David Glass collection.)

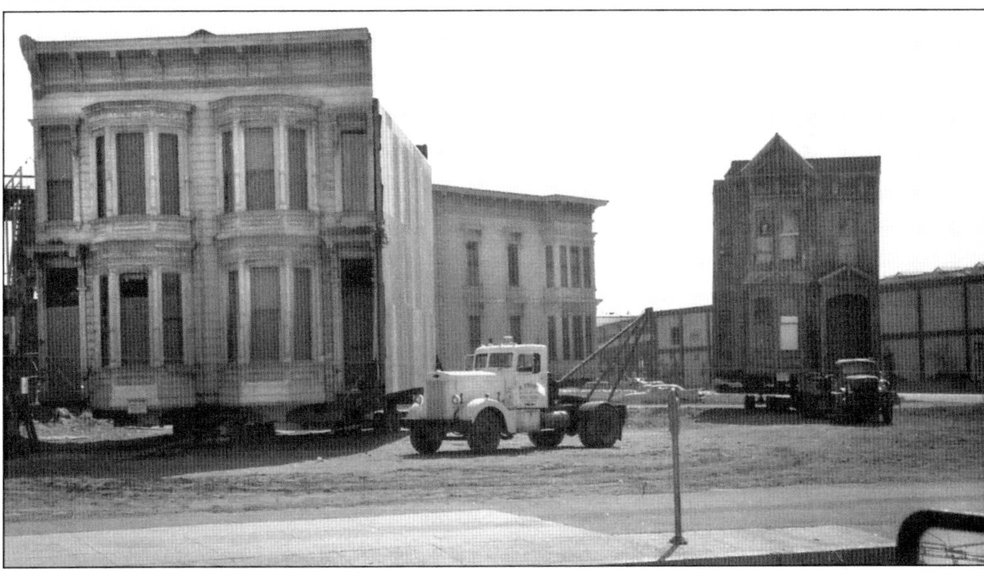

Fillmore and Sutter Streets saw much activity in 1976 as the demolition deadline grew near. Here, three Victorians are prepared to move (nearly simultaneously) to their new locations. There was a method to the moving madness—houses had to be moved in the proper order because there was no passing room. The buildings now sit on the 1700 block of Fillmore Street, part of a neat row of restored Victorians. (Courtesy of the David Glass collection.)

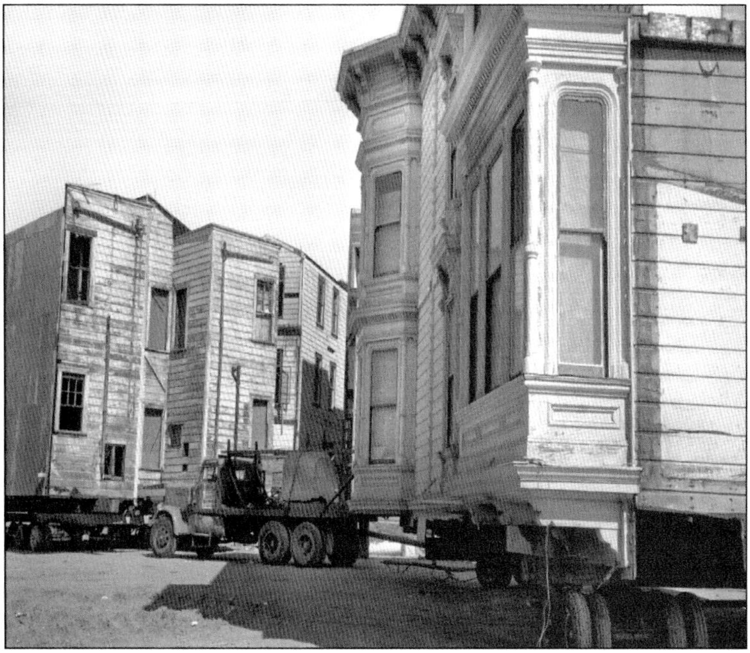

While most building moves are carefully orchestrated, only a few cities in the country have had massive simultaneous structural moves. This group of houses was moved from Japantown a few blocks away. Before it became Marcus Books on Fillmore and Post Streets, one building from this group once housed the infamous jazz joint Jimbo's Bop City. (Courtesy of the David Glass collection.)

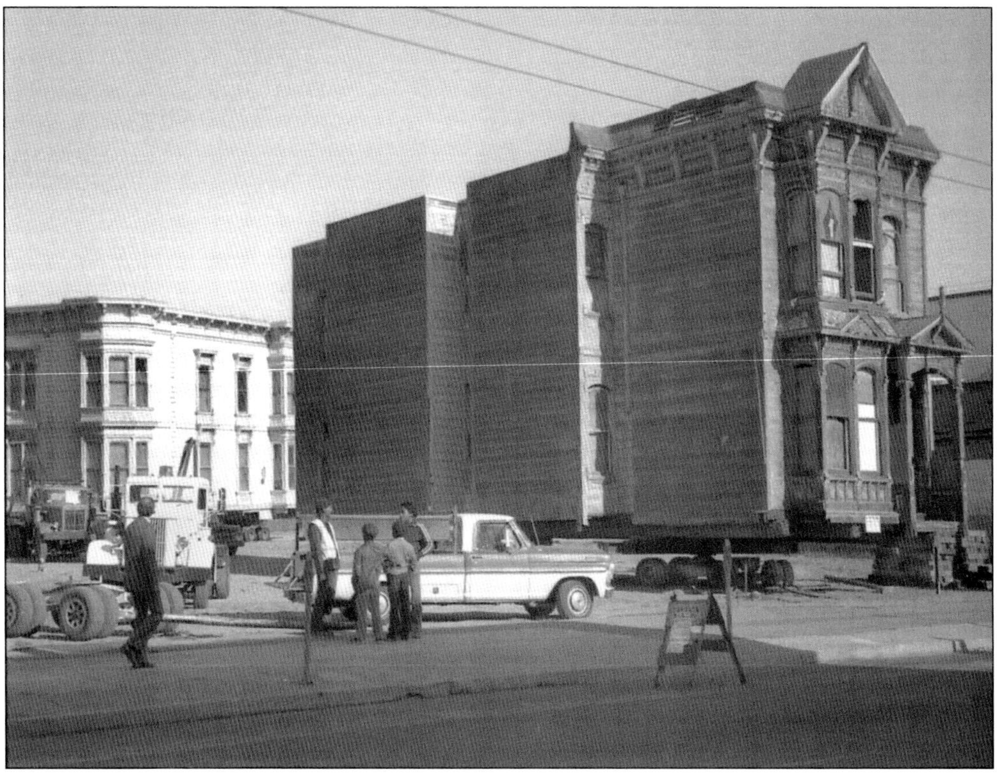

This side view of a building moved from Fillmore and Sutter Streets in 1976 shows just how long these Victorian structures were. The other structures on the same block are all ready to go, too. A dozen century-old buildings had to be moved across freeway on-ramps at night to minimize any traffic impact. (Courtesy of the David Glass collection.)

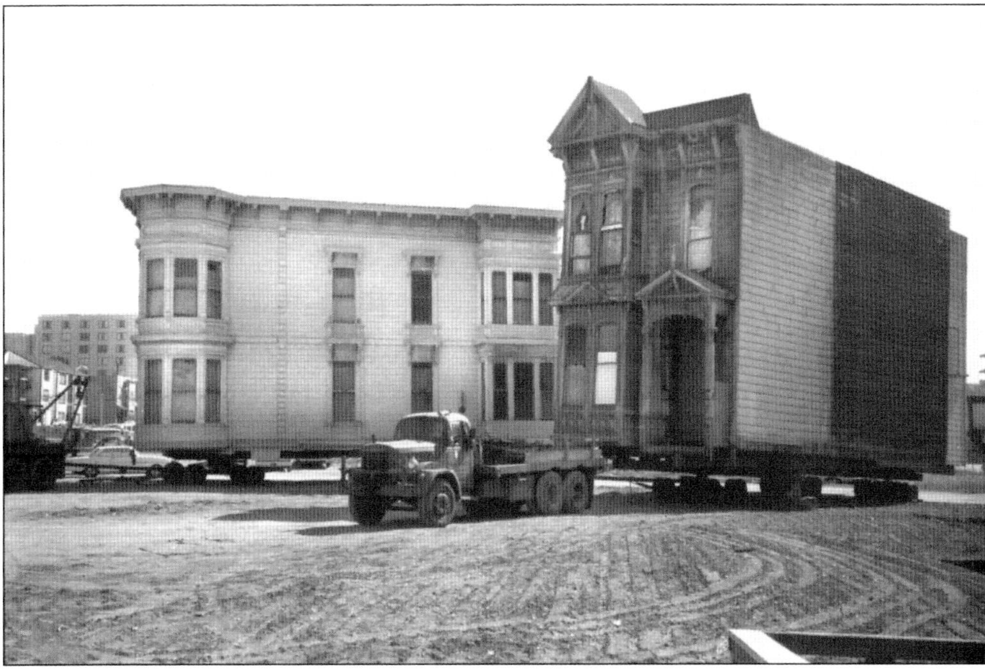

This 1976 photograph shows the Fillmore and Sutter Streets building hooked up and ready for its journey. The effort involved not only structural engineers, but also required utility crews to accompany the moving houses to remove and then re-string power lines, streetlights, and trolley lines. An escort cavalcade of 30 motorcycle police cleared the streets once the houses were underway. (Courtesy of the David Glass collection.)

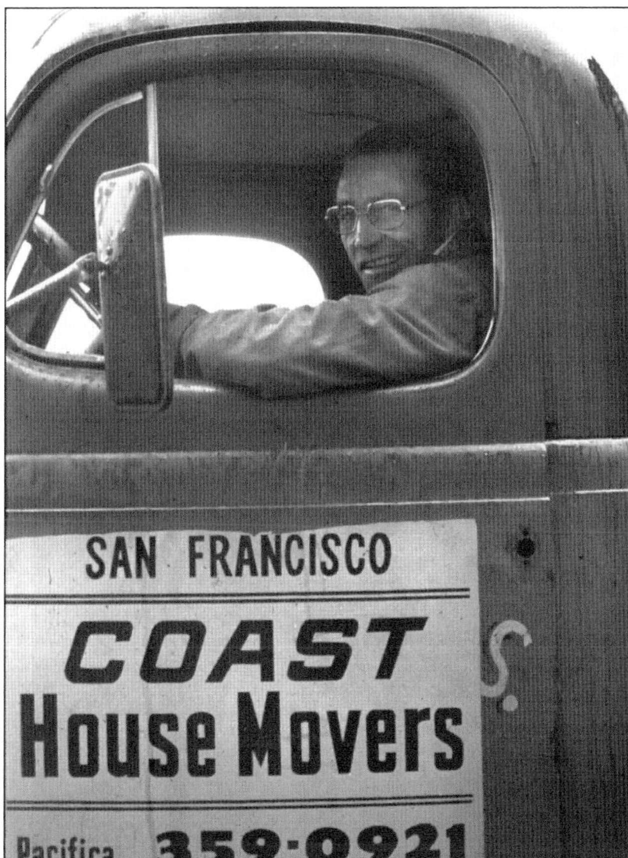

Coast House Movers (located just south of San Francisco) was just one of a number of house-moving professionals involved with the project. Here is an old Coast House Movers truck driven by mover Manuel Pereira, waiting his turn. This man broke his back in 1973 and was never supposed to walk again, but here he is, moving buildings. (Courtesy of the David Glass collection.)

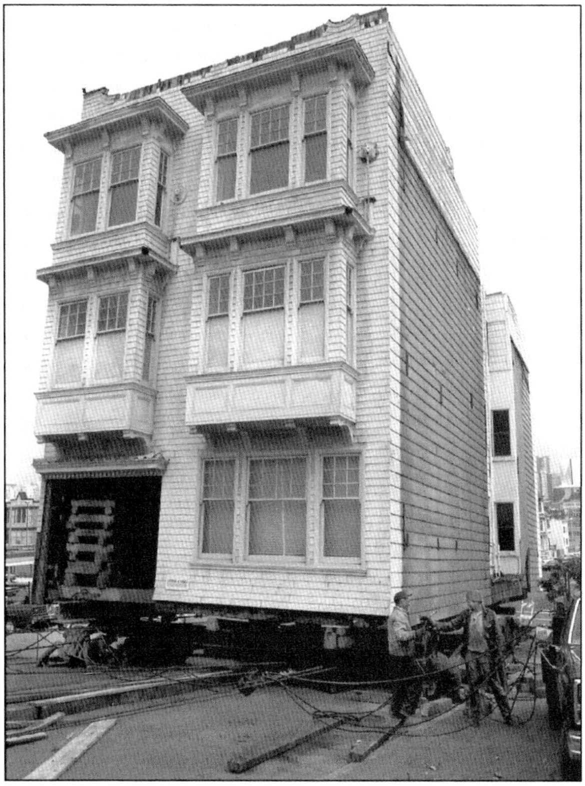

Workers prepare a shored-up Ellis Street house for the arduous physical move to its new home. Note the cribbing in place. Hydraulic lifts raise the house slightly, and three dollies are used (two at the rear and one in the front) to ultimately roll the house along the street, towed via truck. (Courtesy of the David Glass collection.)

Here, workers attempt to back a three-story Victorian apartment building up a fairly steep hill. Planks are placed in front of the various wheels. If a set of wheels drops during a move, the entire house could topple over. The planks help prevent this. (Courtesy of the David Glass collection.)

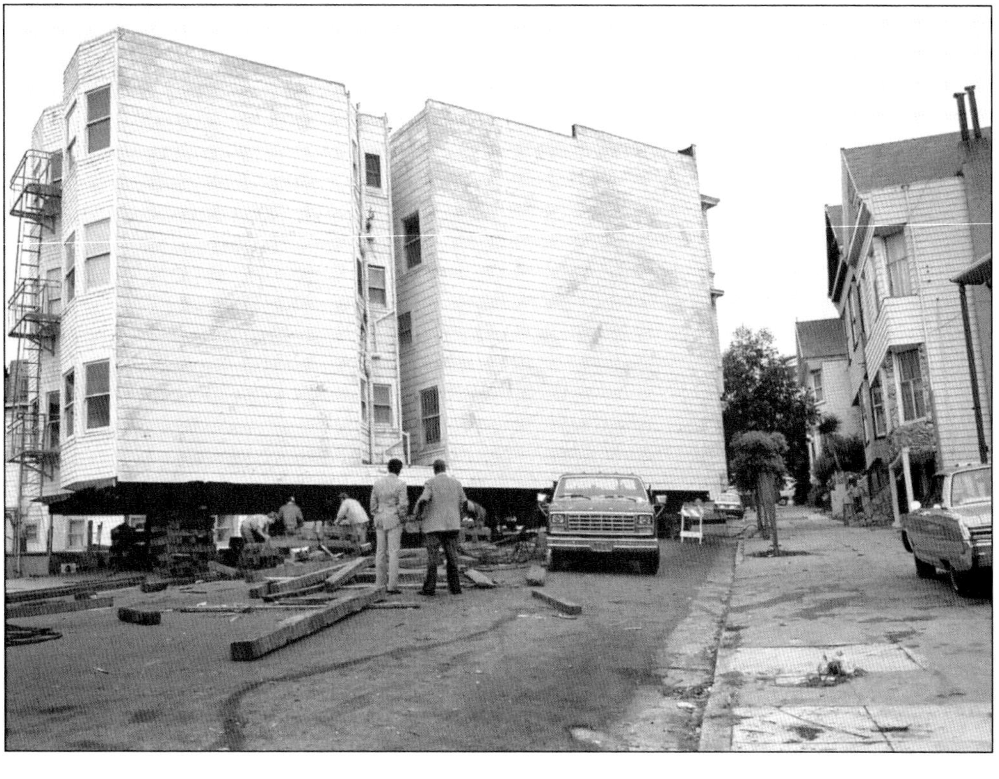

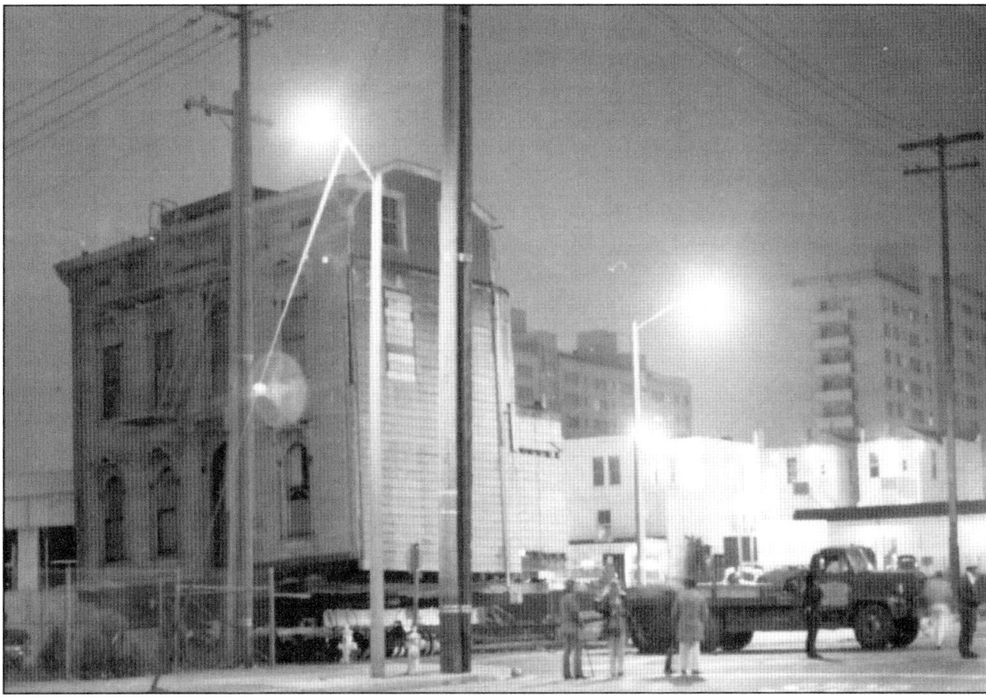

Hubert Trost, a longtime Bay Area mover, had quit the local business and was in Alaska moving buildings when he got the call to consult on the Western Addition moves. This photograph was shot at night; the trolleys closed at 2:00 a.m., and the movers had two to four houses ready to go in a convoy. The other house movers would pull them to their lots, and Trost's team would place them. (Courtesy of the Hubert Trost collection.)

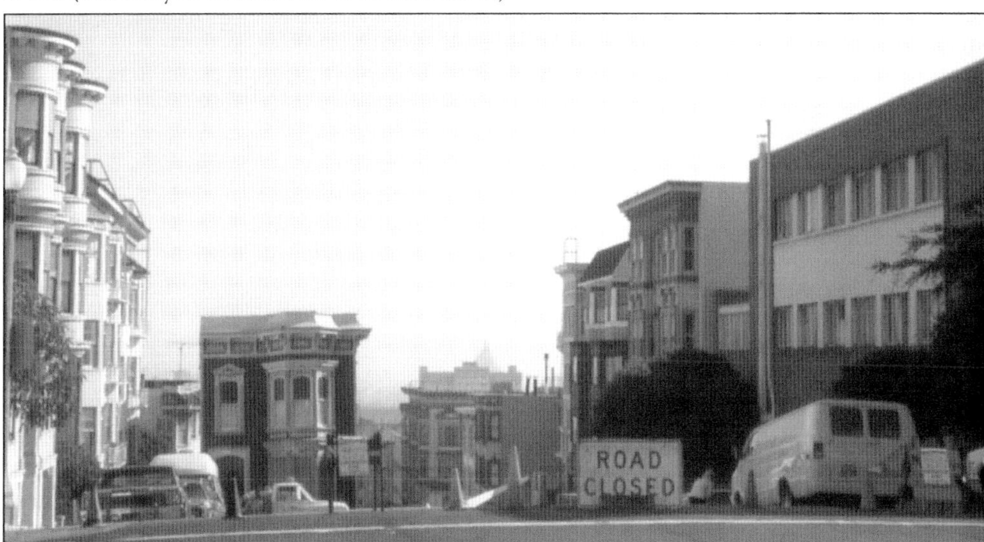

Trost is hauling a building at Golden Gate Avenue near Broderick Street. Hubert Trost helped Coast House Movers with this historic endeavor. It is no mean feat moving a 110-ton house up or down a hill. Two trucks were often stationed uphill during the move, with steel cables embracing the house. If it got out of control, the trucks theoretically could hold it back. (Courtesy of the Dennis O'Rorke collection.)

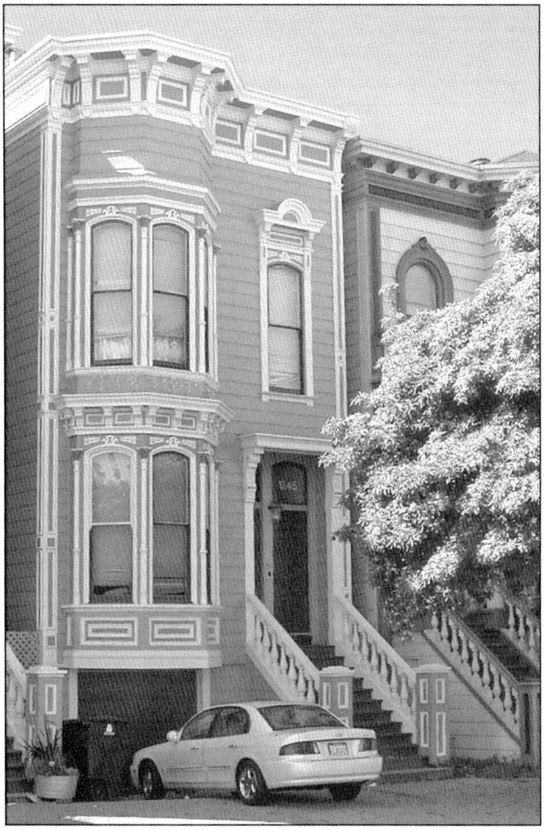

This Scott Street building was one of eight buildings moved onto a two-block development within the Western Addition Area No. 2 and is listed in the National Register of Historic Places. A house like this could be purchased from the San Francisco Redevelopment Agency for $1 plus relocation and restoration costs. (Courtesy of the Alvis E. Hendley collection.)

Ayen House Movers of San Leandro was one of several companies involved in the Western Addition moves. They led the parade of Victorians across town and used a flatbed truck to pull the first 100-ton Victorian home. The company is no longer in business today, but its legacy lives on in the houses that were moved in the 1970s. This three-story building is moving at Ellis and Divisadero Streets. (Courtesy of the David Glass collection.)

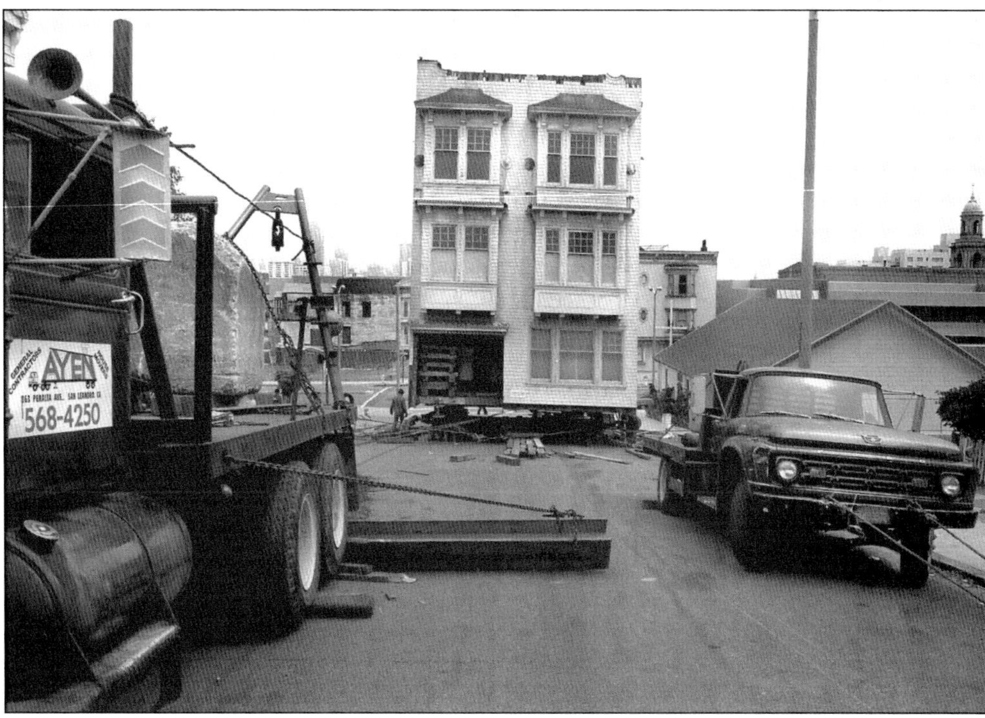

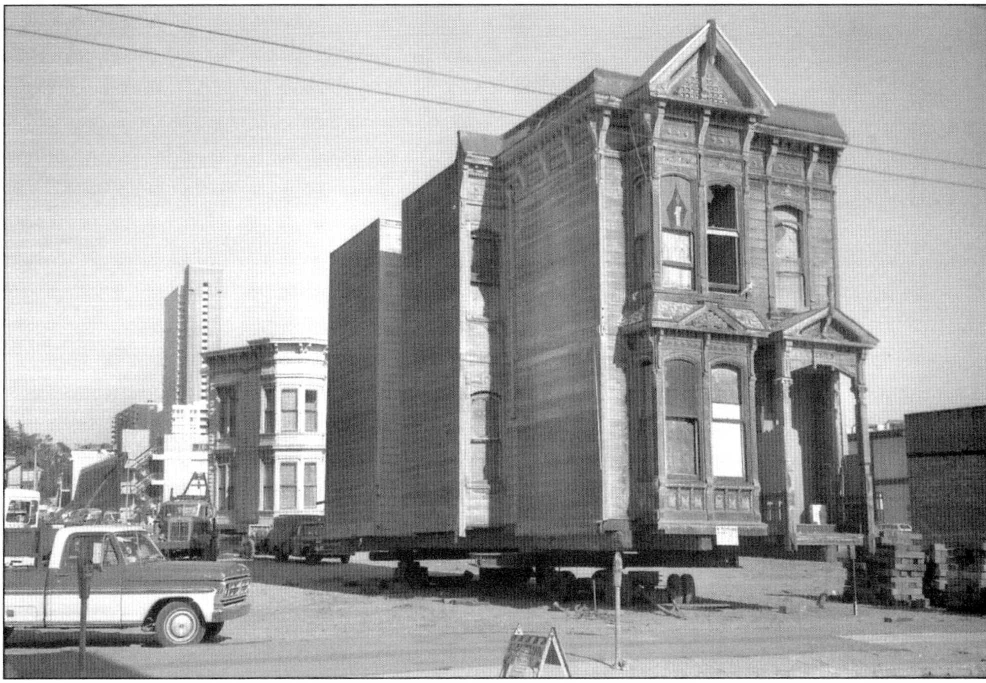

A line-up of buildings waiting to be moved on Fillmore Street gives evidence of the coordination required for such a massive building-moving endeavor. Unlike a single building's move, the evacuation of several structures at once required precise measurements, a coordinated effort between all city agencies, and the cooperation of several building-moving experts who had won bids to move the houses at an average of $12,000 per house. (Courtesy of the David Glass collection.)

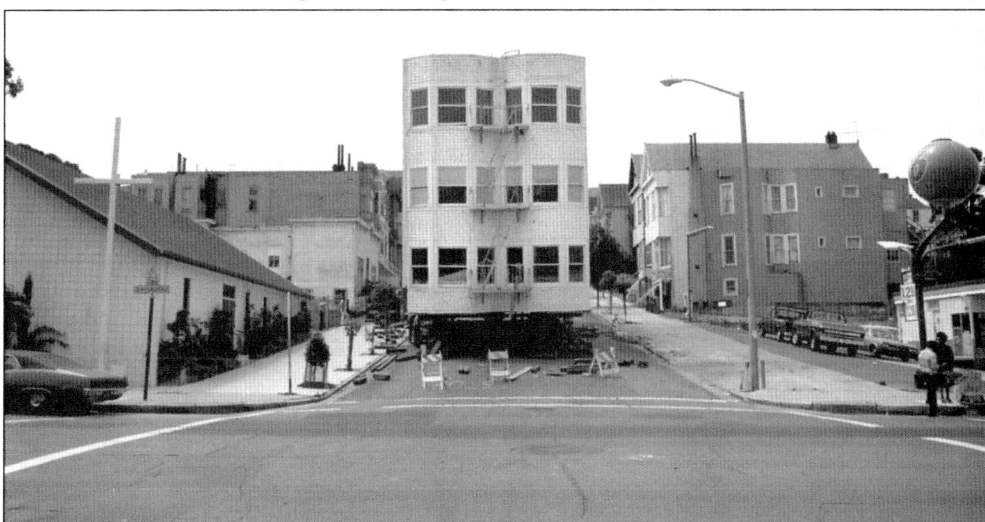

One moved building rests at Divisadero and Ellis Streets. In 1971, San Francisco Heritage was formed to identify 12 Victorian houses that were scheduled for demolition but could be saved. The Redevelopment Agency agreed to sell the houses only if they were moved to a new location. At a public auction in the summer of 1972, San Francisco Heritage entered minimum purchase bids, gained ownership of the houses, and identified new homeowners to rehabilitate them. (Courtesy of the David Glass collection.)

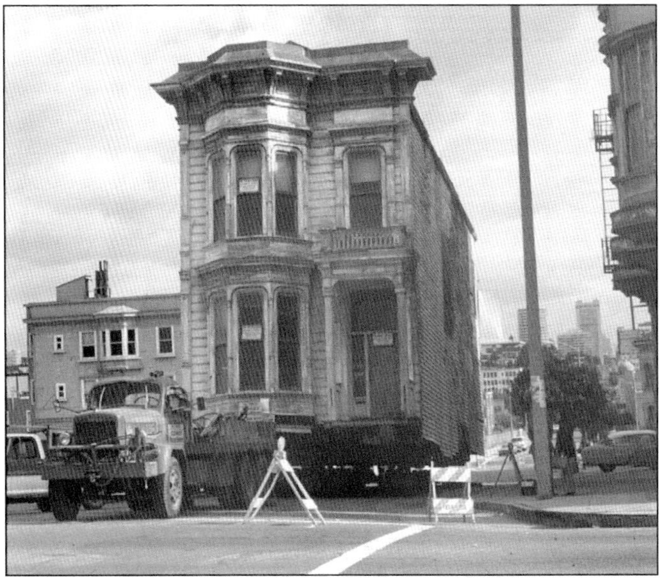

Some 2,500 Victorian homes were demolished in the name of urban renewal when the city's redevelopment agency razed the predominately black Fillmore area in the 1970s in a move that destroyed San Francisco's largest African American community. Over 800 businesses were closed, and well over 4,000 households were displaced. This photograph captures Coast House Movers as they tow a building down the street between Divisadero and Ellis Streets. (Courtesy of the David Glass collection.)

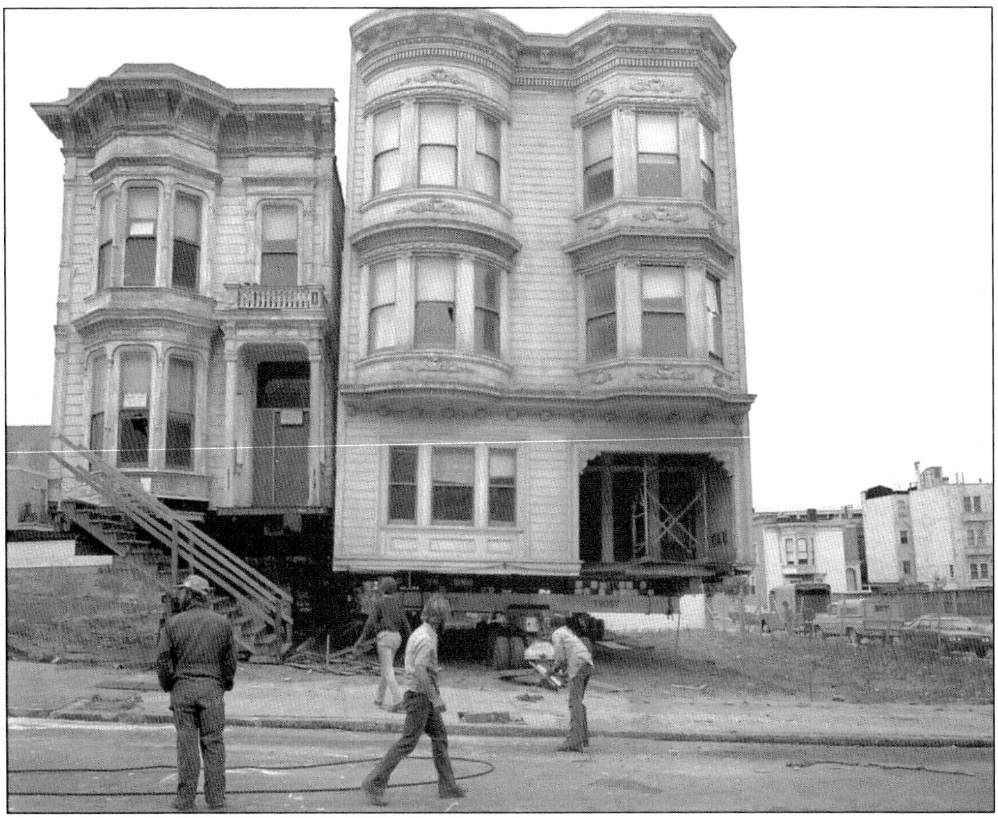

Before a building can be moved, it has to be jacked up. Here, a Trost mover prepares a huge Victorian building. Once the building is cut loose from water, sewage, and utilities, holes are drilled through the foundation, steel beams are slid underneath, and hydraulic jacks lift it up. If it is not high enough, it is jacked up and supported on cribbing, and then the jacks are repositioned on cribbing to raise it further. (Courtesy of the David Glass collection.)

Seven

The Last Movers
The Waning of an Era

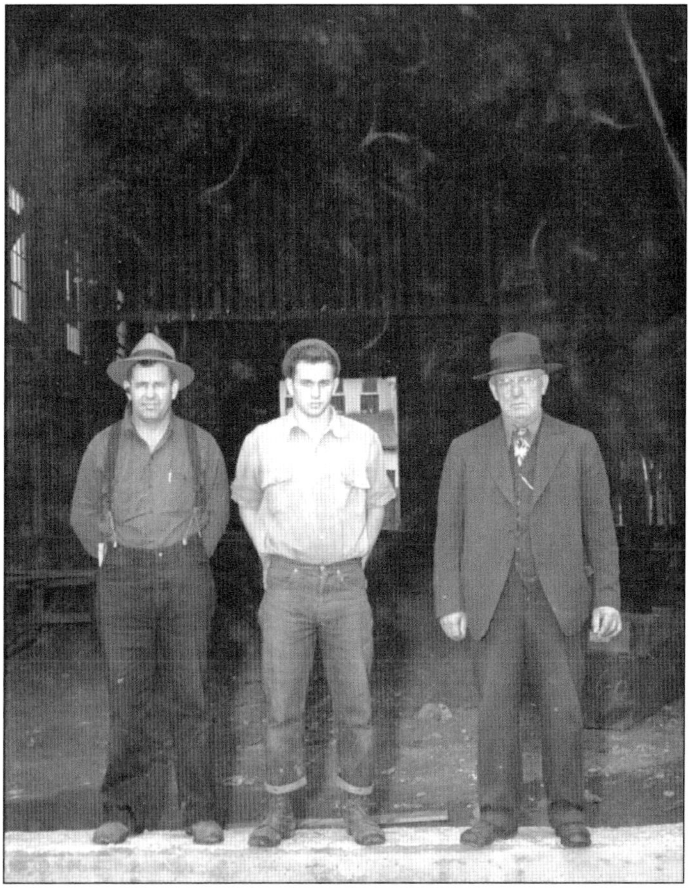

Three generations of Montgomery movers stand together here. They are, from left to right, Richard Barr "R.B." Montgomery, Norman Montgomery, and Walter Montgomery. In 1875, one Walter Suell opened Suell House Moving. His son D.J. took over when he retired and elevated and moved many historic homes over San Francisco's steep hills. When Suell foreman R.B. Montgomery married Alice Suell (D.J.'s great-granddaughter), he took over the business and named it R.B. Montgomery House Movers. Upon R.B.'s retirement, his son Norman moved the business to Sacramento in 1955. (Courtesy of the Steve Montgomery collection.)

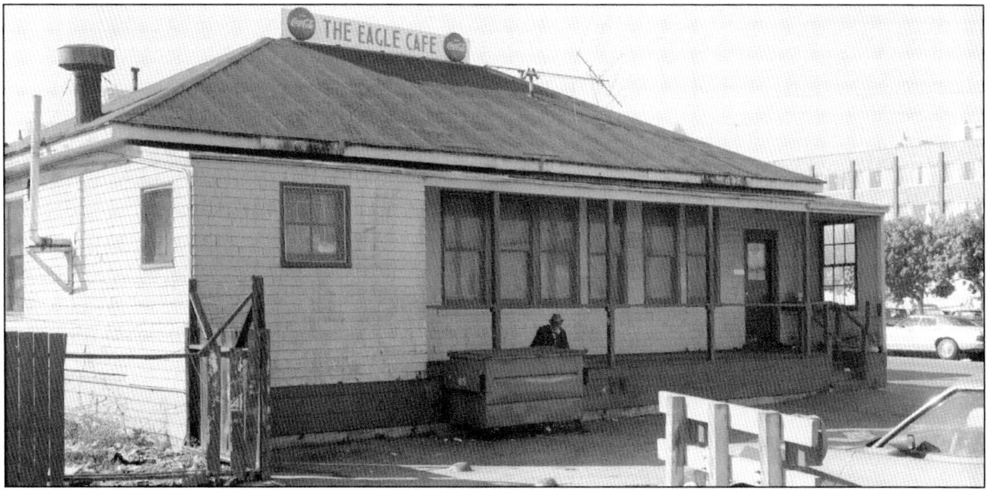

The Eagle Café was a ticket office for passengers traveling from San Francisco to Mendocino and Humboldt Counties before it became a restaurant and bar in the 1920s. In 1978, it faced demolition. Lou Andreotti inherited the Eagle from his father and pushed for the building to be moved from its original location (now the Pier No. 39 parking garage) to the new Pier No. 39 tourist development, where it stands today. Aaron Gallup took this photograph. (Courtesy of the Library of Congress.)

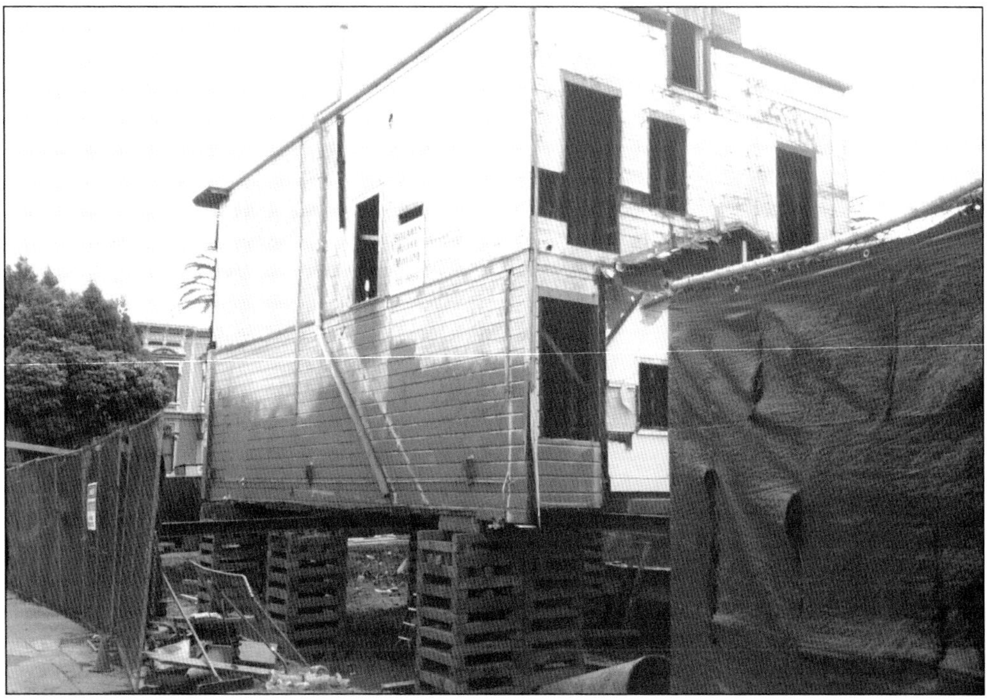

The corner of Fifteenth and Dolores Streets was occupied by the Swedish Evangelical Lutheran Ebenezer Church in 1903, with a parsonage next door. Over the decades, the church changed denominations and burned in 1993, leaving only the parsonage. A bid to demolish the rectory and construct a 13-unit building resulted in assignment of its historic status as a survivor of the 1906 earthquake. The parsonage rests on cribbing. (Courtesy of LisaRuth Elliott, Shaping San Francisco/Foundsf.org)

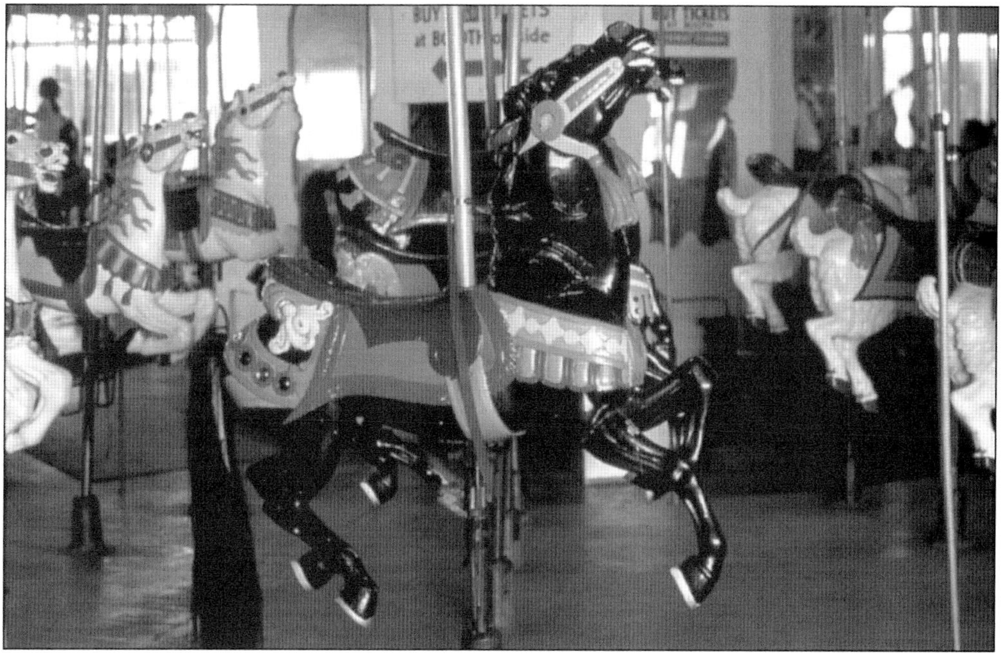

This Looff carousel moved five times during its history. Built in Rhode Island, it moved to Seattle and lived there for 5 years, then resided in San Francisco for 59 years, wound up in storage in Roswell, New Mexico, for 11 years (until 1984), moved to Long Beach, California, for 15 years, and finally moved back to San Francisco, where it has been for the last 16 years. (Courtesy of the Dennis O'Rorke collection.)

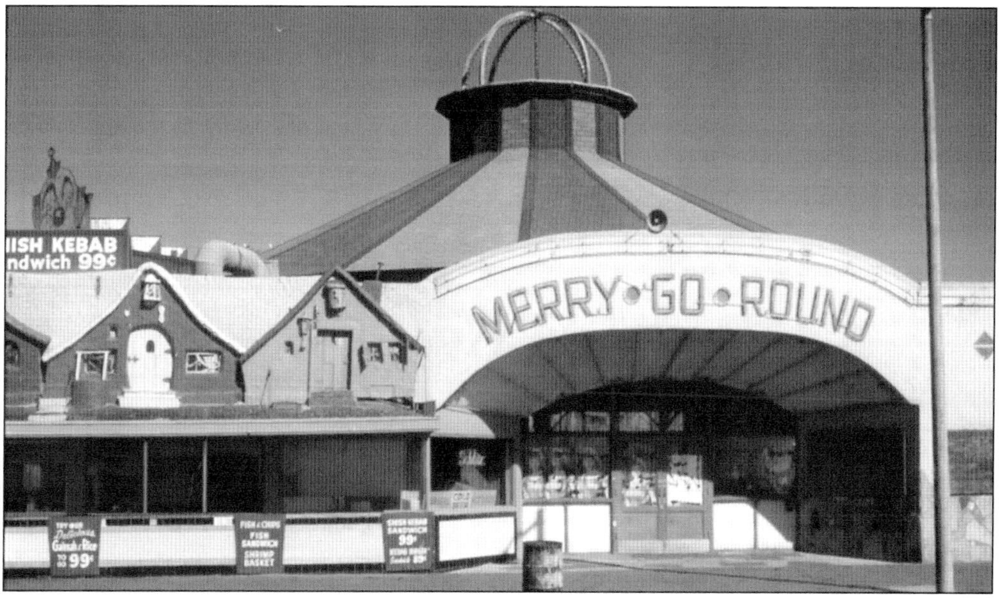

The Looff carousel was temporarily sent north to Luna Park, Washington, via boat around Tierra del Fuego when the 1906 earthquake prevented its delivery to San Francisco. The carousel finally moved to its intended home in 1913, six years after the city was rebuilt. In 1972, Playland closed, and its carousel was purchased by a private collector and moved to Roswell, New Mexico, to be refurbished. In 1983, it moved to Long Beach, California. (Courtesy of the Dennis O'Rorke collection.)

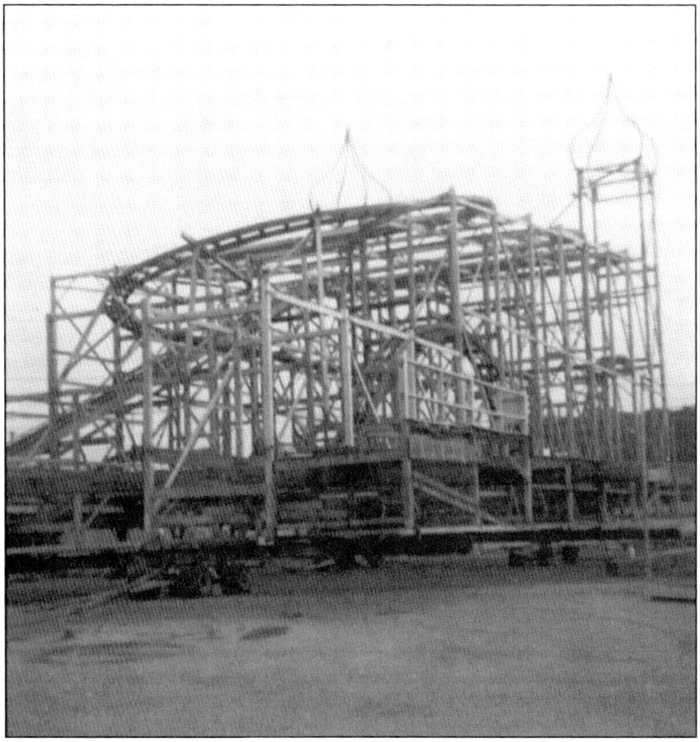

The Alpine Racer roller coaster was located at the corner of Fulton and LaPlaya Streets before it moved to Balboa Street and the Great Highway in 1968. When Playland began to experience vandalism, a big fence was erected to protect its attractions, but the Alpine was left outside the fence, likely due to property boundaries. When it was eventually vandalized, it needed to be moved inside the fence. (Courtesy of Hubert Trost collection.)

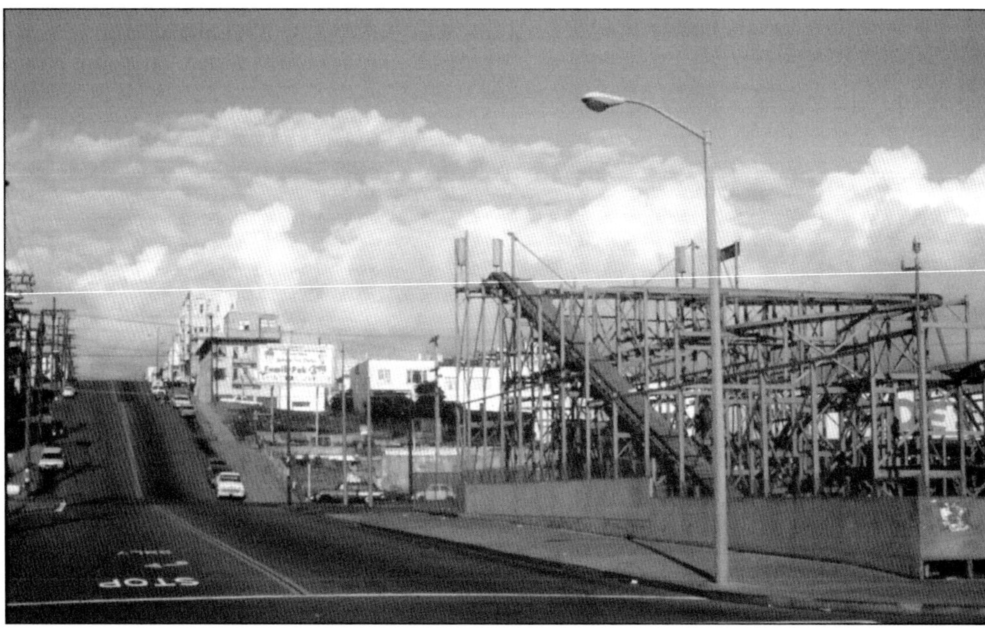

Professional mover Hubert Trost said, "We [didn't] take [the roller coaster] apart: it moved all in one piece. That makes it easier, quicker, and you don't have to take anything apart or put it back together." It was moved on a three-point suspension system on house-moving dollies, a notable achievement for an old wooden structure, especially considering that attractions were almost always disassembled for moves. Playland closed in 1972. Several attractions were moved and saved, but the Racer had finished its journeys. (Courtesy of the Dennis O'Rorke collection.)

This 1998 Union Street restoration site illustrates the final era of San Francisco's building-moving history—the vertical move. These moves usually involve elevating a building in place on its lot. Reasons range from adding a garage or parking under the building to creating commercial or living spaces beneath an existing structure. In this case, the sign advertises retail space to be built underneath. (Courtesy of the David Glass collection.)

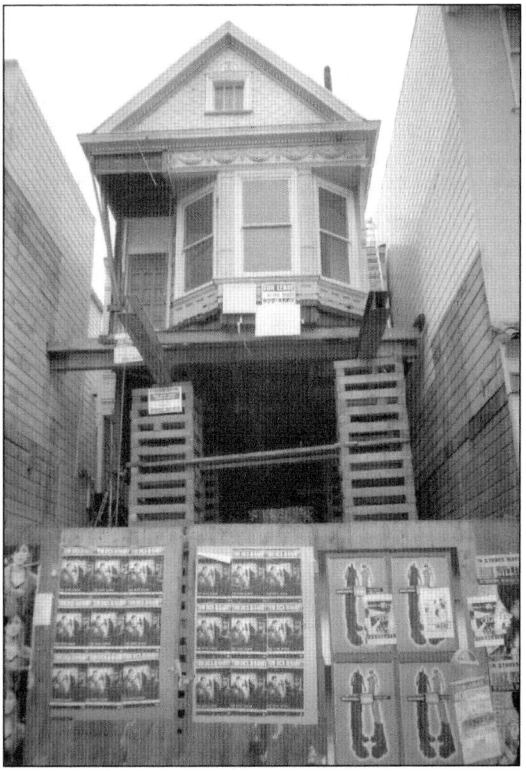

The historic Building Halleck No. 201 has moved twice in its lifetime. The first move occurred in the 1930s when nearby Doyle Drive was constructed next to the Army Presidio, requiring the building to be moved several yards by the Army. Images of that move do not exist. The second move took place in August 2013. The long 1897 Halleck Building No. 201 is shown here raised on cribbing in preparation for its journey. (Courtesy of the Steve Montgomery collection.)

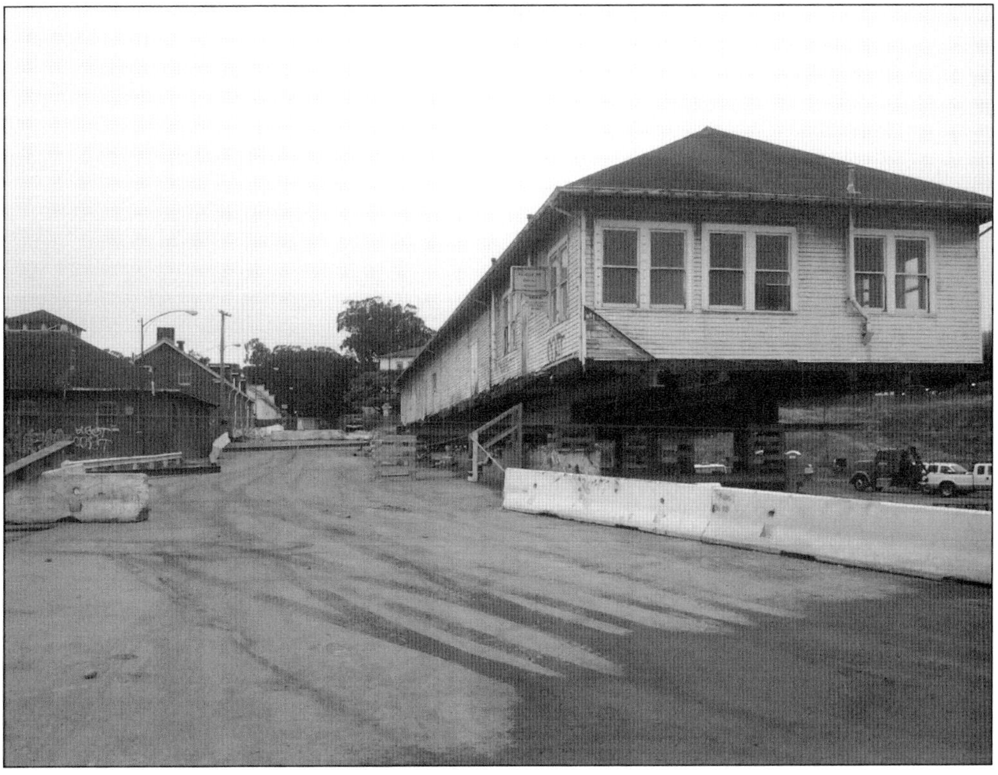

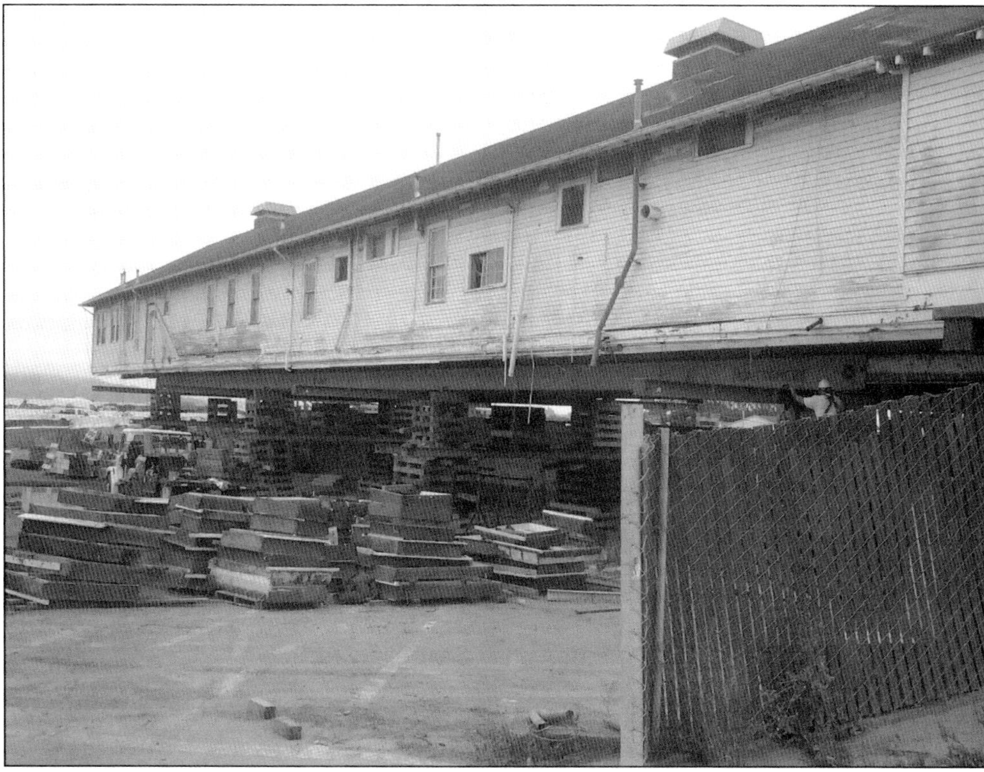

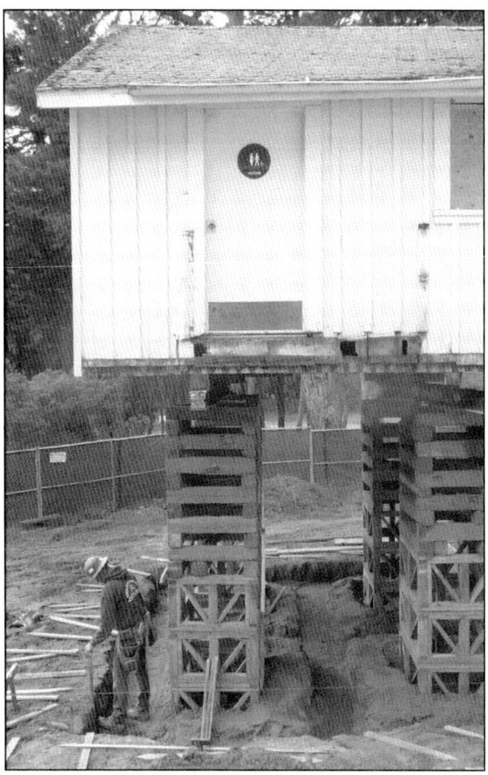

Upon walking the 4,000-foot proposed move route, Steve Montgomery observed there were buildings on the left and ahead, as well as a basement. The building had to make a 90-degree right turn when it was moved. There was an 18-foot difference in the 400-foot moving route. Halleck Building No. 201's length is supported by cribbing and bracing here. (Courtesy of the Steve Montgomery collection.)

Men at work under Halleck Building No. 201 are building up the piers. The building had to be moved first downhill and then back up the hill. Raising it was the first step of its journey. The 10-by-12-foot section had a 6-inch-thick concrete floor. In order to support this added weight, two 40-foot-long 14-by-68-foot beams and two 15-foot-long 21-by-50-foot beam stiffeners had to be installed. The building was raised four feet, six inches. (Courtesy of the Presidio Trust.)

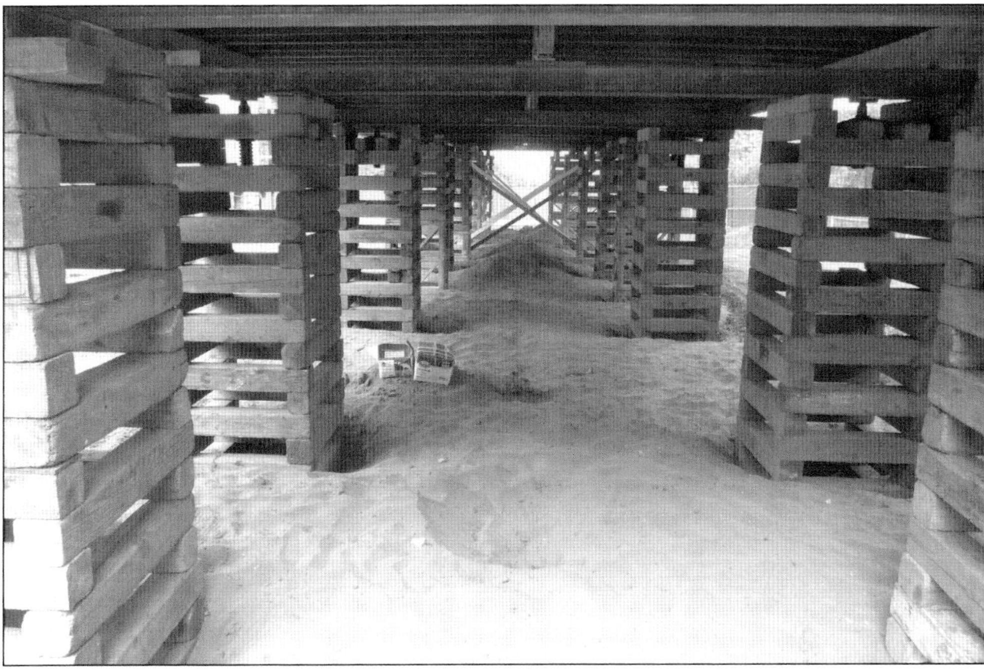

Two trucks lowered the building down the hill, backfilling and compacting the basement to allow for a gradual turn and incline. When they were cutting the dirt down, they discovered a 20-inch mortar shell. The bomb squad from the nearest Air Force base detonated it; Steve Montgomery was surprised to find dirt all over his trucks from the explosion when he returned to the job site after lunch. (Courtesy of the Presidio Trust.)

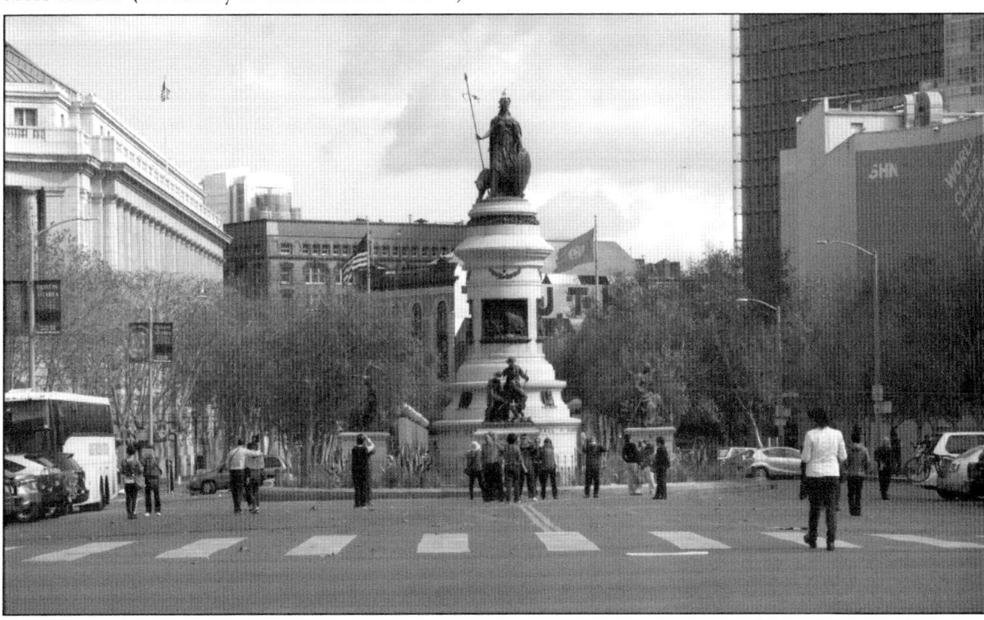

San Francisco's venerable but controversial 1894 Pioneer Monument needed to be moved in 1991 to make way for a new library. The weighty old relic required 20 heavy-duty, steel-carrying beams on hydraulic dollies to drag the bronze behemoth 700 feet (one city block). The monument is shown in its new home, safe and restored. (Photograph by Beni C. Bacon.)

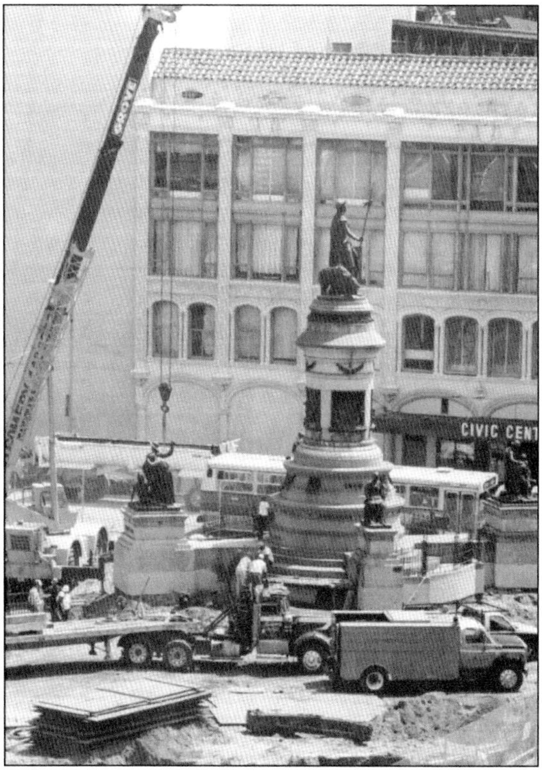

The first phase of moving the massive monument involved removing its outer granite ring. The city's sandy soil led to building everything close to the streets and close together. As a result, one side of the monument was only four feet from the street and needed to be shored up to keep the sandy road bed from caving in during the move. (Courtesy of *Structural Mover Magazine* and the Steve Montgomery collection.)

Before cribs could be used, digging had to be done five feet along each side of the structure, and four steel mats were placed to provide a stable foundation. Each mat supported two 200-ton jacks and two blocks of cribs. Then, 60-foot steel listing beams, weighing 500 pounds per foot, were placed along each side of the monument, while 40-foot-long tunnels were bored under it so that 12-ton cross beams could be positioned. (Courtesy of *Structural Mover Magazine* and the Steve Montgomery collection.)

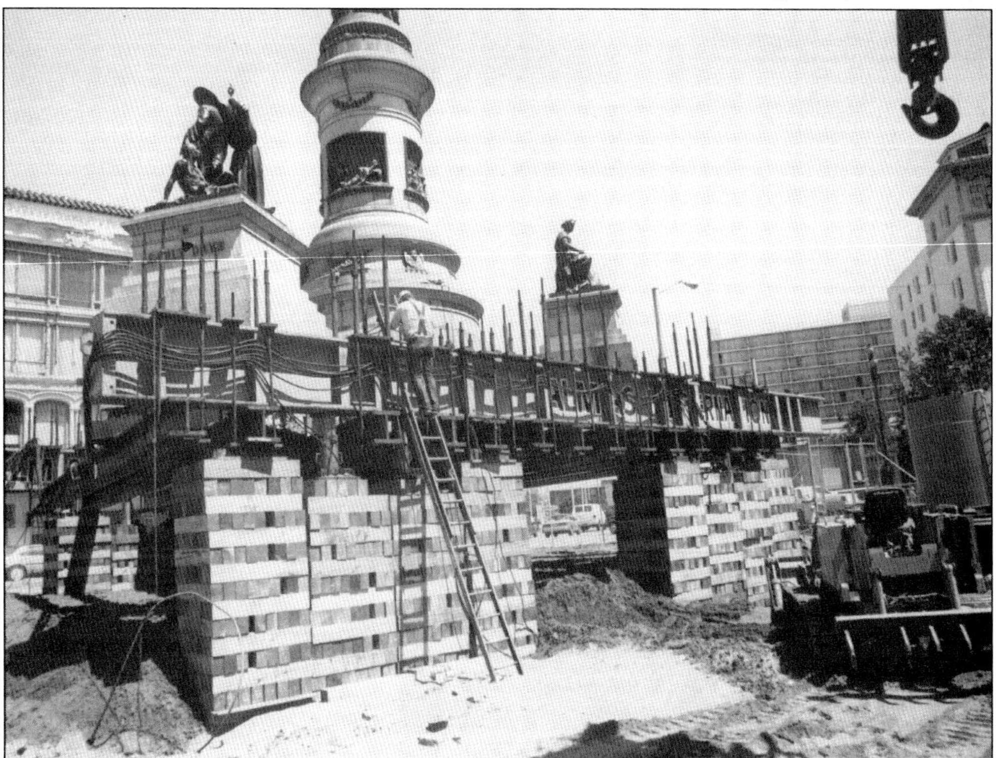

After 14 cross beams were placed and tightened, six men were able to raise the monument 10 feet in five hours using eight 200-ton jacks welded to the lifting beams. Next, 16 solid cribs were built, with sand helping to match the monument to street level, and 28 dollies were set on the now-solid foundation to roll the monument to its new home. (Courtesy of *Structural Mover Magazine* and the Steve Montgomery collection.)

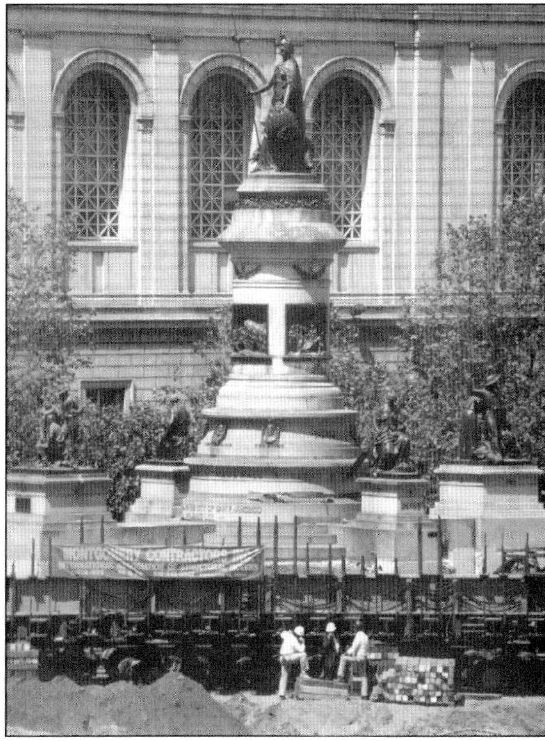

The first moving day was spent pulling the structure off at the corner location by rotating it 180 degrees and moving it 300 feet. As part of the job, Montgomery Contractors helped oversee the accompanying $350,000 restoration project. The total project cost was over $800,000, making it one of the city's largest historic moving projects ever. (Courtesy of *Structural Mover Magazine* and the Steve Montgomery collection.)

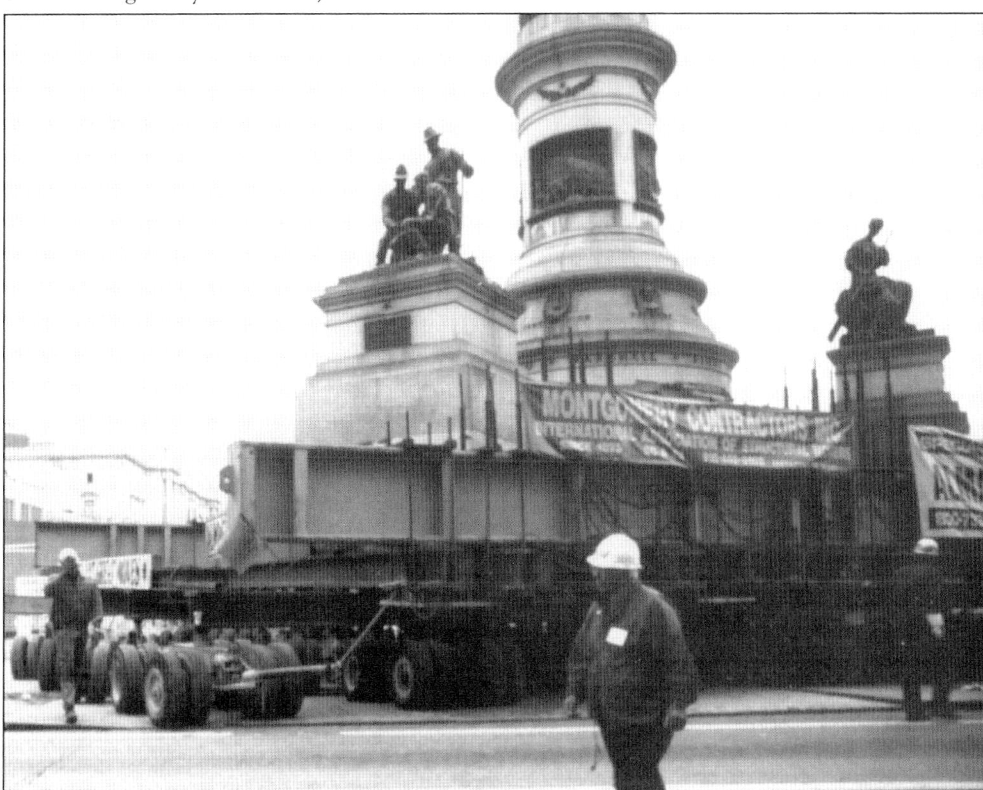

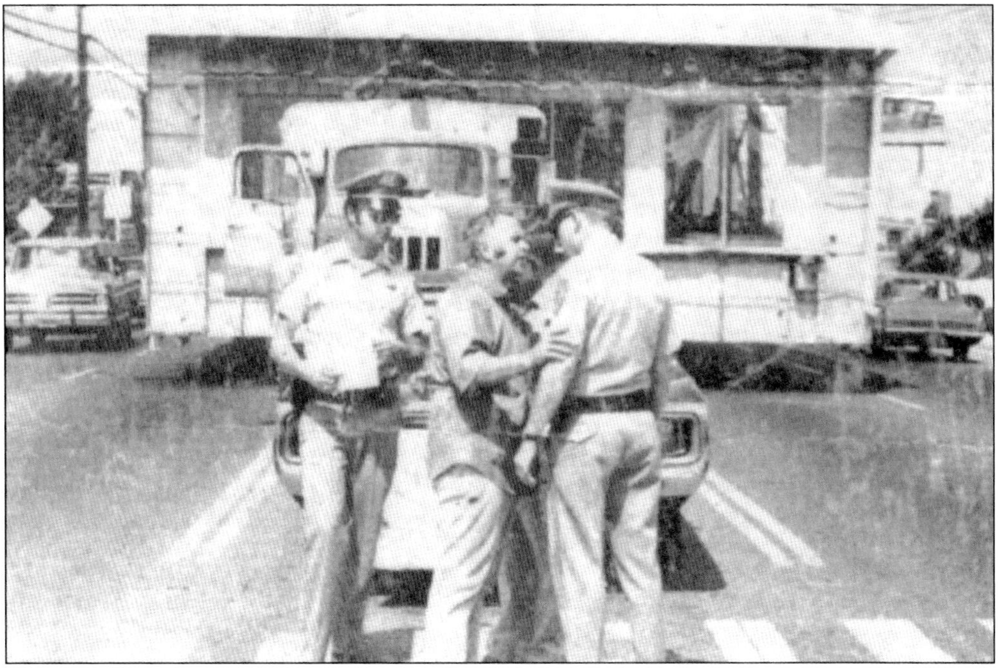

Not all building moves receive the blessing of public agencies despite the permit process. In 1972, R.B. Montgomery House Movers was moving a building over Highway 99. The California Highway Patrol stopped R.B. Montgomery and asked to see the transportation permits. Since the building was crossing the freeway, a county permit was needed, and the Sacramento City permit was not enough. A discussion ensured, which eventually went to court. (Courtesy of the Steve Montgomery collection.)

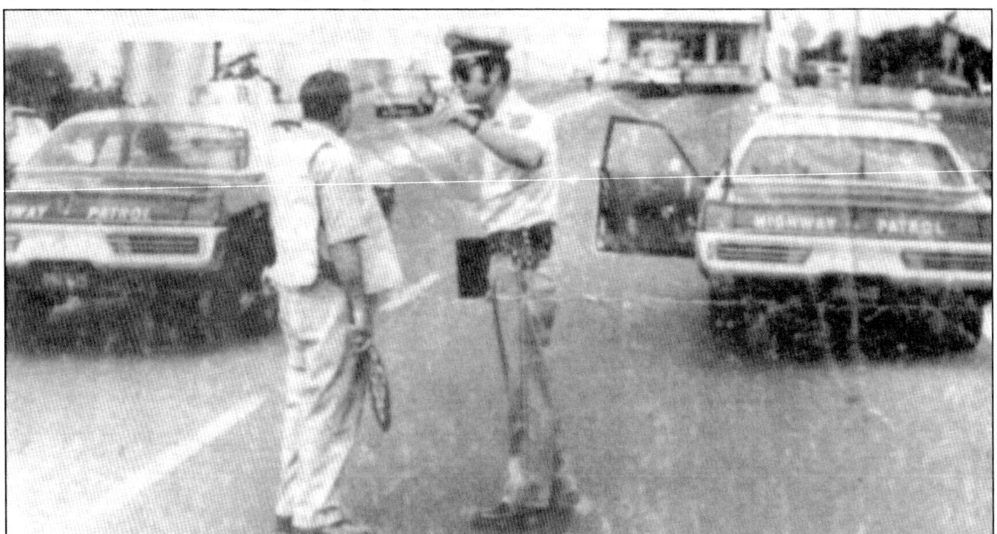

A county permit was eventually shown, and the court case was dismissed; however, R.B. Montgomery House Movers often got into arguments with the police over moving buildings on public streets and highways. As San Francisco is both city and county, the permit process was a little easier, but once a mover took a building over county lines, other county permit systems were involved in the process. (Courtesy of the Steve Montgomery collection.)

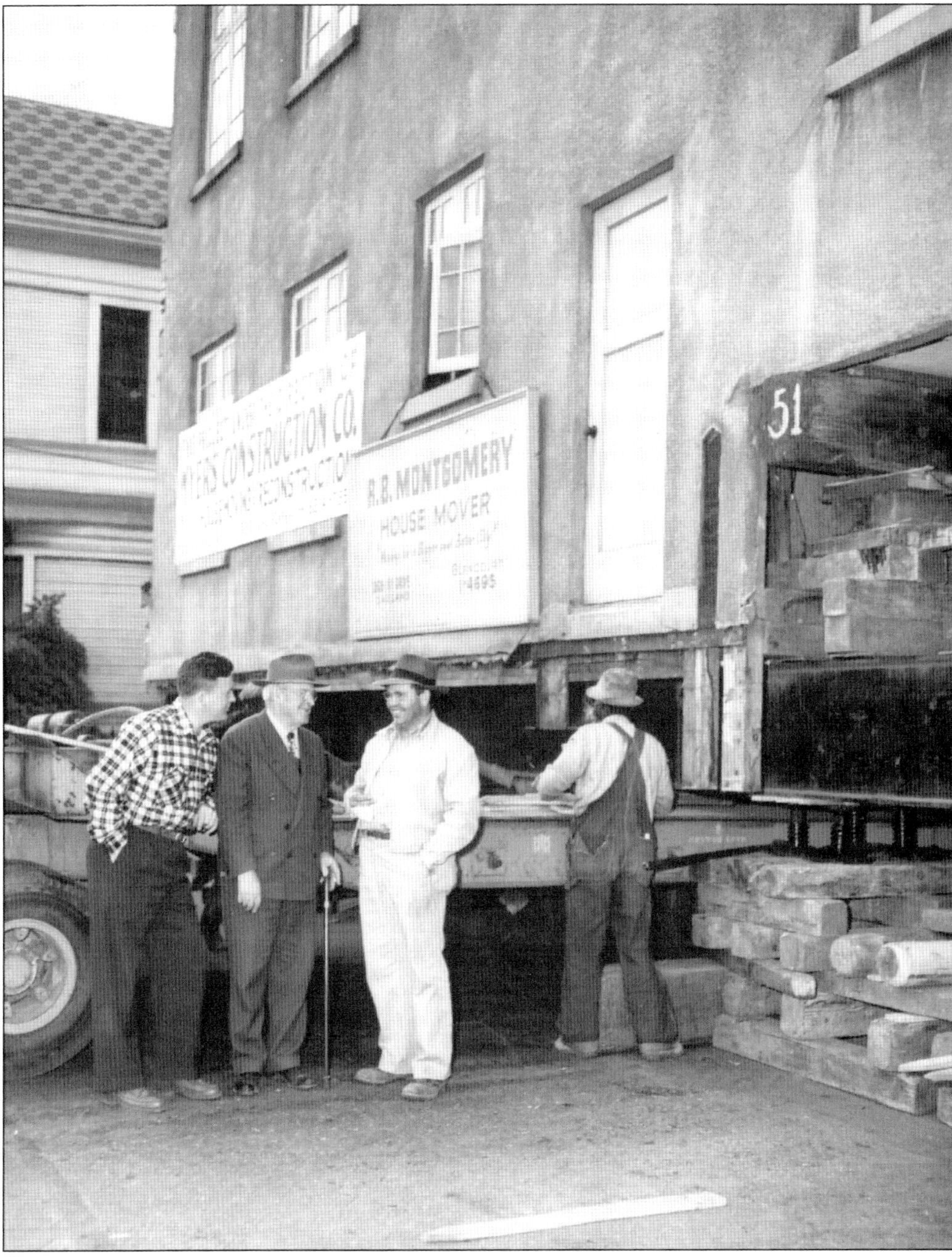

Key employees make for successful house moves. The owner of the moved building stands in the center with a cane, the young man is the general contractor Meyers (left), and R.B. Montgomery, home mover, is speaking to them. The man on the far right is unidentified. When moving houses, a three-man crew is a minimum, and a four-man crew is optimum. Many workers are devoted to the building-moving industry and will take unemployment and temporary jobs while they wait for house-moving projects. (Courtesy of the Steve Montgomery collection.)

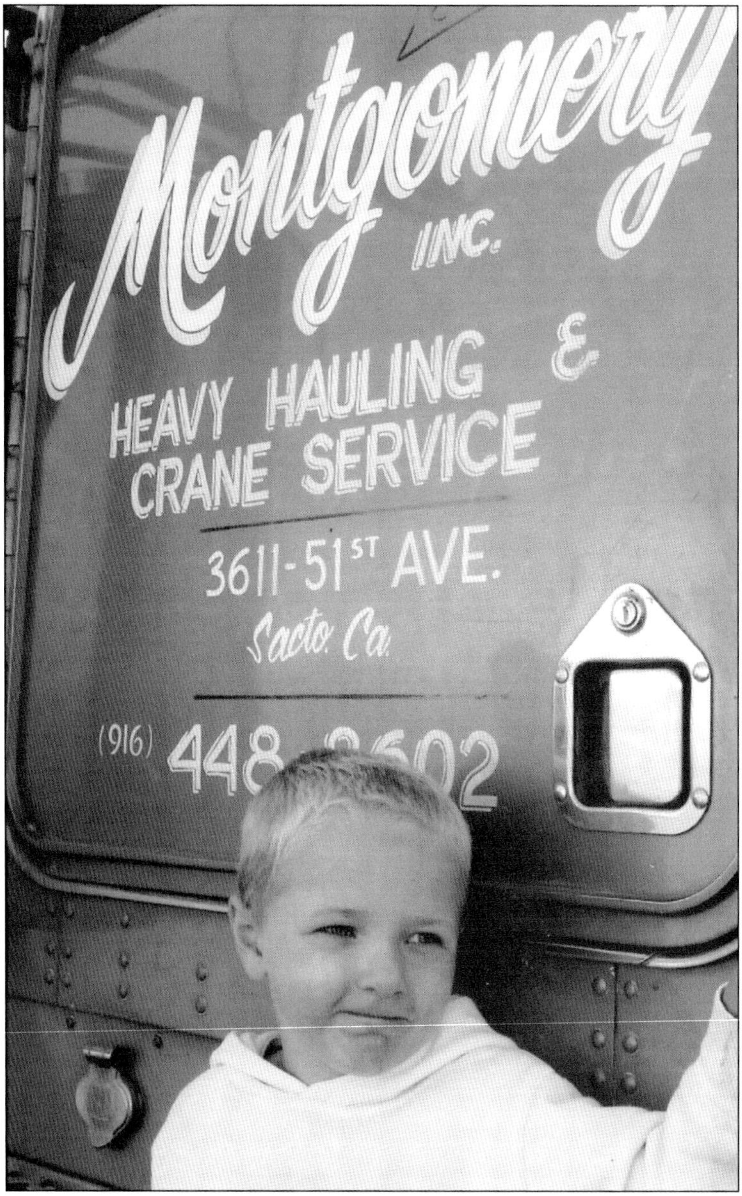

Meet Kelynn Montgomery, Steve Montgomery's nephew's son, potentially the seventh generation to be involved in the Montgomery family's moving business. The opportunities for moving houses in the United States has diminished due to utility lines, traffic signals, and urban density. In California, the permit process takes a long time and is expensive. Houses have to be brought up to code, and land costs are high. New York, New Jersey, and Louisiana are seeing much of the building-moving action due to storms and flooding, but if the oceans rise, California could be looking at as many as 75,000 building elevations. In the last five years, four California house moving firms have gone out of business despite the fact that house moving has become an easier job with unified hydraulic machines capable of handling 100 jacks. In the past, 100 men were required to move a large structure. Now, a three-to-six-man crew can do everything. Despite this, the younger generation is not willing to work as hard, and moving houses is much harder work than plumbing or electrical contracting. (Courtesy of the Steve Montgomery collection.)

INDEX